Meeting
the Buddha

On Pilgrimage
in Buddhist India

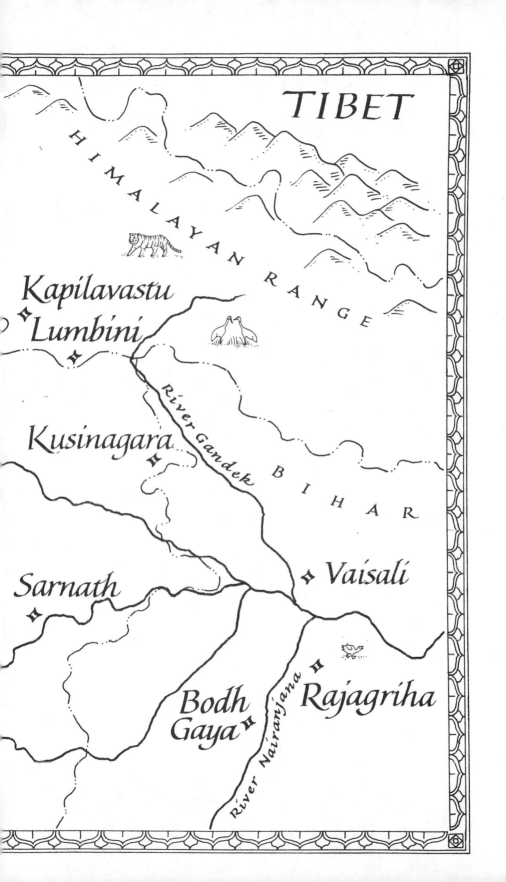

Meeting the Buddha

On Pilgrimage in Buddhist India

A Tricycle Book

Edited by
Molly Emma Aitken

With an Introduction by
Andrew Schelling

Photographs by
Simon Chaput

RIVERHEAD BOOKS, NEW YORK

RIVERHEAD BOOKS, NEW YORK

Published by The Berkley Publishing Group
200 Madison Avenue
New York, New York 10016

Book design by **Caroline Rowntree**
Cover design by **G. C. Potter Associates**
Photography by **Simon Chaput**
Maps by **Elinor Holland**

First edition: November 1995

Library of Congress Cataloging-in-Publication Data
Meeting the Buddha: on pilgrimage in Buddhist India/edited by
    Molly Emma Aitken. — 1st ed.
        p.   cm.
    Includes bibliographical references.
    ISBN 1-57322-506-1 (pbk. : alk paper)
    1. Gautama Buddha—Shrines—India. 2. Buddhist
pilgrims and pilgrimages—India.   I. Aitken, Molly Emma.
BQ6460. M44   1995
294. 3'435'0954—dc20   95-17218
                                                             CIP

Printed in the United States of America
10 9 8 7 6 5 4 3 2 1

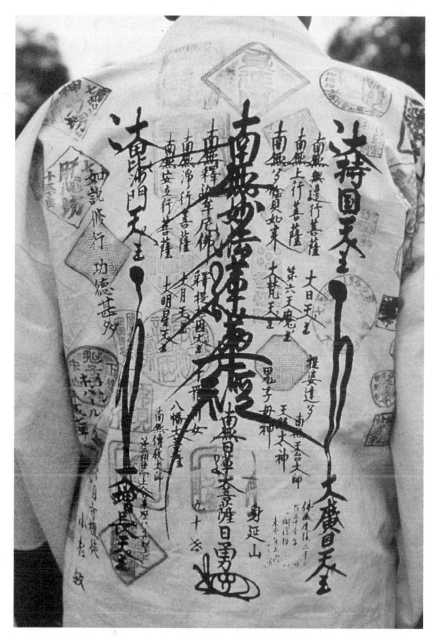

A Japanese pilgrim wearing a robe stamped with the symbols of Buddhist shrines he has visited.

Contents

Sarnath:
Where the Buddha First Taught 137

Rajagriha: Where the Buddha
Tamed the Elephant Nalagiri 187

Sravasti and Sankasya: Where the Buddha Performed the Great Miracles and Where He Descended from the Trayastrimsas Heaven

Introduction

by Andrew Schelling

"*T*he householder's life," says old Buddha's docu-
ment *The Digha Nikaya*, "is full of dust and hin-
drance." And immediately you feel it, right in
your shoes. From the start, Buddhism showed a sharp
impatience for stay-at-home habits. It has spread out
from India, traveled to China and Japan, Southeast Asia,
Europe and America, and in twenty-five hundred years
hasn't shaken that fine old skepticism.

The impulse to ramble is as old as humankind.
We have ample testimony of a close ancestral connection to migratory animals, and it appears that the earliest calendars were incised animal bone, small enough to
slip in a pocket as the human clan arranged its year by
traveling to seasonal food sources. Archaeologists are
uncovering routes of migration our human forebears followed, keeping herds of reindeer and antelope, bison
and sheep in sight. For most human beings, for tens of
thousands of years, home was quite literally "on the
hoof." The hunter, the nomad, the rambler, and finally
the pilgrim. Perhaps it is no more than the swift human
intellect and our proud, strong legs following a primordial hunger to see what's around the bend, over the next
hill, or just upriver.

Every child grows up in a landscape both seen
and imagined. Parents, relatives, and friends bring home
tales of marvelous places. The elderly revisit their childhood landscapes by turning them into further stories.
These brilliant outward-looking eyes never quite catch

up with that shimmering ability to see things and locations within. Poems, journals, hagiographies, the diaries of merchants and seekers, accounts of sailors and soldiers — traditions of storytelling never disappear. How many records do the libraries hold now of visits to India — a continent known in its own treasury of tale and legend as Jambudvipa, the Rose-Apple Island?

Tale and legend? Stations of pilgrimage, like stories, get more, not less rich as the generations roll past. The earliest human art — cliff walls pecked with meaningful designs or pictographs — caves delicately and inspirationally peopled with ocher and manganese animal forms—were not undertaken at places of permanent residence. They were at locales to which people journeyed, passing by on migratory circuits, or at a later date making special efforts to visit: they were ceremonial centers, shrines, locations of brave human deeds and brilliant supernatural occurrences. Peerless art and innovative architecture arise to commemorate the old stories, and in their wake spring up field tents, or little guest lodges, to make the sites hospitable for visitors. Everyone hungers to visit and revisit the locales associated with legend. To some, this life of rambling and migration takes such hold of the imagination that it comes to seem the one life worth leading — if only for some brief period. If only once in a lifetime.

❁

The early Buddhists were an order of "wandering alms-seekers." A ragtag bunch, they could be found at crossroads and river fords, along highways, camping in city parks, or sheltering in forest groves. India would scarcely offer such a range of destinations for the Buddhist pilgrim had Shakyamuni Buddha settled into a secluded ashram like a Brahman priest, or lived out his days as a philosopher king in his father's palace. The model he took for himself and his followers — that of philosophical rambler, beggar of food, tatter-robed paraclete, inveterate pilgrim — was an old one. Others before him had gone to the forests and highways for centuries, tired of rigid social forms and a predictable religion of the kitchen and bedroom. India's great casteless community of the homeless was already ancient in Buddha's day.

The pilgrim, the wanderer, the forest dweller, figures so familiar to the old epics, to poetry and legend, that the arts of India seem charged with them. The Buddha's resolve as a young man to leave his father's palace, what the annals call his Great Going-Forth, came after seeing the Four Signs. On successive days he encountered an old man, a sick man, a corpse and, lastly, a wandering mendicant on perpetual pilgrimage to the source of life. You meet similar mendicants on every pilgrimage route in India today, at all the temples and riverbanks. You see them on trains, in taxis and rickshaws, traveling by private cars. But mostly they have gone and continue to go forth by foot.

How can we separate the notion of pilgrimage from the primal instinct to set out on a walk, shake off the householder's dust, and simply see something new? Our bones ache with it. The word *pilgrim* along with its Latin original, *peregrine*, simply means a person who wanders "across the land." The old Sanskrit words from India spring from the same irresistible source. A *yatrika* is a rambler, a *thirthayatrika* a wanderer who frequents crossroads and riverbanks. You may think the world of nation states, superhighways, and rigidly drawn borders no longer accommodates such folk, but in India they ramble as they have for millennia — a tradition that traces itself back to a prehistoric pan-Asiatic shamanism.

It was near Taxila in 323 B.C., after fording the Indus River, that Alexander the Great's army encountered a community of spiritual goers-forth. The fierce, ragged, skull-carrying mendicants they met were not Buddhists but sadhus — on pilgrimage into the Himalayan foothills holy to Siva. But before the Greek soldiers were done with India they would bring back accounts of a Buddhist civilization that took for its principal emblem the *shramana* or homeless wanderer, who owned only a patchwork robe, begging bowl, and razor to tonsure the head. The Greeks coined their own term, *gymnosophist* — naked philosopher — to describe these figures. And ever since, homeless men and women of religion, perpetual pilgrims, have exerted the strongest fascination over foreign travelers to India — probably because nowhere else has such a community so durably established itself. Buddhism picked the archaic tradition up from epic and wisdom book, and placed the wanderer at the core of its discipline.

Even the initial settling in of the *bhikkhu* and *bhikkhuni* (ordained monk and nun), which occurred during Buddha's lifetime, did not spell an end to the wandering life. It arose as a provisional response to cycles of weather. July and August are India's monsoon season. Every year torrential rains pour from the sky, rivers overflow, and water makes the roads nearly impassable. Sakyamuni Buddha counseled his students to sit out the periodic downfalls as specified "rain retreats." Certain of these shelters developed over time into permanent centers. Some received donations of land and used financial gifts to raise walls and spires, meditation halls, stupas, and libraries. With the blossoming of Buddhist civilization, the vast *viharas* of north India came into existence — centers of meditation, art, learning, philosophical debate, and trade. The one at Nalanda, founded in present-day Bihar state in the fourth century C.E., accommodated up to ten thousand resident yogins, scholars, and artists at a time. Yet for all

4

the massive walls, the kitchens and libraries, the halls of worship, no concept of "staying put" ever fully caught on. Etymologically, the word *vihara* means "a place to wander about." To consider these way stations colleges or monasteries misses something crucial. You'll see, if you visit the expansive courtyards and long, covered arcades of Nalanda, that its residents thought the best seeking and most subtly colored thinking was still to be done on foot.

What is this thinking done on foot? Ask any pilgrim, you'll get the same answer: You only find out by going. It is an attitude toward life, not a catechism had from some book. Old Buddha ancestor of North America Henry David Thoreau gets as close as I've seen. In his essay "Walking" he tracks the word *saunter* to Old French *Sainte Terre* — holy land. A saunterer is a holy-lander, a walker to sacred places and storied locations. "We should," he admonishes, "go forth on the shortest walk, perchance, in the spirit of undying adventure, never to return — prepared to send back our embalmed hearts only as relics to our desolate kingdoms." It's here he gives a taste of that adventurous urge that forms the pilgrim's resolve. "If you are ready to leave father and mother, brother and sister, and wife and child and friends, and never see them again, — if you have paid your debts, and made your will, and settled all your affairs, and are a free man, then you are ready for a walk."

Only the walker who sets out toward ultimate things is a pilgrim. In this lies the terrible difference between tourist and pilgrim. The tourist travels just as far, sometimes with great zeal and courage, gathering up acquisitions (a string of adventures, a wondrous tale or two) and returns the same person as the one who departed. There is something inexpressibly sad in the clutter of belongings the tourist unpacks back at home.

The pilgrim is different. The pilgrim resolves that the one who returns will not be the same person as the one who set out. Pilgrimage is a passage for the reckless and subtle. The pilgrim — and the metaphor comes to us from distant times — must be prepared to shed the husk of personality or even the body like a worn out coat. A Buddhist dictum has it that "the Way exists but not the traveler on it." And when you peruse the journals, books, and poems left behind by travelers of the Buddhist world — to India, China, Japan, or Tibet — you find a strange thing. For the pilgrim the road is home; reaching your destination seems nearly inconsequential.

No pilgrim to Buddhist India has left more compelling an account than seventh-century Chinese monk Hiuen Tsiang. I'd call him the patron saint of the pilgrim. His own record of the twenty-year journey describes in vivid terms the elemental recklessness you need if you would become a pilgrim, you must be as much rogue as saint, as much buccaneer as contemplative. Simply to get out of T'ang Dynasty China, Hiuen Tsiang had to break an imperial decree, bribe a series of border guards, and slip off toward barbarian lands in disguise. And that was the easy part. From there his way was beset by bandits, fierce desert storms, unscalable mountains, savage beasts. Fearsome supernatural creatures would lurk at every turn of the road, but over the border he goes like a convict over the wall, and never looks back. Wu Ch'eng-En's delightful book *Monkey* provides Hiuen Tsiang with a rascally, trickster monkey alter ego and guardian, giving the tale a fabulous coloring: pilgrim and irrepressibly mischievous monkey, bound to each other as they pursue a supernatural journey into old India. Everyone heading off to the Buddhist sites of India should read it. For on that vast subcontinent, your own mind, so similar to the silly, aggressive rhesus monkeys you meet on the road, will be your greatest nemesis. That same mind is also your only protector.

What I mean is that excessive piety does not prove particularly useful to the Buddhist practitioner. What an impediment it is to the pilgrim! If your temperament impels you toward the sites of the Buddhist world, especially those spread across the Gangetic Plain, you're going to need to be loose, spontaneous, charitable, open-eyed, humorous, and unsentimental as you encounter India's endless string of beggars, cripples, lepers, dirty children, imploring mothers, avaricious merchants. You need generosity but not lavishness, determination but not rigidity. You need a dry wit, even a trace of irreverence. It helps the inner organs, assists the appetite, and certainly makes more tolerable Bodh Gaya's scorching winds or those aggressive flies in the teashops of Lucknow.

Chuckling demons are likely to strew your path with impediments. If you take the pilgrim's route to India, you must be prepared for nearly anything — for misguided companions, bad food, crowded trains, for pickpockets, unreliable buses, filthy toilets. And most of all, for that companion's monkey: your own peevish egoism.

Going to India in 1992, my third trip, I expected to visit the Buddhist sites of the north. Some I'd not seen in twenty years, some not at all. Bodh Gaya, Sarnath, Nalanda, Lumbini . . . I intended to bow my head at each. But in Calcutta my companion and I found our plane tickets no good — the airlines on strike. No one had warned us. Refugees from religious riots that were flaring in Bombay and Lucknow choked all the trains. Even a taxi could not get over the bridges that might lead us west. We raged and worried, we raced about town. But through some baffling string of events we landed on a train winding south, and in a few days found ourselves outside Bhubaneswar, from which Buddhism had been brutally driven twelve hundred years earlier. On a massive rock overlooking the field where Buddhist king Asoka had vanquished the Kalinga empire, we found his first edicts carved in the archaic script: "One must feed and give shelter to wanderers."

❁

*Here, within this body, is the Ganges and Jumna . . .
here are Prayaga and Banares — here the sun and
moon. Here are the sacred places, here the* pithas
and upa-pithas. *I have not seen a place of pilgrimage and an abode of bliss like my own body.*

So sang Saraha, eighth-century arrow-smith and tantric adept from Orissa. His words add an unexpected twist to the pilgrim's journey, but he is not alone in his sentiments. Renowned contemplatives, fearsome yogis, and reckless poets have always interpreted pilgrimage in similar ways. They've mocked it as futile, belittled it, reviled it for ignorance. Sixteenth-century bhakti poet Mirabai, her tongue full of barbs for mechanically heed-less modes of worship, declared "Banares and Ganges are found at a holy man's feet!" And in Japan, Dogen Zenji told his students, "No need to wander the dusty coun-tries." A long-standing tradition in India discounts pil-grimage as one of the "easy" practices, contrasted to the notably tough disciplines of yoga, meditation, renuncia-tion, and celibacy. And Saraha and others of his tem-perament insist that Buddha himself is hidden in the practitioner's body. What use all this traveling, to pray at a monument built over a litter of bones?

Yet, having pushed our way through the rigors and austerities, the tough inward labors, the meditations and koans and visualizations, all those dharma combats

8

and the countless Vajrayana prostrations, some of us still burn with a profound hunger we know we can only satisfy by actually journeying to the legendary sites. Mirabai, it turns out, was an avid pilgrim; Saraha wandered so much no one knows quite where he practiced; and Dogen spent twenty years marking the dusty countries with his foot soles before exhorting his students to stay home. These adepts and poets, do not forget, are using a wry topsy-turvy language meant to get under your skin. "Upside-down language" it's called in some sects of tantra. Gary Snyder has pointed out how in the literature of Zen blame is often praise in disguise. In tantra, interdiction regularly serves as the secret goad. Upside-down speech, twisted utterance, hidden teachings.

As so, alert to the ironies, the Buddhist practitioner heads for north India.

Buddhism flowered in India for fifteen hundred years. It grew from a small band of wandering mendicants into a vast civilization. Princes and kings, merchants and philosophers, poets and courtesans, bandits and streetsweepers — all contributed voices and acts to a continent that was already thick with old stories. Architects and sculptors and painters played their roles. The splendid Mahayana sutras of India conjure Buddha worlds "numerous as the grains of sand on the Ganges," and today with a map you can visit thousands of unexcavated ruins. Renowned Buddhist sutras like the Vimalakirti or *Lankavatara* open with a survey of those in attendance: *bhikkhus* and *bhikkhunis* by the thousands, bodhisattvas by the tens of thousands, the nearly numberless gods and goddesses known to Hinduism; and "*devas, nagas, yaksas, gandharvas, asuras, garudas, kinnaras,* and *mahoragas"*— supernatural beings of every conceivable sort. Animals and ghosts appear, warlords and lepers — all are in some sense interchangeable. Thus Ambapali, former courtesan of Vaisali and disciple of the excellent Buddha, fashioned a song:

> *Once I had the body of a queen*
> *Now it's lowly, decrepit, an old house*
> *plaster falling off*
> *Sad but true*

Partly it's this perception of splendor and squalor rubbing against each other that draws you to India: sites where Buddha "turned the wheel of dharma" such as Vulture Peak, Magadha, Anathapindika's garden, or Sravasti, other sites, intimately associated with Buddha's life — Lumbini, his birthplace, Bodh Gaya, where he heroically attained enlightenment, Sarnath, where he first taught, and Kusinagara, where he entered the great nirvana. But if you go with open eyes, there is more — charnel grounds, orphanages, sumptuous palaces, nuclear power plants, devastating slum sectors, holy rivers. How could you pass up an opportunity to visit the Ajanta caves, with their murals that make you weep at past splendor? The pillar-edicts set up by King Asoka? And what of those splendid temples down south?

Yet a thousand years ago the Buddhist civilization that created so much grandeur disappeared. When Hiuen Tsiang visited Bodh Gaya to pay homage to the legendary Bodhi tree under which Buddha had attained enlightenment, a statue of Avalokiteshvara stood alongside it. The pilgrim recounts an old prophecy, that the earth will swallow this statue completely when Buddhism vanishes from India. And with a sharp unsentimental eye Hiuen Tsiang notes that the statue has already sunk in the dirt to its breast, and he gravely observes that in India Buddhism can't last longer than another 150 or 200 years.

He wasn't far off. Except for Magadha and distant Kashmir, between the eighth and ninth centuries Buddhism was driven from India. Twelve hundred years of Moslem then British rule have given it little room to return. The orange robe of the Buddhist pilgrim really only reappeared in our own lifetime. So of that extensive, now legendary civilization, what remains in India on the eve of the twenty-first century? Shattered buildings and sculptures by the thousands, a few careful archaeological renovations, dozens of underfunded regional museums, and a million Buddhist refugees from Tibet. Yet, the sites remain tender and animated. The stories associated with Buddha have lost none of their vibrancy. You have to believe that the *lokapalas* — tutelary deities that guard the local sites — have kept to their job.

Above all, there is India herself — a teeming Buddha world. It draws pilgrims like no other nation. At the Buddhist mountain of Udhayagiri, sitting inside a hermit cave hewn from one massive boulder into the shape of a tiger's head (you go in through the jaws), I wrote in a 1993 journal:

> *I sat here once*
> *a hundred years*
> *and all the women I ever knew*
> *were like a vapor*

Even if you can't get out of Calcutta or Bombay, even if the Buddhist sites prove beyond reach, you can sit in a doorway or hermit cave, or wander on Nimtalla Ghat while corpses turn to ash and vapor over slow stacks of firewood. You can ponder terrible environmental destruction, or the collapse of great empires. Everything, everyone you've ever known, may seem a vapor. During Shakyamuni Buddha's lifetime, his disciple the poet Mahakala composed this terrible song:

This lady who cremates the dead
black as a crow —
she takes an old corpse and breaks off a thighbone,
takes an old corpse and breaks off a forearm,
cracks an old skull and sets it out
like a bowl of milk
for me to look at.

Witless brain don't you get it —?
whatever you do just
ends up here.
Get finished with karma, finished with rebirth —
no more bones of mine
on the slag heap.

It's the same meditation, twenty-five hundred years from Mahakala to Allen Ginsberg's "A body burning in the first ash pit." To sit in a charnel ground and brood on impermanence — "the Way exists but not the traveler on it." To feel the skull under your face. To envision yourself the Old One, the Sick One, the Corpse. To take to the road, spurred by a Buddha's insight. To visit places others have wandered before you, they also spurred on by old stories. Maybe none of this so accommodated into life's daily round as in India these many thousand years.

And so, in your hand — a book: the accounts of what a few travelers found there.

Meeting
the Buddha

On Pilgrimage
in Buddhist India

Lumbini: The tank of Queen Maja

LUMBINI
AND KAPILAVASTU

Where
the Buddha
Was Born and Raised

A noble person is hard to find;
one is not born everywhere.
Wherever such a wise one is born,
that family attains felicity.

What not even a mother, a father, or any other
relative will do, a rightly directed mind does do,
even better.

— *The Dhammapada,*
5th–1st c. B.C.E.,
translated from the Pali by Thomas Cleary

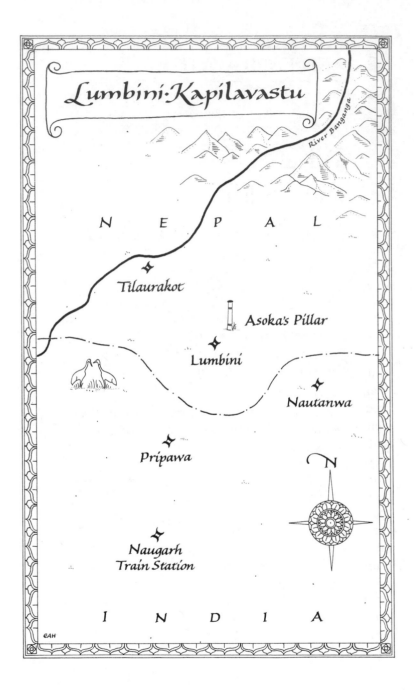

Lumbini·Kapilavastu

River Banganga

N E P A L

Tilaurakot

Asoka's Pillar

Lumbini

Nautanwa

Pripawa

N

Naugarh
Train Station

I N D I A

eAH

*T*he land where Siddhartha the Buddha was born and raised is a place of dreams. Before giving birth to Siddhartha, Queen Maya, it is said, dreamt of a large white elephant entering her body. She related her dream to a pandit, who interpreted its significance before the court at Kapilavastu. The elephant, the pandit explained, was her son Siddhartha, the future Buddha, and the elephant's entrance into her, her son's conception.

The legends describe the Lumbini and Kapilavastu of Siddhartha's youth as beautiful places — verdant and prosperous. But the legends tell us, in Siddhartha's eyes, their beauty and luxuries were as evanescent as dreams. Indeed, while Lumbini has faded into an unspectacular flatness, the site of Kapilavastu, razed at the end of the Buddha's lifetime, has altogether disappeared. Today the region's past beauty lives on only in Buddhist stories, and in the imaginings of inspired pilgrims.

At Lumbini and Kapilavastu, no one has suc-cumbed to dreams of the past more than the area's schol-ars and archaeologists. In 1897, the British government hired Anton Führer to find the ancient town of Kapilavastu, which had been lost for centuries. Führer went to the Nepalese Terai, where the town was believed to exist and, within a short time, began to send reports to his superiors of fantastic successes in the field; he was digging up Buddhist stupas, inscriptions, and relics. His reports were precise. His careful measurements and minute descriptions left no doubt that he had found the real Kapilavastu. Excited, Führer's supervisor paid him an unexpected visit. To his shock, the archaeological site bore no resemblance to Führer's reports. Maddened by his search for fame and facts, Führer had invented nine-tenths of his concrete historical evidence. What he did not invent he had destroyed in a futile search for relics.

In 1976, the site was discovered again, this time

in Piprahwa, a town in India's Uttar Pradesh. Evidence at Piprahwa was more convincing. Archaeologists had found monasteries, seals labeled "Kapilavastu," and a stupa thought to contain a portion of the Buddha's relics. Unfortunately, the evidence at Piprahwa was not conclusive and debates about Kapilavastu's real location continue.

Lumbini undergoes new development even as Kapilavastu waits to be fixed on the map. Lumbini's planners intend to adorn the area with monasteries, a moat, and a nature sanctuary on the one hand, shops, banks, hotels, and a golf course, on the other. Dreams of the past mingle with dreams of the future as the area's planners attempt to evoke Lumbini's ancient glory, while creating a new center of international Buddhist activity.

Queen Maya was on her way to her parents' home when she stopped to give birth in the Lumbini Grove. Her baby son, it is said, bore the thirty-six distinguishing marks of a future Buddha, including webbed fingers & toes and a circle of hair between his brows. Shortly after her baby's birth, Maya's husband, the king of Kapilavastu, invited seers to foretell the prince Siddhartha's future. Recognizing the thirty-six marks, the seer predicted that the baby would become either a universal monarch or a great religious leader.

As the future Buddha or Bodhisattva grew older, his father watched anxiously for signs of spirituality in his son. Hoping to keep the boy at his side, he arranged his son's marriage, built pleasure palaces for Siddhartha, and surrounded him with seductive courtesans. His wife, Yasodhara, bore the Bodhisattva a son named Rahula, further tying the young man to home. Fearing the sequestered prince would remain too naive to fulfill his destiny, the gods placed first an old man, second a sick man, third a dead man, and finally an ascetic on the road outside the city, where they would catch the Bodhisattva's eye on his pleasure rides into the countryside. Disturbed by these sights, Siddhartha resolved to leave the city and look for a solution to the sorrow of impermanence (dukka). Despite his father's best efforts, he turned away from home and family and, exiting Kapilavastu's East Gate, entered upon the life of a wandering ascetic.

I. LUMBINI

Peter Matthiessen, 1978 C.E.

I sit on the top level of the wall, my feet on the step on which the loads are set and my back against a tree. In dry sunshine and the limpid breeze down from the mountains, two black cows are threshing rice, flanks gleaming in the light of afternoon. First the paddy is drained and the rice sickled, then the yoked animals, tied by a long line to a stake in the middle of the rice, are driven round and round in a slowly decreasing circle while children fling the stalks beneath their hooves. Then the stalks are tossed into the air, and the grains beneath swept into baskets to be taken home and winnowed. The fire-coloured dragonflies in the early autumn air, the bent backs in bright reds and yellows, the gleam on the black cattle and wheat stubble, the fresh green of the paddies and the sparkling river — over everything lies an immortal light, like transparent silver.

In the clean air and absence of all sound, of even the simplest machinery — for the track is often tortuous and steep, and fords too many streams, to permit bicycles — in the warmth and harmony and seeming plenty, come whispers of a paradisal age. Apparently the grove

Lumbini: Prayer flags under the Bodhi Tree

of *sal* trees called Lumbini, only thirty miles south of this same tree, in fertile lands north of the Rapti River, has changed little since the sixth century B.C., when Siddhartha Gautama was born there to a rich clan of the Sakya tribe in a kingdom of elephants and tigers. Gautama forsook a life of ease to become a holy mendicant, or "wanderer" — a common practice in northern India even today. Later he was known as Sakyamuni (Sage of the Sakya), and afterward, the Buddha — the Awakened One. Fig trees and the smoke of peasant fires, the greensward and gaunt cattle, white egrets and jungle crows are still seen on the Ganges Plain where Sakyamuni passed his life, from Lumbini south and east to Varanasi (an ancient city even when Gautama came there) and Rajgir and Gaya. Tradition says that he traveled as far north as Kathmandu (even then a prosperous city of the Newars) and preached on the hill of Swayambhunath, among the monkey and the pines.

Queen Maya Gives Birth in the Lumbini Grove

From Asvagosha, **The Buddha-Karita,** *first century* C.E.

Verily the life of women is always darkness, yet when it encountered [Mahamaya], it shone brilliantly; thus the night does not retain its gloom, when it meets with the radiant crescent of the moon.

"This people, being hard to be roused to wonder in their souls, cannot be influenced by me if I come to them beyond their senses,"— so saying Duty abandoned her own subtile nature and made her form visible.

Then falling from the host of beings in the Tushita heaven, and illumining the three worlds, the most excellent of Bodhisattvas [the future Buddha] suddenly entered at a thought into her womb, like the Naga King entering the cave of Nanda.

Assuming the form of a huge elephant white like Himalaya, armed with six tusks, with his face perfumed with flowing ichor, he entered the womb of the queen of King Suddhodana, to destroy the evils of the world. . . .

Maya . . . holding him in her womb, like a line of clouds holding a lightning-flash, relieved the people around her from the sufferings of poverty by raining showers of gifts.

Then one day by the king's permission the queen, having a great longing in her mind, went with the inmates of the gynaeceum into the garden of Lumbini.

As the queen supported herself by a bough which hung laden with a weight of flowers, the Bodhisattva suddenly came forth, cleaving open her womb.

At that time the constellation Pushya was auspicious, and from the side of the queen, who was purified by her vow, her son was born for the welfare of the world, without pain and without illness.

Like the sun bursting from a cloud in the morning, — so he too, when he was born from his mother's womb, made the world bright like gold, bursting forth with his rays which dispelled the darkness.

As was Aurva's birth from the thigh, and Prithu's from the hand, and Mandhatri's, who was like Indra himself, from the forehead, and Kakshivat's from the upper end of the arm, — thus too was his birth [miraculous]. . . .

Unflurried, with the lotus-sign in high relief, far-striding, set down with a stamp, — seven such firm footsteps did he then take, — he who was like the constellation of the seven rishis.

"I am born for supreme knowledge, for the welfare of the world, — thus this is my last birth,"— thus did he of lion gait, gazing at the four quarters, utter a voice full of auspicious meaning. . . .

When he was born, the earth, though fastened down by [Himalaya] the monarch of mountains, shook like a ship tossed by the wind; and from a cloudless sky there fell a shower full of lotuses and water-lilies, and perfumed with sandalwood.

On the Road to Lumbini

Major Rowland Raven-Hart, 1956 C.E.

It was a hot and dusty journey; but I was very fortunate in my travelling-companions. There was a local lawyer, and a doctor (I think the Railway Doctor), and the Sub-Divisional Officer, travelling second-class with us for the sake of company. They were all very interested in my plans. . . . [T]he doctor offered to borrow an elephant for me, but added (advice which I had already received from other sources) that I should do better to relinquish the romance and take a pony: "unless you are a good sailor. When you watch an elephant walking, it looks so smoo-ooth, like floating on soap. But when you are up on it, all the legs are walking as if they hated each other, and you may think there are sixteen legs."

The countryside was disappointingly flat. I had hoped to get into hillocks at least, heralding the Hills, and to see these in the distance; but the Indian plains continue well into Nepal before the foothills rise suddenly from them; and clouds curtain the snows except in the mornings or rarer evenings. Sugar was the main dull crop of those dull plains, but relieved by patches of forest and by fine groves at the stations: mango, rose-apple, mahua, neem chiefly. . . .

Except for the Himalayas to the north it was not a picturesque route. Except for them; but, oh Lord! the glory of those pearl-polished eternal snows, rising to twenty-six thousand feet behind their wine-purple foothills a mere twenty-five miles away, and backed by a shrill blue sky which seemed nearer than the peaks. We had them for a few morning hours only, after the sun had licked up their level garlands of mist: then billows of white cloud swamped them. One must live in flatlands for years, as I had done, to realise at the sight of the Hills how one has missed them; and to add to my joy in them was the thought that here, at least, was a sight that the Buddha must also have loved as a boy.

Perhaps, too, something of the keen crystal of those peaks has entered into Buddhism: as the endless, implacable desert into Islam, or the labyrinthine magnificence of the forests into Hinduism. . . .

We had many rivers to cross. I kept no log, but would estimate that there were four big ones, although the last of them, the nearest to Lumbini, was almost dry; and another four smaller streams; and a dozen or more of irrigation-watercourses, often only a couple of yards across but surprisingly deep — I crossed most of them on pony-back, and often had to hoist my long legs up onto his neck to keep my sandals dry. One or two had remnants of bridges, over which I teetered in trepidation: the guide would not trust his pony to them but forded the channels. . . .

The ferry, at the one river that was too deep to ford, was a proud and ancient craft, some twenty-five feet long, poled to and fro, with a raised decking at the stern. Most of the planks of this decking were loose, and some were missing: after distributing the baggage so as to block the larger holes, the pony was persuaded aboard, to my surprise and somewhat to the alarm of two country-women who crossed with us. . . .

This ferry was at a village. Our course lay, in fact, from village to village, the cool-shady mango-grove of the next-to-come always visible as we left each. It is traditional for the Indian village to have a grove, though in the days of the Buddha they were more probably of sal up here, clumps deliberately left when clearing the virgin forest. Such a grove was (and is) also traditionally the meeting place . . . where the Buddha so often preached to villagers.

We made a couple of short halts in those mango-groves. . . . They give a solid shade, but the leathery, dead-green leaves are crowded at the ends of the branches, so that one looks up into bare boughs of an interwoven complexity like the ribs of a futuristic umbrella, as hypnotic as a Cretan labyrinth-ornament. Often, when my eyes had been enmeshed there, a slant of sunlight below was the Lord's yellow robe, as he passed through the shade on the

24

way to his daily Alms-round for his one daily meal.

Apart from the mango-groves, there was no temptation to linger in the villages. Nepalese villages are rarely attractive. The standard "eligible residence" is a windowless, smoke-filled hovel, the once-whitewashed mud walls ornamented with cow-dung cakes, drying there for use as fuel, further impoverishing the land. Pumpkin vines did their best here to cover walls and roofs, their yellow flares welcome patches of brightness. There was of course no sanitation, and the neighbourhood of watercourses and ponds stank to Beelzebub, who provided the serried cohorts of flies that they demanded. . . .

John Blofeld, 1956 C.E.

At the time of my visit to Lumbini, the road had not quite been completed, so I decided to make the journey from the rail-head on horseback, starting at dawn. I set off on a thin, hired nag along a sandy track which led me through the rice-fields and across several streams where the villagers were performing the ablutions with which each Hindu day begins. They were standing up to their waists in water, laving themselves from brass pots, India's inevitable *lotas* [water pots]. The men's bodies, burnt copper by the sun, glistened as the water slid over them; the women were fully dressed as if they had been standing on dry land. If the ford lay far from a village, instead of bathers there would be brightly plumaged birds pausing in their morning drink to stare superciliously at the clumsy human intruder on a strange, four-legged beast and the tattered figure (my guide) who slouched beside. Presently the green vegetation grew sparser; I could almost see the implacable advance of the yellow sand which, by a process of erosion, is rapidly turning this part of hungry India into a desert. By now the sun stood high in a brazen sky and the temperature had almost reached its peak for that day — I learnt later that it had been 116 degrees in the shade. A burning wind sprayed me with coarse particles of sand, clogging eyes and nostrils and rasping my throat. I had never in my life experienced such cruel discomfort, but I knew the worse would follow, for the blisteringly hot ride back to the rail-head would have to be accomplished that afternoon. Foolishly I had brought no hat and was wearing a short-sleeved bush-shirt, so that my lower arms were in danger of having all the skin burned off their upper surface.

Barbara Crosette, 1994 C.E.

On an initial visit to the archaeological center, I went by taxi (arranged with advance notice by the hotel). Next day, I switched to a bicycle, and that made all the difference. Pedaling along still-earthen roads that traverse the site on its north-south axis — lanes more jarring to cars than bikes — makes it possible to listen to those zephyr breezes and see small pictures of life that would otherwise be missed: a village boy fishing with a bamboo pole in water that will soon be channeled into the park, a woman and her little son eating lunch in the shade of Buddha's trees. The people who live around Lumbini are mostly Hindus and Moslems, said Nirmala Nanda Bhikku, the abbot and only resident monk at the Theravada temple. "There's not a Buddhist in sight," he reassured me. The Bhikku allows families from the neighborhood to harvest and sell the mangoes from more than a hundred trees in his monastic grove; it brings them a welcome added income.

In the Lumbini Grove

From the Introduction to the Jataka, 5th–1st c. B.C.E.

[T]here was a pleasure-grove of sal-trees, called

Lumbini Grove. And at this particular time this grove was one mass of flowers from the ground to the topmost branches, while amongst the branches and flowers hummed swarms of bees of the five different colors, and flocks of various kinds of birds flew about warbling sweetly. Throughout the whole of Lumbini Grove the scene resembled the Cittalaka Grove in Indra's paradise, or the magnificently decorated banqueting pavilion of some potent king.

Hiuen Tsiang, mid-seventh century C.E.

To the northeast of the *arrow well* about 80 or 90 li, we come to the Lumbini . . . garden. Here is the bathing tank of the Sakyas, the water of which is bright and clear as a mirror, and the surface covered with a mixture of flowers.

To the north of this 24 or 25 paces there is an *Asoka-flower* tree, which is now decayed; this is the place where Bodhisattva was born on the eighth day of the second half of the month called Vaisakha, which corresponds with us to the eighth day of the third month. . . .

East from this is a *stupa* built by Asoka-raja, on the spot where the two dragons bathed the body of the prince. When Bodhisattva was born, he walked without assistance in the direction of the four quarters, seven paces in each direction, and said, "I am the only lord in heaven and earth; from this time forth my births are finished." Where his feet had trod there sprang up great lotus flowers. Moreover, two dragons sprang forth, and, fixed in the air, poured down the one a cold and the other a warm water stream from his mouth, to wash the prince.

To the east of this *stupa* are two fountains of pure water, by the side of which have been built two *stupas*. This is the place where two dragons appeared from the earth. When Bodhisattva was born, the attendants and household relations hastened in every direction to find water for the use of the child. At this time two springs gurgled forth from the earth just before the queen, the one cold, the other warm, using which they bathed him.

Maha Sthavira Sangharakshita (D. P. E. Lingwood), 1949 C.E.

During the couple of days that we spent at Lumbini our feelings were divided between joy at being at the very spot where the future Buddha had first seen the light of day, and a sense of regret, even outrage, at the desolate and neglected appearance of the sacred place. It was as though the tide of Buddhist revival, which flowed strongly at Sarnath, and none too feebly at Kusinara, had as yet hardly touched Lumbini. The only modern building to be seen was the Rest House erected by the Government of Nepal for the benefit of pilgrims, where we installed ourselves soon after our arrival, and where the caretakers provided us with a meal. Those other than pilgrims found it convenient to use the Rest House, however. Either because there was no other accommodation, or because in the land of autocracy even the lowest representative of authority was accustomed to behave in a high-handed manner, touring government officials regularly treated it as a sort of caravanserai. On the evening of our arrival a police inspector turned up with twenty of his men and soon the peace and silence of the place were lost in uproar. Next day it was even worse. While their master was busy squeezing money from the local landlords, who from time to time arrived on elephants, bearing with them the customary gifts, some of the inspector's men slaughtered a goat in the compound and without removing its hair, hide or anything else cooked it whole over an open fire. Though Munindra, Arun Chandra and Thaung Aung were by no means vegetarians, on seeing this gruesome sight all five members of our little party felt like making a strong protest. But on reflection we decided not to do so. The police inspector had been drinking since early morning, and to judge from the way in which he was behaving with the landlords he was not the sort of person who would be amenable to reason. All the same, we could not help thinking how sad it was that the First Precept, the precept of abstaining from injury to any living being, should be so flagrantly violated in the very birthplace of the Buddha.

V. S. Naravane, 1965 C.E.

[T]hroughout our journey to Lumbini we pass through a backward, undeveloped area. As we drive from Gorakhpur to the border town of Nautanwa, and then again as we cover the ten miles from Nautanwa to Lumbini on elephant-back, we find that neither nature nor human ingenuity has anything exceptional to offer us. And yet, in spite of the uninteresting landscape, the drabness all around, and the utter absence of any architectural remains, we cannot help being stirred to our depths at the very sight of Asoka's pillar. A saffron-robed *bhikku* stands serenely in a corner with a dreamy, far-away look in his eyes. There is no bustle, no persuasion, no supplication. Beggars do not remind us of the rewards awaiting the charitable in heaven; priests do not solicit our co-operation in the task of saving our own souls; double-locked doors do not hide the deity. All we have here is the pillar of Asoka, two tiny mounds of earth to mark the excavation of some relics, and a small temple with an image of Queen Maya delivering Siddhartha. The legends we have heard or read do the rest, and we are satisfied.

John Blofeld, 1956 C.E.

After tethering my horse and resting awhile, I went in search of the stump of a stone commemoration

29

pillar erected there almost two thousand three hundred years ago by the Emperor Ashoka who, having conquered all India by fire and sword, lived to become a devoted peaceful servant of the Compassionate One and the leading Buddhist missionary of all time. The remaining stump was too meagre to be at all impressive except on account of its history. Yet, mindful that I was on pilgrimage, I seated myself nearby, composed my mind reverently and entered upon a discursive meditation, trying to evoke the scene of the sacred birth which had taken place on or very near the spot indicated by the base of the Ashokan pillar. Presently, I entered upon a vivid daydream.

Before me stood a deliciously cool and shady forest of sal trees all laden with scarlet flowers and surrounded by mile upon mile of fertile fields. In the distance, a glittering cavalcade was approaching. Messengers rode before, proclaiming that Her Majesty Queen Mayadevi was returning to her father's house, there to await the birth of her royal child, whom the astrologers had foretold might one day rule the earth. The cavalcade drew near. I saw warriors in snow-white *dhoti*, [cloth worn around the waist] behelmeted and mailed in chain of silver; courtiers in coloured silks with graceful curved swords supported by golden chains worn across their naked breasts; women unveiled in the ancient style, but with the outlines of their figures modestly concealed beneath fold upon fold of their gold-bordered saris. Chariots followed, drawn by white oxen with gilded horns, and at last a palanquin carried upon the shoulders of three score bearers, its heavy silken canopy hiding the lovely Queen who sat within. Presently a tiny hand emerged and gestured lightly to a courtier riding a white and strawberry horse close to the palanquin's left. A word of command was barked down the line and the procession halted. Women hastened forward from their places behind the royal palanquin, their saris aflutter;

and from within stepped down a lady, her outer garment a simple sari of silver-edged white silk gauze; her lovely docile face full with the fullness of approaching mother-hood; her eyes alight with pleasure as she gazed at the scarlet clusters upon the sal trees. Smiling to her ladies, she walked slowly towards the welcoming shade of the forest, moving cautiously lest she stumble and hurt her precious burden. Beneath the finest tree of all, which flaunted its scarlet beauty as though contemptuous of mere human adornment, she stopped and raised her hand, supporting the weight of her body upon a heavily laden branch. That which was about to befall no man dare even try to imagine. I knew that her child would be born even as she stood upright leaning upon that lov-ingly offered branch. Hurriedly I turned away my head — or, rather, I opened my eyes to the hot glare.

Gone were forest, smiling fields, thrice-blessed Queen and cavalcade. There was nothing in sight but the burning ugliness of the present. Yet I felt beautifully refreshed. I was smiling and inclined to sing. What I had seen had been neither dream nor vision. I had merely shut my eyes and deliberately induced a picture of the events which have made Lumbini a place ever to be remembered. But either the magic of the place itself as the repository of sublime thoughts proceeding from the hearts of generation upon generation of pilgrims, or else the state of mind which the mere thought of being in Lumbini induced, had clad my imagining in such rich colours that I felt like a man awakened from a delicious dream — a dream so real that even the lotus-shaped henna stain upon Queen Mayadevi's palm remained imprinted on my memory. Though the journey back to the rail-head proved as physically painful as I had feared, there was such a sense of gladness in my heart that bod-ily fatigue had no power to distress me. I knew that my journey to that grim-looking place had not been in vain, for "neither poppy nor mandagora" could have induced such vivid and lovely thoughts in any other setting than sacred Lumbini.

Lumbini's Monuments

In 1896, the German archaeologist Anton Führer found a broken Asokan pillar and identified the site where it lay as the Lumbini Grove. Sixty-two years later, in 1958, King Mahendra of Nepal donated money for the site's rehabilitation. Around this time, the United Nations was funding excavations in the area as well. Established in 1970, the Lumbini Development Committee sketched out extensive plans for the Grove's further development. Though work is ongoing at the site, progress, under the committee's aegis, is slow.

TILLAR NADI — THE RIVER OF OIL

Known as the river of oil, the Tillar Nadi, where Queen Maya bathed after giving birth to the future Buddha, lies to the southeast of the Asokan pillar.

From Tibetan Works in the Bkah-Hgyur *and* Bstan-Hgyur, 8th–14th c. C.E.
In accordance with what happens at the birth of every Buddha, there fell on his head a stream of cold water and one of warm, which washed him, and at the spot where he had been born there appeared a spring in which his mother bathed.

Hiuen Tsiang, mid-seventh century C.E.
[There] is a little river which flows to the southeast. The people of the place call it the *river of oil*. This is the stream which the Devas caused to appear as a pure

and glistening pool for the queen, when she had brought forth her child, to wash and purify herself in. Now it is changed and become a river, the stream of which is still unctuous.

THE ASOKAN PILLAR

King of the Mauryan Empire, Asoka ruled over most of what is now present-day India. In the early years of his reign, Asoka waged war against the Kalingas of Orissa. Though victorious, he was repulsed by the war's brutality and decided to embrace nonviolence and the Buddhist dharma. He proclaimed his change of heart to the public in a number of stone inscriptions engraved on cliff faces and pillars throughout his empire. Asokan pillars erected at or en route to several Buddhist pilgrimage sites fed legends, like the Asokavadana, *which portrayed the king as an ideal Buddhist ruler and pilgrim. An inscription appears at the base of the Asokan pillar in Lumbini recording Asoka's pilgrimage to the Grove.*

From the Asokavadana, second century C.E.
Upagupta took [Asoka] to the Lumbini Wood, and stretching out his right hand he said: "In this place, great king, the Blessed One was born."
And he added:

This is the first of the caityas
of the Buddha whose eye is supreme.
Here, as soon as he was born,
the Sage took seven steps on the earth,
looked down at the four directions,
and spoke these words:
"This is my last birth
I'll not dwell in a womb again."

Asoka threw himself at Upagupta's feet, and getting up, he said, weeping and making an anjali:

They are fortunate and of great merit
those who witnessed
the birth of the Sage
and heard his delightful voice.

Now for the sake of further increasing the king's faith, the elder asked Asoka whether he would like to see the deity

who witnessed in this wood the birth
of the most eloquent Sage,
saw him take the seven steps,
and heard the words he spoke.

Asoka replied that he would. Upagupta, therefore, stretched out his right hand toward the tree whose branch Queen Mahamaya had grasped while giving birth, and declared:

Let the divine maiden who resides in this asoka tree
and who witnessed the birth of the Buddha
make herself manifest in her own body
so that King Asoka's faith will grow greater still.

And immediately, the tree spirit appeared before Upagupta in her own form, and said, making an anjali:

Elder, what is your command?

The elder said to Asoka: "Great king, here is the goddess who saw the Buddha at the time of his birth."
Asoka said to her, making an anjali:

The Asokan Pillar at Lumbini

You witnessed his birth and saw
his body adorned with the marks!
You gazed upon his large lotus-like eyes!
You heard in this wood
the first delightful words
of the leader of mankind!

The tree spirit replied:

I did indeed witness the birth of the best of men,
the Teacher who dazzled like gold.
I saw him take the seven steps,
and also heard his words.

"Tell me, goddess," said Asoka, "what was it like
— the magnificent moment of the Blessed One's birth?"
"I cannot possibly fully describe it in words,"
answered the deity, "but, in brief, listen":

Throughout Indra's three-fold world,
there shone a supernatural light,
dazzling like gold and delighting the eye.
The earth and its mountains, ringed by the ocean,
shook like a ship being tossed at sea.

Hearing this, Asoka made an offering of one
hundred thousand pieces of gold to the birthplace of the
Buddha [and] built a caitya there.

King Asoka, the Rummindei Pillar Edict, an inscrip-
tion in Brahmi found at the base of the Asokan pillar
in Lumbini, 274–232 B.C.E.
Twenty years after his coronation, King Priyadarsi
[Asoka], Beloved of the Gods, visited this place in person
and worshiped here because the Buddha, the Sage of the
Sakyas, was born here.

He ordered a stone wall to be constructed
around the place and erected this stone pillar to commemorate his visit.

He declared the village of Lumbini (now
Rummindei) free of taxes and required to pay only one-
eighth of its produce (about half the usual amount) as
land revenue.

Hiuen Tsiang, mid-seventh century C.E.

In Hiuen Tsiang's day, the Asokan pillar had already fallen in two. During his visit, Tsiang saw

. . . a great stone pillar, on the top of which is the figure of a horse, which was built by Asoka-raja. Afterwards, by the contrivance of a wicked dragon, it was broken off in the middle and fell to the ground.

Maha Sthavira Sangharakshita (D. P. E. Lingwood), 1949 C.E.

[T]he Asokan Pillar nearby . . . stood beneath the open sky behind a low railing. On its highly polished surface the ancient Brahmi letters were cut deep and clear, and we could still spell out the announcement "Here the Blessed One was born." For some reason or other, I felt even more deeply moved here than I had done at either Sarnath or Kusinara. The truncated stone shaft stood so calmly and so simply beneath the cloudless blue sky; it seemed so unpretentious, and yet to mean so much. Lingering behind when Buddharakshita and the others had moved on in the direction of the mounds, I gathered some small white flowers and with a full heart scattered them over the railing at the foot of the column. As I did so I heard Buddharakshita's voice. "What are you messing about with those flowers for?" he shouted roughly. "Come on, we can't wait for you all day!"

THE TEMPLE OF QUEEN MAYA

Queen Maya's temple is said to rest on the foundations of an Asokan monument and the temple's relief sculpture to have been commissioned by the Mall kings of the Naga Dynasty, rulers of southern Nepal between the eleventh and fifteenth centuries.

Maha Sthavira Sangharakshita (D. P. E. Lingwood), 1949 C.E.

Apart from the two mounds, which rose like two volcanic islands out of a perfect sea of loose bricks, and seemed to have once formed the lower half of twin stupas, the only ancient building of which any trace remained above ground was the Rumindei Temple. This was so small as to be a chapel rather than a temple, and in an extremely dilapidated, not to say ruinous, condition. On our first visit to the place, soon after our arrival, we found the door locked, and it was not until the evening of our second day at Lumbini that it was opened by the old Hindu woman who kept the key and was responsible, so it seemed, for the rudimentary worship that kept alive the religious traditions of the place. The interior of the temple was disappointing. The only object of interest was a stone slab so well worn, and so thickly smeared with vermilion, that the figure of Mahamaya holding onto the branch of a sal tree as she stood giving birth to the future Teacher of Gods and Men was barely discernible. On our questioning the old woman it soon became clear that she had not even heard of the Buddha or of Buddhism and that she was under the impression that the temple was dedicated to a Hindu goddess.

S. R. Wijayatilake, 1963 C.E.

Adjacent to the Asokan pillar is the *Maya Devi temple.* It is obviously a recent structure, crude and incongruous. However, this temple contains a significant piece of sculpture depicting the birth of the little Siddhartha. Queen Maya Devi is shown holding the branch of a sal tree and the baby prince emerging from a side. Unfortunately, misguided devotees have daubed the place with oil and paint. . . .

Let us pause for a moment and take our minds

back to that day of nearly 2,600 years ago. We could see the caravanserai making its way from Kapilavastu on its way to Devadeha — the home of Queen Maha Maya. Here is an oasis of sal trees with a beautiful pool of fresh water with the Vesak lotus in full bloom. The Queen looks out of her palanquin and is delighted. The order goes out that Her Majesty would like to rest here a while and enjoy the beauty of the scene with the snowcapped mountains of the Himalayan range in the dim distance. . . .

Maha Maya could feel the pangs of birth come one after another. Maha Prajapathi helps her on and the attendants hurriedly make an enclosure with their colourful sarees in the sal grove.

Maha Maya inclines on a sal tree for support and with ease she delivers herself of the Prince who is Siddhartha. . . . Never was there so much joyousness in Lumbini. The full moon showed itself slipping out from a dark cloud and lit up the countryside with a radiance that was seen for miles around. It is curious that a little of this radiance is still in the air even now. This is singular about this little hamlet of Lumbini.

II. KAPILAVASTU

The mind is restless, unsteady, hard to guard,
hard to control. The wise one makes it straight,
like a fletcher straightens an arrow.

Like a fish out of water, cast on dry ground,
this mind flops around trying to escape
the realm of bedevilment.

> — *The Dhammapada,*
> *5th–1st c. B.C.E.,*
> *translated from the Pali by Thomas Cleary.*

Kapilavastu: Ruins of the Palace

From Asvagosha, The Buddha-Karita, *first century C.E.*

There was a city, the dwelling-place of the great saint Kapilaa, having its sides surrounded by the beauty of a lofty broad table-land as by a line of clouds, and itself, with its high-soaring palaces, immersed in the sky.

By its pure and lofty system of government it, as it were, stole the splendour of the clouds of Mount Kailasa, and while it bore the clouds which came to it through a mistake, it fulfilled the imagination which had led them thither.

In that city, shining with the splendour of gems, darkness like poverty could find no place; prosperity shone resplendently, as with a smile, from the joy of dwelling with such surpassingly excellent citizens.

With its festive arbours, its arched gateways and pinnacles, it was radiant with jewels in every dwelling; and unable to find any other rival in the world, it could only feel emulation with its own houses.

There the sun, even although he had retired, was unable to scorn the moon-like faces of its women which put the lotuses to shame, and as if from the access of passion, hurried towards the western ocean to enter the [cooling] water. . . .

After mocking the water-lilies even at night by the moonbeams which rest on its silver pavilions, — by day it assumed the brightness of the lotuses through the sunbeams falling on its golden palaces.

Attachments:
Growing Up in Kapilavastu

THE LAND

From *Sir Edwin Arnold*, Light of Asia, 1879 C.E.

Arnold's verses are full of rich Victorian descriptions of Buddha's India. Here, Arnold imagines Kapilavastu's king taking his son on a tour of the kingdom. He hopes young Siddhartha will become attached to the bounty and beauty of the realm:

> *"Come, Sweet son! and see the the pleasaunce of the*
> *spring,*
> *And how the fruitful earth is wooed to yield*
> *Its riches to the reaper; how my realm —*
> *Which shall be thine when the pile flames for me —*

Feeds all its mouths and keeps the King's
chest filled." . . .

All things spoke peace and plenty, and the Prince
Saw and rejoiced. But, looking deep, he saw
The thorns which grow upon this rose of life:
How the swart peasant sweated for his wage,
Toiling for leave to live; and how he urged
The great-eyed oxen through the flaming hours,
Goading their velvet flanks: then marked he, too,
How lizard fed on ant, and snake on him,
And kite on both; and how the fish-hawk robbed
The fish-tiger of that which it had seized;
The shrike chasing the bulbul, which did hunt
The jewelled butterflies; till everywhere
Each slew a slayer and in turn was slain,
Life living upon death. So the fair show
Veiled one vast, savage, grim conspiracy
Of mutual murder, from the worm to man,
Who himself kills his fellow; seeing which —
The hungry ploughman and his labouring kine,
Their dewlaps blistered with the bitter yoke,
The rage to live which makes all living strife —
The Prince Siddhartha sighed. "Is this," he said,
"That happy earth they brought me forth to see?
How salt with sweat the peasant's bread! how hard
The oxen's service! in the brake how fierce
The war of weak and strong! I' th'air what plots!
No refuge e'en in water. Go aside
A space, and let me muse on what ye show."

THE PALACE

From the **Abhiniskramanasutra,** *circa 70* C.E.

And now the Prince, growing up by degrees,
reached his nineteenth year. And when at this age, the

father Suddhodana Raja caused three Palaces to be constructed for him, each of them for a different season of the year. The first a warm palace, calculated for the winter; the second a cool palace, for the summer; the third fit for the spring and autumn. . . .

Moreover, the prince was surrounded by servants both male and female, brought up on the purest food. The Prince himself partook only of the daintiest fare, and every sort of luscious fruit. Thus every day and every night brought him some fresh joy and pleasant diversion, protected by a beautiful white umbrella during the day, and sleeping under the finest gauze canopies by night.

MARRIAGE

From Asvagosha, The Buddha-Karita, *first century* C.E.

[The king] sought for him from a family of unblemished moral excellence a bride possessed of beauty, modesty, and gentle bearing, of wide-spread glory, Yasodhara by name, having a name well worthy of her, a very goddess of good fortune.

Then after that the prince, beloved of the king his father, he who was like Sanatkumara, rejoiced in the society of that Sakya princess as the thousand-eyed [Indra] rejoiced with his bride Saki.

THE OLD MAN, THE SICK MAN, THE DEAD MAN, AND THE ASCETIC

From Tibetan Works in the Bkah-Hgyur *and* Bstan-Hgyur, *8th–14th c.* C.E.

One day the prince told Tchandaka [his charioteer] that he wanted to go drive in the park, and while there he saw an old man, and the charioteer explained what old age was and how all were subject to it. . . . Deeply impressed, the prince turned back and went home.

A short time after, while out driving, he met a dropsical man . . . emaciated, weak, with faculties impaired . . . and Tchandaka told him what disease was . . . and again he turned back.

Another time he came across a procession bearing along on a litter, with burning torches, something wrapped in many-coloured stuffs. [T]he women accompanying it had dishevelled hair and were crying piteously. It was a corpse, Tchandaka told him, and to this state all must come. . . .

And yet on another occasion he met a deva of the pure abode who had assumed the appearance of a shaved and shorn mendicant, bearing an alms-bowl and going from door to door. The charioteer told him that he was one who has forsaken the world, a righteous, virtuous man, who wandered here and there begging wherewith to satisfy his wants. . . . So the Bodhisattva drove up to him and questioned him about himself, and received the same answer. Then pensively he drove back to the palace.

From the Introduction to the Jataka, *5th–1st c. B.C.E.,* to *1st century C.E.*

And the Future Buddha entered his palace in great splendor and lay on his couch of state. And straightway richly dressed women, skilled in all manner of dance and song, and beautiful as celestial nymphs, gathered about him with all kinds of musical instruments, and with dance, song, and music they endeavored to please him. But the Future Buddha's aversion to passion did not allow him to take pleasure in the spectacle, and he fell into a brief slumber. And the women, exclaiming, "He for whose sake we should perform has fallen asleep. Of what use is it to weary ourselves any longer?" threw their various instruments on the ground and lay down. And the lamps fed with sweet-smelling oil continued to burn. And the Future Buddha awoke, and

Kapilavastu: Stupa where relics of the Buddha were found

seating himself cross-legged on his couch, perceived these women lying asleep, with their musical instruments scattered about them on the floor, — some with their bodies wet with trickling phlegm and spittle; some grinding their teeth, and muttering and talking in their sleep; some with their mouths open; and some with their dress fallen apart so as plainly to disclose their loathsome nakedness. This great alteration in their appearance still further increased his aversion for sensual pleasures. To him that magnificent apartment, as splendid as the palace of Sakka, began to seem like a cemetery filled with dead bodies impaled and left to rot; and the three modes of existence appeared like houses all ablaze. And breathing forth the solemn utterance, "How oppressive and stifling is it all!" his mind turned ardently to retiring from the world. "It behooves me to go forth on the Great Retirement this very day," said he; and he arose from his couch, and coming near the door, called out, —

"Who's there?"

"Master, it is I, Channa," replied the courtier who had been sleeping with his head on the threshold.

"I wish to go forth on the Great Retirement to-day. Saddle a horse for me."

"Yes, sire." And taking saddle and bridle with him, the courtier started for the stable. There, by the light of lamps fed with sweet-smelling oils, he perceived the mighty steed Kanthaka in his pleasant quarters, under a canopy of cloth beautified with a pattern of jasmine flowers. "This is the one for me to saddle to-day," thought he; and he saddled Kanthaka. . . .

Now Kanthaka was eighteen cubits long from his neck to his tail, and of corresponding height; he was strong and swift, and white all over like a polished conch-shell. If he neighed or stamped, the sound was so loud as to spread through the whole city; therefore the gods exerted their power, and muffled the sound of his neighing, so that no one heard it; and at every step he took, they placed the palms of their hands under his feet.

The Future Buddha rode on the mighty back of the mighty steed, made Channa hold on by the tail, and so arrived at midnight at the great gate of the city. . . .

Thus the Future Buddha . . . departed from the city in great splendor on the full-moon day of the month Asalhi, when the moon was in Libra. And when he had gone out from the city, he became desirous of looking back at it; but no sooner had the thought arisen in his mind, than the broad earth, seeming to fear lest the Great Being might neglect to perform the act of looking back, split and turned round like a potter's wheel. When the Future Buddha had stood a while facing the city and gazing upon it, and had indicated in that place the spot for the "Shrine of the Turning Back of Kanthaka," he turned Kanthaka in the direction in which he meant to go, and proceeded on his way in great honor and exceeding glory.

The Rediscoveries of Kapilavastu: Tilaurkot or Piprahwa?

Purna Chandra Mukherji, 1899 C.E.

In 1898, Mr. Mukherji was hired to conduct archaeological surveys in the Nepalese Terai in order to pinpoint Kapilavastu's location. He was taking over the job from the German archaeologist Anton Führer, who appears to have lost his mind looking for the ancient site. Falsifying his data, Führer damaged important monuments in his mad search for relics.

[Dr. Führer] went from Nigliva to Rummin-dei, where another Priyadarsi *Lat* [Asokan pillar] had been discovered; and an inscription, about 3 feet below surface, had been opened by the Nepalese. The inscription recorded the fact of King Priyadarsi's visiting Lumbinigrama, where Buddha was born, in the 21st year of his reign. This fact, with the name of Rummin-dei, — the corruption of Lumbinidevi, — at once set at rest all doubts as to the exact site of the traditional birth-place of Gautama Buddha. The key to the site of Kapilavstu being thus found, Dr. Führer went north-west and very vaguely located the site amidst jungles and the villages of Ahirauli, Siunagar, and Ramapura on the south, and Jagdispur on the north. . . .

In 1898, Dr. Führer was again deputed to the Tarai to assist the Nepal Government with advice and suggestions as regards the best course to be followed in the excavation on the sites of Kapilavastu; for which purpose the Darbar had sanctioned a sum of Rs. 2,000. Finding some ruined mounds in the forest of Sagarva, and near the tank Sagar, from whence the village-name is derived, the Doctor halted here for about two months, superintending the excavations, which had been commenced in the previous year. . . . Excavations were started on 22nd December 1897, and continued till the beginning of March 1898; about 200 coolie, mostly *Tharus*, being employed for a week at a time, who returned to their villages; and then a fresh relay of labourers took their place. Several Stupas were found and ruthlessly destroyed. The large number of the Stupas, which he identified as the "Massacred of the Sakya," were no sooner traced than destroyed in the hope of finding relics, which, however, were very poor, consisting of a few carved bricks, relic-vessels or caskets, containing some gold *Nagas*, greenish crystals, beads, ruby, and pieces of bones. His alleged discovery of several inscriptions in "pre-Asoka" characters has been proved to be not based on facts. Altogether his results were very unsatisfactory and not less conflicting.

Mr. Vincent Smith, 1899 C.E.

Vincent Smith, Führer and Mukherji's supervisor, visited Führer in the field, only to discover that Führer's fabulous discoveries were wholesale fabrications. In volume 26 of the Archaeological Survey of India, *Smith touches on Führer's misinformation.*

[Dr. Führer']s fictions about the Konagamana *stupa* and pillar do not stand alone. The inscriptions of the Sakyas alleged to have been found in the small *stupas* at Sagarwa are impudent forgeries, and when Dr. Führer supplied the Burmese priest U Ma with sham relics of Buddha, he endeavored to support the imposition by a forged inscription of Upagupta, the *guru* of Asoka. In the course of my official duty the whole case was investigated by me, and no doubt as to the facts is possible. I find that the reserved language used in previous official documents has been sometimes misinterpreted, and it is now necessary in the interests of truth to speak out plainly. . . .

[R]easons will be given for believing that the pillar lying at the Nigali Sagar has been moved about eight or thirteen miles from its original position which was probably either at Sisania or at Palta Devi. It is impossible Konagamana's *stupa* should have stood anywhere near Nigliva. The belief that it ought to have been found near that village was so strongly held by Dr. Führer that it induced him to invent the *stupa* which he could not discover; and to place at the basis of the pillar a foundation "of imagination all compact."

Purna Chandra Mukherji, 1899 C.E.

By the time Mukherji began his surveys, the site of Lumbini was well established. Assuming Kapilavastu to lie near Lumbini (known in the nineteenth century as Rummindei), Mukherji began his search in Queen Maya's grove.

Since there is no map of the Tarai, it is not easy to examine the region of the ancient and now forgotten Sakya-kingdom. There is no road in any direction, the pedestrians travelling in the fields and across *nullahs* and streams, which are seldom bridged. The cart track is so circuitous, that it takes at least double the direct distance before the bullock carts reach their destination.

The Tarai is a flat country, crossed by mountain streams, which flow from north to south, and at short distances from one another. . . . The Tarai (literally *Talai* from Sanskrit *Tala* — below or lower region) is generally cultivated, excepting those parts, which are covered with forests. . . . Since the forests are all reserved by the Nepal Government, nobody being allowed to cut even for fuel, they are full of wild animals, which generally intrude upon the neighbouring villages; as I saw one tiger almost attacking me one day near the ruins of Tilaurakot; so that exploration of the ruins was not altogether without risks and difficulties. . . .

To map out this tract, which was the first duty entrusted to me, required a good deal of travelling in different directions, for which purpose I had insufficient time. I had only one or two marches, while removing my camp. . . . I had therefore to consult the little compass attached to my watch, or the sun, while journeying, — and thus took the bearings. And counting the distance by the hours of march, and from what I heard from the villagers, I jotted down from memory what I saw when I reached camp. . . .

I marched, on 11th March, towards Rummin-dei, the Lumbini-vana of the Buddhistic geography, which I reached the next day.

After clearing the jungles, I minutely examined the big mound and set the Nepalese coolies to excavate at the promising places. From the very commencement, the diggings brought out to light several remains. . . . The principal find was the anterior temple of Mayadevi, of which the beautifully ornamented plinth in brick exists. Remains of several small Stupas and other edifices were also exposed.

On the 19th, I visited the ruins of Saina Maina at the foot of the hills and hidden in the thick forest of sal. The days became so hot now that the Nepalese Captain and his men left for the hills; and myself and my draftsman fell sick. Finishing, therefore, my survey, and taking photographs, as quickly I could, I left Rummin-dei on the 29 March. . . .

In my late tour I was rather badly equipped; for both the Survey and Drawing implements and the photographic apparatus were old and not in good order, which gave me a great deal of trouble in my work. I was allowed only one draftsman, and he joined me late. And my work grew so much in exploration, direction, supervision of excavations and taking notes, that I hardly found time for drawing on the spot. I took several sketches with detailed measurements. And latterly my draftsman and I fell sick. Though labouring under these disadvantages, I succeeded in gathering a mass of information and illustrations and made a lot of discoveries, of which the identification of Kapilavastu might be the most important.

Putting Kapilavastu on the Pilgrimage Map

With two major (and several minor) locations being identified as Kapilavastu, travelers looking for authenticity rarely attempt to visit any of the contending sites. Among those who have made the trip, John Huntington chose to visit the Tilaurkot Kapilavastu and Noeyal Peiris, Piprahwa.

TILAURKOT

John Huntington, 1985 C.E.
As immigration regulations permit foreigners to cross the border only at Saunali, one goes to Lumbini first and then follows the new highway in progress to Kapilavastu. (On the day of this author's trip to Kapilavastu in December 1984, the highway was indeed still very much "in progress" and, on several occasions, impromptu fordings, detours and repairs to the road surface had to be made to facilitate progress along it. Once at the Kapilavastu site, however, staff from the Royal Nepalese Department of Archaeology showed the greatest courtesy and were immensely helpful in making sure that the most important features of the site were visited.) Two *stupa* bases . . . both much damaged by flooding of the Banganga River . . . are on the west side of the ruins of the site. These two *stupas* have been identified by recent finds of Gupta period seals as the *stupas* of Suddhodana and Mayadevi, the parents of the Buddha. While these seals do not constitute conclusive proof of

the identification of the early site, they provide identification of what was, in effect, the *de facto* site for several centuries, presumably most of the pre-Christian era and early Christian era periods.

What remains of the palace area . . . is the brick foundations of the relatively modest structures in the centre of a walled enclosure. While the bricks are of the Kusana period, they rest on Maurya remains, which in turn (presumably) rest on pre-Maurya (Sakya) remains. If this is the case, the structure is small by standards for even modest Asian palaces but in keeping with the remains of structures at Rajagrha . . . of approximately the same period. Ultimately, it is the eastern gate of the walled area . . . the gate of the Great Departure (Mahabhiniskramana), that is the most important spot of the site. It is through this portal that the Bodhisattva, with his groom Chandaka and mounted on the horse Kanthaka, departed the material world of sense-desire. As one looks at this gate, one has to envision what this action must have meant for the young prince who had never known anything but the luxury of the palace, and whose infant son was yet to be born, and whose profound family ties to his father and aunt could only have beckoned him back.

PIPRAHWA

Noeyal Peiris, 1976 C.E.

A Sri Lankan Buddhist, Noeyal Peiris took a vow to bring relics of the Buddha back to Sri Lanka. The discovery of Kapilavastu in northern Uttar Pradesh was announced in the paper during Peiris's trip to India, and he immediately went to visit the excavations, arranging to bring several relics from the site back to Sri Lanka, and, later, organizing a celebration of Vesakha, the Buddha's birthday, to be held at the newly unearthed Kapilavastu.

Mr. Siriwardene showed me a paper cutting of the Times of India, New Delhi, dated 24th January, 1976. There were in big letters, the words, LOST CITY OF KAPILAVASTU FOUND. Mr. Siriwardene gave it to me and said, "Give some publicity to it as it is very important to us Buddhists in Sri Lanka." I thanked him and took the paper cutting and seeing it, I said, "What? To give publicity? Not only publicity, I must go to this place and see it for myself before going back to Sri Lanka. I must see it and try and develop it so that all other Buddhists of the world may be able to pay their respects to the place where Prince Siddhartha spent 29 years, at Kapilavastu. It was in this place that he got the idea to go all out to see what could be done to stop Suffering, disease, old age and death. . . ."

On the 1st of February, 1976, we left by the 7 A.M. bus from Naughar to Birdpur, a distance of 9 miles, and from there we took a Cycle-Rickshaw to Kapilavastu which is in India, and not in Nepal — a distance of another 6 miles. We met one of the Archaeological Department employees walking to Kapilavastu; we got him also into the Rickshaw as we were all going to the Piprahwa Camp site where all the officers and men were working. We could go only 3 miles by Rickshaw as the road was not yet built. We all had to get down from the Rickshaw and walk because the road was sandy. When I wanted to walk my American friend told me not to get down and walk because I had with me another Robe and the Relics Casket. He made me sit in the Rickshaw and he pushed it along with the other 2 persons and we reached the Piprahwa Camp site, a distance of another 3 miles, shortly afterwards.

Seeing the canvas tents I was overjoyed; there were about 300 men working and 15 officers of the Archaeological Survey of India. We all went to the site and met Mr. Lal Chand Singh, the Technical Assistant, who greeted us and was very happy to see us. He was also very happy to hear that I was a Buddhist from Sri Lanka and that my friend, Mr. Alexander Rybalkin, was from the USA. He served us with tea and was very happy to take us round the ruins excavated so far, and explained all that they had excavated. . . . It was really a moving experience to see such a vast place being excavated; the whole area was about 25 square miles. This was the Holy Land where our Prince Siddhartha had lived for 29 years and left to find a way to save all humanity from Suffering, old age, disease and death. . . .

We went down 24 feet to the Relic Chamber, which they had excavated and where they found the Soapstone Casket with the charred bones of Lord Buddha, the one-eighth portion of the Corporeal Relics of the Buddha given to the relations of the Buddha, who were the Sakya people. I went down the ladder to the very place where the Casket was unearthed by Mr. Srivastava. I placed the sacred Robe that I had brought all the way from Sri Lanka, lighted 7 coconut oil lamps I had also brought with me, placed the small silver casket I had brought on the Robe I had brought to be offered at Bodhgaya, and started chanting Pirith, with my friend Alexander by my side.

I could not finish chanting, when tears started pouring down from my eyes; I could not even chant the Karaniya Metta Sutta halfway. I just could not chant. There was no sound. I was spellbound as the Spiritual Vibrations were so very powerful in that place. I have no words to explain the feelings about that Holy Place as I have never visited such a place before. Not only did tears come to my eyes, but my whole body was vibrating with that Spiritual Force which developed in that place. . . .

I had the most exciting experience of my whole life when I went down the ladder to the Relic Chamber of the Nigrodhaya Chaithiya built by King Kanista. I placed the Yellow Robe and my own Relic Casket, and lighted the 7 oil lamps which I had been doing all along at all the places that I had been trying to develop in Sri Lanka — the ancient irrigation tanks, the ruins of ancient monuments, including the colossal Buddha Statue at Maligawila. I made an Aditthana (resolution) and searched for some Relics, and to my utter surprise and overwhelming joy I was able to find and obtain two Relics from the very place the Casket of the Relics of the Buddha had been found. My request and Aditthana were that if I get some Relics I will come back and observe Ata-Sil at this Stupa, and light oil lamps and chant Pirith and observe the 2600th Birth Anniversary of Prince Siddhartha at the very site of this Stupa, with some Buddhist Monks from Sri Lanka. It was with this Aditthana that I was able to find the two Relics of the Buddha at that very place where the Relic Caskets were placed thousands of years back, by the relations of the Buddha, the Sakyawansa people. I placed the two Relics I was able to find, inside my Silver Casket wherein I had some other Relics which had helped and given me the opportunity to go all the way to India, to find this valuable and most spiritually powerful place in the world — Kapilavastu — Piprahwa.

The Mahabodhi temple

BODH GAYA
(Bodhgaya; Buddha Gaya)

Where the Buddha Attained Enlightenment

*I have gone through many repeated beginnings
seeking without finding the maker of this house;
it is miserable to start over again and again.*

*You have been seen, maker of the house;
you will not rebuild again.
Your framing is all broken,
your ridgepole destroyed.
The mind set on detachment from created things
has attained extinction of craving.*

— *The Dhammapada,*
1st–5th c. B.C.E.,
translated from the Pali by Thomas Cleary

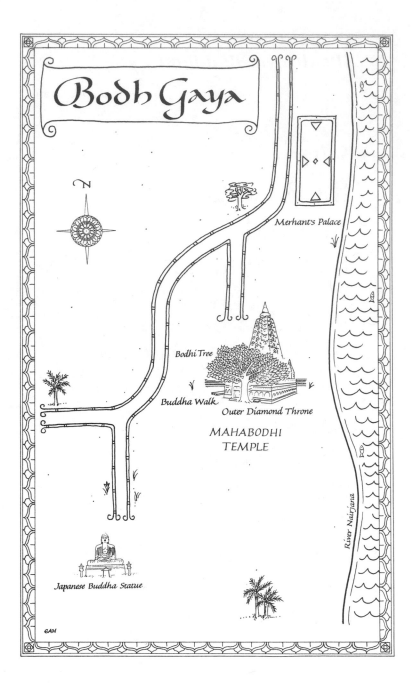

Bodh Gaya

N

Merhant's Palace

Bodhi Tree

Buddha Walk

Outer Diamond Throne

MAHABODHI
TEMPLE

River Nairjana

Japanese Buddha Statue

EAH

*T*he Bodh Gaya Temple complex lies in a depression. Approaching the area from a high vantage point, travelers see at first glance all the site's principal features spread out before them — the Bodhi tree, the diamond throne, the soaring temple, whose floor E. M. Forster describes lit up by candlelight like "a lake of fire." To the reader, the image of fire may suggest an arrival at night. Yet, most travelers will arrive at Bodh Gaya, where the Buddha attained enlightenment, in broad daylight, under a hot sun, and most will enter the town on a bus. Indian buses are always interesting but never calming. Landscapes are unfamiliar, children whisper *"angrezi"* (English person!), women are brilliantly clothed, men wear fascinating headdresses, pilgrims appear out the left window, and the vehicle lurches and heaves in complicated road traffic.

Compared to the problems of the early pilgrims, these distractions are nothing. The modern traveler need not walk all the way and fight off armed bandits as the Chinese pilgrim I-Tsing did. To honor the Buddha's enlightenment, a testimony to the powers of mental discipline, pilgrims often prepare themselves to enter Bodh Gaya with an altered state of consciousness, walking the distance on foot, reciting prayers at every step, even prostrating themselves hundreds, sometimes thousands, of times. From pilgrimage accounts, it becomes apparent that many people have been affected by this extraordinary place and have succeeded, despite the distractions of the journey, to prepare themselves for their own moment under the Bodhi tree.

Six years passed between Siddhartha's departure from Kapilavastu and his arrival in Bodh Gaya. After leaving his home and family, Siddhartha cut off his hair, traded his fine clothes for the plain garb of a hunter whom he had met in the woods, and entered upon the "homeless life." As he passed into the forests outside Kapilavastu, Siddhartha became one of many wanderers and ascetics in India who had, like him, left home and family to seek or teach unorthodox beliefs and practices. Still a young novice, Siddhartha hoped to find among these wanderers older and wiser teachers who could show him an escape from the cycle of death and suffering. He consulted two teachers famous in the region, Alara and Kalampa. When they were unable to answer all of his questions, he turned to asceticism. Perhaps, he thought, through self-mortification and intense meditation, he would gain the understanding of suffering which his teachers had failed to impart. For six years, he lived with five ascetics, eating, in a full day, no more than a grain of rice or a berry. His flesh fell away and his body became ghastly, skeletal and weak. Still he did not attain the enlightenment he was seeking. He was too frail, he realized, to progress on the path to perfect wisdom. "This is not the way to passionlessness, nor to perfect knowledge, nor to liberation." Giving up the ascetic's life, Siddhartha accepted a bowl of milk from a young girl named Sujata. Strengthened, he sought the shade of a large fig tree, sat down, and resolved to remain in that position until he had achieved enlightenment. When he sat down, he was still what Buddhists call a bodhisattva. With his enlightenment, he became for his followers the Buddha.

The spot under the fig or Bodhi tree where the Buddha attained nirvana is a kind of geographical omphalus or axis mundi for the Buddhists. Buddhism was conceived under the Bodhi tree, the only spot on earth, the texts tell us, which was perfectly stable. Despite Bodh Gaya's importance to Buddhists, the area fell into decay for hundreds of years. During this time, the Mahabodhi Temple became the residence of a Saivite priest, and the

Bodhi tree an object of Hindu worship. The area came to Buddhist attention in the early 1900s when the author of The Light of Asia, Sir Edwin Arnold, made a plea for its restoration. Bodh Gaya has since been transformed into an important Buddhist center of meditation and devotion. Its decay and resurrection are chronicled in pilgrim accounts from the seventh to the twentieth centuries.

On the Road to Bodh Gaya

Through the efforts of two men, Sir Edwin Arnold and the Sri Lankan Angarika Dharmapala, Bodh Gaya's restoration became a Buddhist cause celebre. The area was not only dilapidated, it had fallen under Hindu control. Efforts to wrest the Mahabodhi Temple from a Saivite priest, in addition to British archaeological investigation of the site, brought Bodh Gaya to the attention of Western travelers and British colonists. The site's pilgrimage record, broken in the thirteenth century, was resumed at the end of the 1700s.

From the Introduction to the Jataka, 5th–1st c. B.C.E.

[T]he Future Buddha took his noonday rest on the banks of the river, in a grove of sal-trees in full bloom. And at nightfall, at the time the flowers droop on their stalks, he rose up, like a lion when he bestirs himself, and went towards the Bo-tree, along a road which the gods had decked.

I-Tsing, 671–695 C.E.

At a distance of ten days' journey from the Mahabodhi Vihara [in Bodh Gaya] we passed a great mountain and bogs; the pass is dangerous and difficult to cross. It is important to go in a company of several men, and never to proceed alone. At that time I, I-Tsing, was attacked by an illness of the season; my body was fatigued and without strength. I sought to follow the company of merchants, but tarrying and suffering as I was, became unable to reach them. Although I exerted myself and wanted to proceed, yet I was obliged to stop a hundred times in going five Chinese miles. There were there about twenty priests of Nalanda, and with them the venerable Teng, who had all gone on in advance. I alone remained behind, and walked in the dangerous defiles without a companion. Late in the day, when the sun was about to set, some mountain brigands made their appearance; drawing a bow and shouting aloud, they came and glared at me, and one after another insulted me. First they stripped me of my upper robe, and then took off my under garment. All the straps and girdles that were with me they snatched away also. I thought at that time, indeed, that my last farewell to this world was at hand, and that I should not fulfil my wish of a pilgrimage to the holy places. Moreover, if my limbs were thus pierced by the points of their lances, I could never succeed in carrying out the original enterprise so long meditated. Besides, there was a rumour in the country of the West (India) that, when they took a white man, they killed him to offer a sacrifice to heaven (Devas). When I thought of this tale, my dismay grew twice as much. Thereupon I entered into a muddy hole, and besmeared all my body with mud. I covered myself with leaves, and supporting myself on a stick, I advanced slowly.

The evening of the day came, and the place of rest was as yet distant. At the second watch of night I reached my fellow-travellers. I heard the venerable Teng calling out for me with a loud voice from outside the village. When we met together, he kindly gave me a robe, and I washed my body in a pond and then came into the village. Proceeding northwards for a few days from that village, we arrived first at Nalanda and worshipped the Root Temple (Mulagandhakuti), and we ascended the Gridhrakuta (Vulture) mountain, where we saw the spot on which the garments were folded. Afterwards we came to the Mahabodhi Vihara. . . .

Hye Ch'o, 724 C.E.

. . . I arrived at the Mahabodhi monastery. I was very happy as my long cherished wish had been fulfilled. I expressed my humble wishes in a five-word poem:

> *Untroubled by the distance to Mahabodhi*
> *Unafraid that the Deer Park is so far,*
> *Only the dangerous path worried me.*
> *Not caring how the evil wind blows.*
> *To visit the eight stupas is truly not easy.*
> *All places were burnt.*
> *How then could one's desire be fulfilled?*
> *With my eyes I saw it this very day.*

Paul Deussen, 1893 C.E.

[We] got into the most miserable of country carts, to have ourselves jolted along a fine broad road, through wooded fields, to Buddha-Gaya, a distance of about one hour and a half. The place consists of a cluster of houses by the wayside; to the left of the road lies a monastery of Brahman *Sadhus*, while to the right lies a great temple of Buddha in a hollow, care having been taken to prevent the debris of ages raising the level of the soil. This is surely the spot where the sublime one sat under a fig tree in that great night in which he received his Buddhahood, for Buddha lived long enough to point out the exact spot to his numerous disciples. . . . In Buddha-Gaya, as everywhere else in India, there was not a single Buddhist to be found, with whom we might have exchanged impressions.

Eliza Ruhamah Scidmore, 1903 C.E.

It was a raw January morning, with the yellow dust whirling in clouds, when I reached Gaya station on my pilgrimage to the Tree of Knowledge, and it was a cold, dull, prosaic drive of a mile in a rattling gharry to Gaya town and the dak bangla, where the government provided chill cheer for the few European travelers who ever rest there. One elephant passed by on the station road, — a touch of the ancient East, the Hindu India, that did not accord with the background of barbed-wire fences, telegraph poles, and railway tracks, nor with the well-metaled highway of British India that the creature trod upon. A string of dusty brown camels filed across the neutral, dusty distance, and turbaned folk sped by in bullock-carts or gay *ekkas*, the native cabs, mere curtained canopies hung with balls and bells, and the ponies caparisoned to match, with high, peaked collars and blue bead necklaces. . . .

The road southward for seven miles to Buddha-Gaya was broad, smooth, and well made, shaded with tamarisk- and bo-trees, strung along with little hamlets and mud huts, and following the banks of the Phalgu River. Each group of dwellings had its common well, and, under some wide-spreading tree, a plastered-up terrace or altar supported a tiny shrine, or the greasy image of a Hindu god, — this the same pagan, heathen India, the life little changed since the all-perfect Gautama Buddha used to pass this way in his yellow robes, with his golden begging-bowl and a glory of six cubits height extending around his head. Brown fields stretched on either hand; brown hills bounded the view; and narrow streams loitered here and there among the stones of the broad, sandy river-bed. A few bare-footed people moved by in silence, and the brown monotony, the comforting warmth of the hot midday sun, and the quivering heat-rays in the air, soon gave an eerie, unreal look to things, a strange, hazy, hypnotic effect, a sense of dreamy spell.

We turned from the Gaya road to a massive white gateway, where sheeted Brahmans and turbaned folk lay in leisured wait for us, and noble white bullocks rested beside tilted carts that had brought priestly visitors to this Sannyasi or Saivite college of Buddha-Gaya. A much-marked Brahman, with the sacred white thread across his shoulder, led us off by a sandy path toward the pinnacle of a temple roof just showing beyond some tree-tops, when suddenly all Mahabodhi, the Place of Great Intelligence, was revealed to us.

Gary Snyder, 1962 C.E.

Riding the "Up Doon Express" — Joanne slept on newspapers in the aisle, I sat crosslegged over bundles. 6 a.m. in the town of Gaya, Joanne and me off. Still six miles to Bodh Gaya, the place where Sakyamuni Buddha achieved enlightenment. Outside the Gaya station, first sight of Tibetans, camped in the shelter of an old building under a verandah roof. Droopy wine-red coats tied up at the waist, felt and leather boots. They have indeed the famous warm "rancid yak butter" smell, mixed with old leather — not unpleasant! And they are dirty with long greasy hair and heavy jade or turquoise jewelry. The weather noticeably cooler here than it was in the south, Joanne was wearing a shawl she'd bought in Calcutta, and me my sweaters.

Bodh Gaya: Rickshaws push around — but we want to take the bus from Gaya to Bodh Gaya — after walking a turn round the square before the railway station, and seeing no bus stop, we have tea (next to a man neatly preparing to make up the day's supply of betel to sell — washing off the mixing board, and bronze utensils shiny and ready) — Joanne takes a double portion of milk tea in her tall white enamel cup, then I go look back of the brick shed where the Tibetans are sacked out —

husky ragged-haired kid far taller than me, can't make out if it's a girl or boy — mukluk-like boots, he looks and smiles at me — I walk over a floor of people rising and dressing in hunks of sheep-skin, tattered felt, rough chunks of silver and heavy beads — long hair, the men's uncombed forever; the women's worked into braids or coils. Through them, and beyond, still no sign of where to catch a bus. Then one Indian comes up and asks what I want. I say the bus to Bodh Gaya. He leads me back across the square inside the train depot and up to the tourist information bureau — it is open now. I go in and there is a young fellow behind a desk talking to a pair of yellow-robed Bhikkus. I ask where do you catch the bus for Bodh Gaya? He says: "The bus stand. And that is about a mile away, pay 4 annas for a cycle-rickshaw." I go back outside and ask the first cycle-shaw boy that comes up how much to the bus stand? 4 annas? He says o.k. But he gets lost as I push over to the tea-stand where I left Joanne and our two rucksacks perched on an upturned bench spotted with crow-droppings from the tree above, a rookery. (Why do crows like trains? The third train station I've seen since Ceylon with a rookery nearby.) We pick up our gear and start arguing about fare with another cycle-shaw. A Tibetan Lama suddenly appeared with a huge smile saying "six annas." Then I spied the boy who tagged me as I came out of the station, and he again said 4 annas, so off we go with him, Joanne and me both, and two rucksacks. Finally the bus stand. The bus (with all signs written in the Devanagari script, hence incomprehensible) is empty. We get in. The time is now about 7 a.m. The bus is supposed to leave at 7:30, but at 7:10 the bus pulls out (we are eating funny sweet cakes), and after a bit of wriggling about town we are pulling in at the railway station again! 10 or 15 Burmese Bhikkus load aboard. Back then to the bus stand and 7:30 departure. Passing along the road, and along the Lilajan river. Pony cartloads of Tibetans. At the edge of Bodh Gaya village the bus stops and the driver says "Burmese temple" — the Bhikkus clamber out. A long discussion, Burmese laymen interpreting, between the Bhikkus and the driver — at length the driver climbs back aboard. A Bhikku comes back up to his window asking "are you satisfied?"

A short ways to Bodh Gaya village, narrowing and dirty, houses and road turn and up a hill the bus halts under a tree. Mahabodhi temple tower on one side, a tent-camp of Tibetans on the other.

Joanne Kyger, 1962 C.E.

Got off train in Gaya at 6 a.m. Gary chilled and angry because I am wearing his parka; my clothes too fancy to get dirty on a train trip. Here we catch our first glimpse of Tibetans camped around. A pedicab driver, magnificently mild mannered in comparison to the others, leisurely and blandly takes us a mile away to the bus to Bodhgaya — pointing to the wrong bus when we ask him which one. The bus then goes back to the RR station and picks up a troupe of yellow robed Burmese monks. Here I discover the excellent sunglasses I bought in Singapore have been squashed and broken during the night.

Groves of trees with clean swept ground beneath, herd of cows sent through. Pigs with long bristled backs.

Kate Wheeler, 1990 C.E.

I first visited Bodh Gaya in 1990, a time when I had troubling spiritual questions to resolve. After working for thirteen years with Buddhist teachers, I felt a subtle, nagging, profound sense of dishonesty which resulted, as sufferings tend to do, from incomplete realization. Somehow I'd let my teacher's truths supersede my own vision and experience; sometimes I said things to others that I didn't really believe. That first trip to Bodh Gaya, then, was a move toward seeing truly and authoritatively for myself — a move which, ironically, is at the heart of all Buddhist doctrines. At the time I didn't know what I was looking for, exactly, except for hoping there'd be some subtle scent, some clue under the Bodhi tree. Something that would lead me toward freedom from this heart's oppression.

I traveled more or less nonstop from Boston, meeting a friend in London. The last leg of our journey was a 48 hour train ride from New Delhi to Patna in a second class carriage. That ride certainly qualifies among the ordeals that make a pilgrimage worth writing home about. My companion and I had not understood that we needed to pack enough drinking water and food for the trip; instead we drank spiced black tea from vendors' kettles, ate the bananas and glucose biscuits available on station platforms at the longer stops. We also tasted the sweetness of tiny, dark orange, dried apricots, gifts from a passel of giggling maroon-robed Buddhist nuns from Ladakh. We all beamed at each other, delighted to recognize fellow travelers to Bodh Gaya, but soon had to scurry back to defend our seats from scores of ticketless passengers. These piled onto the train at every village, huddling even in the stinking lavatory, like crouching mummies with their heads covered in grimy gray shawls. As night fell, people urged us to abandon our seats, suggesting that Bodh Gaya was the very next stop. We'd better make for the door or we'd miss it, they warned; but we stayed put. Ten hours later, the train still hurtled through the dark, stopping in town after town where these people would have been content to strand us.

An obese Hindu holy man played upon our sympathies. "I am so tired," he wheedled, though he had just boarded the train. "So tired of standing. Please let me sit with you. I will only take little space." As he held up finger and thumb, showing how few millimeters he planned to occupy, my friend whispered, "Don't you dare give up your seat!" If she hadn't been there to scold me into assertiveness, I'd have succumbed to the holy man. Surely he and his thinner, but hardly ill-fed attendant waiting eagerly behind him would have expanded their millimeters until I was on the floor with the majority.

The train arrived at two a.m., 18 hours late, in Patna, a town we had fervently hoped to reach in daylight. Bandits thrive in Bihar, now one of India's poorest, most brutal regions. Cutthroats own the roads after dark. Landowners keep private armies to suppress peasants into virtual slavery. Elections are bloodbaths: the state's reigning prime minister has been convicted of three murders. That night in Patna Station, the waiting room looked like a bomb shelter, crowded with huddled, sleeping human forms. All hotels in visible range were vehemently shut for the night, their facades padlocked behind accordion bars of iron. My friend and I took a chance on a rickshaw driver who promised to find us beds; our hearts pounded as he towed us slowly out of the station's lighted purlieu. Soon, all we could see was the eyewhites and an occasional coppery reflection on a cheek, as people watched us by the glow of tiny dung or charcoal fires. I thought of wolves; but for them, it was simply too cold for sleep. That foggy night, its temperature just above freezing, a hundred people had died of cold in Patna. So we learned a few days after this arrival.

Turning onto a side alley, our rickshaw man stopped below a neon sign proclaiming Hotel Kailash. Loudly he knocked, and was answered by loud, wet, tubercular coughing and hacking. Finally a sleepy landlord poked his head out, and said yes, there was a room, with a large bed into which we gratefully fell. I awoke with the worst headache I'd ever had in my life, the consequence of the sugary, dehydrating diet on the train.

Out we went in search of food — protein! Just down the
alley, a man was squatting in a box amongst lidded alu-
minum pots. As we asked to see their contents, a rat
poked its head out between rice and cold, creamed
spinach. We walked on, and happily found, instead, a
man with a gas burner who fried us numerous fresh
omelets with cilantro and tomatoes.

I don't remember what conveyance took us to
Bodh Gaya, that time, but my memory of the road is
indelible. Its scenes have altered greatly since the
Buddha, but in India, there is something timelessly simple about human relationship to land. This dry, wide
riverbed, its white dust traversed by beaten paths, was
the same river where the milkmaid Sujata offered the
Buddha a meal of rice. One of those distant, humpy hills
is Vulture Peak, site of the famous sermon. These feathery, green, spreading trees, palms and sals and ficus scattered across the flats, must have been the same species
that once constituted the forest groves where, in ancient
times, ascetics loved to practice. Women still carry water,
sometimes in plastic jugs, but sometimes, still, in brass
and pottery jars.

Entering the village, we passed the gates of the
Burmese Vihar, haven beloved of travelers; then, the
white plaster bust of Gandhi, nearly unrecognizable with
his Groucho Marx grin and round eyeglasses freshly painted in shiny black enamel. Suddenly the stupa shot up on
the left, intricately carved stone piercing the sky. All these
sights, and others, have become landmarks in my imagination, instead of the novelties they were then. But when
I returned to Bodh Gaya, I saw them with the same emotions, a fizzy excitement mixed with reassuring certitude,
as if the Vihar, the Gandhi statue, and the stupa, were
unchanging parts of some ancestral home. On that second trip, I understood that even the first time I visited
Bodh Gaya, my feelings were those of a person returning.

Sandy Boucher, 1991 C.E.

The train from Benares was to leave at 5:15 this morning.

We slept badly. Mosquitoes foraged in the room, tormenting us all night. It was too hot to hide completely under the sheet. Out of a light sleep I would hear that grating whine close to my ear, then feel the touch of an insect landing on my neck. Brush it off. Sleep again. Whine. And so on.

The Benares train station looked like a circle of Dante's hell. At 5:00 a.m. the huge lobby was crammed with sleeping people, bodies curled under filthy wraps, a few people sitting up to look dazedly around. Fires sent up smoke. Cows wandered among the sleeping bodies. Chai vendors and newspaper sellers shouted.

We had seen it from the street the night before: a strange, smoky place full of moving bodies, cooking fires. Now we were in it, stepping carefully among the men, women and children on the floor, looking down into large dark drowsy eyes. In this early morning relative quiet, the sounds echoed sepulchrally. My heart lurched; I felt lost, sunk in a space between lives, without direction, without foundation.

For two hours we waited on the train platform. I watched the people around us, men and women huddled in shawls against the dawn chill, and thought how many human histories were embodied here, opaque to me. I imagined spending a month in this station with tape recorder and interpreter. An epic novel lies unwritten in the Benares train station.

Our "deluxe" first-class ticket (at 135 rupees — about $4.50) bought us a pleasant three-hour ride to the city of Gaya, jumping-off place for Bodh Gaya.

We hired a moto-rickshaw in Gaya and set off on a wild ride, sputtering through narrow streets filled with trucks, busses, bicycle rickshaws, moto-rickshaws, taxis,

71

A monk looks through the garlanded railing surrounding the Mahabohdi Temple

bicycles, pedestrians, cows, goats, water buffaloes, chickens and donkeys. I recalled that the biggest cause of tourist fatalities in Asia is traffic accidents. Somehow we threaded our way through it all and arrived safely at Bodh Gaya.

From the Introduction to the Jataka, 5th–1st c. B.C.E.

[T]he Future Buddha turned his back to the trunk of the Bo-tree and faced the east. And making the mighty resolution, "Let my skin, and sinews, and bones become dry, and welcome! and let all the flesh and blood in my body dry up! but never from this seat will I stir, until I have attained the supreme and absolute wisdom!" he sat himself down cross-legged in an unconquerable position, from which not even the descent of a hundred thunder-bolts at once could have dislodged him.

Mara's Temptations

When Gautama sat beneath the pipal tree, temptations assailed him in the form of Mara and his armies. The episode resonates in the minds of Westerners familiar with Christian scenes of temptation. Scholars have sought the origin of the Christian devil in the Buddhist figure of Mara. If Mara is the forefather of Satan, the bloated, toothy grotesques in Mara's armies presage the bands of demons who appear in the West's medieval tympanums and manuscripts. The temptation of Gautama is a more or less metaphorical tale in Buddhist literature. Some descriptions paint a literal picture of malevolent ghouls. Others transform the demons into personifications of Buddhist sins. Excerpted below, the most famous Western biography of the Buddha, Sir Edwin Arnold's nineteenth-century Light of Asia, *takes great care to distance itself from the spectral unreality of the scene, suggesting that Buddha* struggled not with spooks and demons but with the "fell spirits of his inmost heart." However, this "rationalist's" interpretation is nothing new; the temptation of Gautama has always contained a metaphorical dimension.

From the Mongolian Lalitavistara, 1323–28 C.E.

Mara, referred to in this version of the story as the "Simnu," assembles his troops for the attack:

> go [there] with our army, and reduce that monk who is
> going to become Buddha to nothing. "Let us go!"
> [The Simnu] . . . gathered all the Simnus
>
> Who possessed the strength of foremost heroes,
> who had ferocious faces [such as] never before
> were seen,
> who were carrying swords, spears,
> and various knives. . . .
>
> Who had lumpy and bald foreheads,
> who had large bellies and fat bodies,
>
> Who had mouths with thick lips,
> whose faces were on [their] shoulderblades and chests;
>
> Who had protruding and high noses,
> and glowing eyes like fire;
>
> Who had crooked and bared teeth
> and ears like those of deer and elk;
>
> With body hair standing up
> like tridents or awls;
>
> With long and hanging lips,
> with glittering red tongues;

With snouts of sea-monsters and garudas,
with buffalo heads;

With elephant, horse and fox heads,
some [of them] with lion and tiger heads;

Headless and many-headed,
and also, with many arms and many legs;

Such ones [as those] around whose joints of legs and
arms inflated snakes had wound;

Such ones [as those] who made black and green snakes
come out of their nostrils and mouths;

Who had bellies like sacks and jugs,
who had mouths and teeth on their bellies;

Some of them swallowing a whole man,
some of them eating [only] the kidneys and livers;

Emitting shouts [like] "Hulu Bishi,"
uttering evil sounds [like] "Hulu Hulu!"

Who were of motley colors
and had frightening bodies;

He gathered all [such] Simnus,
who were in the three thousand worlds.

Their poisonous evil steam [from their mouths was]
like black rain clouds.

Their knives with sharp blades
[were] like lightning which flashes in the sky. . . .

for a distance of eighty miles, they circled and danced
with no space between them.

"Seize [him], bind [him], chop [him]!"
With [such] evil shouts would they frighten [him]. . . .

They would frighten him
by tearing their bellies open and showing [him] their
intestines.

They would extract snakes from the openings in their
faces,
they would roll their eyes and lips.

Baring their teeth,
they would frighten and startle him, shouting "Take
[this]!"

Shrunken and contracted old women,
clasping their hands and beating their breasts,

Shouted: "My elder, you will be killed,
Ah, get up and flee!"

From Sir Edwin Arnold, The Light of Asia, *1879* C.E.

The "sins" arrive in the shape of demons:

The ten chief sins came — Mara's mighty ones,
Angels of evil — Attavada first,
The Sin of Self . . .
Then came wan
Doubt . . .
Next there drew
Gallantly nigh a braver Tempter, he,
Kama, the King of passions, who hath sway

Over the gods themselves, Lord of all loves,
Ruler of Pleasure's realm. Laughing he came
Unto the Tree, bearing his bow of gold
Wreathed with red blooms, and arrows of desire
Pointed with five-tongued delicate flame, which stings
The heart it smites sharper than poisoned barb:
And round him came into that lonely place
Bands of bright shapes with heavenly eyes and lips
Singing in lovely words the praise of Love
To music of invisible sweet chords,
So witching, that it seemed the night stood still
To hear them, and the listening stars and moon
Paused in their orbits while these hymned to Buddh
Of lost delights, . . .

But Buddh heeded not,
Sitting serene, with perfect virtue walled
As is a stronghold by its gates and ramps;
Also the Sacred Tree — the Bodhi-tree —
Amid that tumult stirred not, but each leaf
Glistened as still as when on moonlit eves
No zephyr spills the gathering gems of dew;
For all this clamour raged outside the shade
Spread by those cloistered stems. . . .

Exploring Bodh Gaya

As the place where the Buddha gained enlightenment, Bodh Gaya is the most important site on the
Buddhist pilgrimage map. In the words of one pilgrim: "If
the Buddha was born in Lumbini, Buddhism was born in
Bodh Gaya." Bodh Gaya has probably drawn more
tourists and pilgrims over the last hundred years than the
other seven sites combined. The area was carefully restored
in the nineteenth century. In the twentieth century, it has

become an international center of Buddhist activity. The traveler's private response to Bodh Gaya is often punctuated by a sense of community, shared with the people who converge there from all over the world.

Anne Cushman, 1993 C.E.

In the hot, dusty countryside on the outskirts of Bodh Gaya, India, not much has changed since a wandering ascetic named Siddhartha Gautama first passed through 2,500 years ago. Men in white dhotis still guide plows drawn by water buffalo through a patchwork of brown and green fields. Golden haystacks shaped like stupas shimmer next to acres of mustard and lentils. Women in saris carry baskets of grain on their heads down crooked dirt alleys roamed by chickens, pigs, and hump-backed Brahman bulls.

Hiuen Tsiang, mid-seventh century C.E.

Rare trees with their renowned flowers connect their shade and cast their shadows; the delicate *sha* herb and different shrubs carpet the soil. The principal gate opens to the east, opposite the Nairanjana river. The southern gate adjoins a great flowery bank. The western side is blocked up and difficult of access *(steep and strong).* The northern gate opens into the great *sangharama.* Within the surrounding wall the sacred traces touch one another in all directions. Here there are *stupas,* in another place *viharas.* The kings, princes, and great personages throughout all Jambudvipa, who have accepted the bequeathed teaching as handed down to them, have erected these monuments as memorials.

Elizabeth Ruhamah Scidmore, 1903 C.E.

The sunken courtyard of the Sacred Bo-tree lay at our feet, and a great nine-storied, pyramidal temple soared one hundred and sixty feet in air, seemingly perfect in every line, from foundation-stone to the gilded pineapple pinnacle, — precisely the temple built in the second or in the third century, as may some time be agreed upon, but certainly the temple that Hiouen Thsang saw. There was, at the first glance, nothing ruinous or hoary or venerable about the apparently well-preserved monument. The good repair was too disenchantingly obtrusive and conspicuous, and for sentiment's sake one would almost rather have seen the temple crumbling and vine-grown in a rubbish-choked court, as it was in 1860. There was a chilling neatness and a forbidding order, too, about the crowded monuments, remains of monuments, and foundations of monuments in that flagged area thirty feet below us, which told of the archaeologist with his tape-measure, his numbers and labels, the restorer with his healing plaster and illusive cement. The view came so suddenly, there was such silence, with no moving object anywhere in sight, that it was as unreal as if a vast drop-curtain had blocked the path. The silence, too, was befitting the sacred place, the actual scene of the great penance and struggle, the illumining of the Light of Asia, the birthplace of India's noblest religious system, a place hallowed by the traditions and associations of twenty-five centuries of religious life. No other visitors, not a pilgrim nor a worshiper, came to that court for hours. Our melancholy Moslem servant, the big, sheeted Brahman, who knew as little as the Moslem of this treasure-spot, and the languid lesser Brahman, more brainless still, were the only moving creatures in all that sunny space. The shrieks of little parakeets, as they flew with flashes of emerald light in and out of the niches of the temple and the branches of the Sacred Bo-tree, were the only sounds in the mellow, slumbering air, that same perfect midday atmosphere that belongs to the ideal days of the East Indian winter, as to the sun-ripe days of the

American Indian summer. All the world drowsed in that golden calm — it was the ideal Mahabodhi.

In Hiouen Thsang's time buildings and monuments were crowded together, almost touching for a mile and a half, all round the Sacred Tree. There remain only what one sees in the single glance at the sunken area; save as archaeologists, digging here and there, have found the remnants of palace and temple and monastery walls, of cloisters and tanks and towers. Where we stood had been the great entrance of the monastery, where three thousand priests once lived, and treasures incalculable accumulated around an inner arcanum, whose solid gold statue was covered from foot to crown with jewel offerings. Instead of the great tower-capped walls stretching a thousand feet either way, and the throngs of yellow-robed priests, there is a very modern little galvanized iron pavilion sheltering a collection of broken images, sculptured and inscribed stones, saved from the pits and rubbish-heaps around, wreckage gathered after centuries of abandonment and final Mohammedan vandalism. The most valuable and interesting stones have been sent to the Calcutta Museum, and some few to London. The guides, of course, knew next to nothing about these relics. "General Cunningham put them there" — "General Cunningham very high esteemed them," etc. The Brahman knew nothing of the history of the temple, the tree, or the place, and was perhaps the most aggravatingly disappointing of all his vampire tribe that fasten upon one in the show-places of India. Our gloomy and monosyllabic Mohammedan — may all travelers in India beware of that professional traveling servant, Faglou Rahman! — knew far, far less. I had to cross-question, call for and demand to be shown this and that; to poke and pry, push and insist and rack my memory for the very little it held of Fahien's or Hiouen Thsang's travels. "He duss-sunt know-ah. People never ask — just memsahib want to know," sighed the melancholy Moslem.

"Where are the caves in the hills where the Buddha lived? Up there?" I asked, pointing. "Is there a cave there with carvings all over the walls?"

The Brahman could not have looked blanker if I had asked for the Eiffel Tower. It took long consultation and visible guesswork by both Brahman and Foglou Rahman for them to answer: "Maybe there are some holes in the hills over there — but — he duss-sunt know, memsahib." One might hope for better things in the next incarnation of the twice-born blockhead, the long-descended Aryan decadent and degenerate — but for the Moslem there ought to be all that the wrath of the Prophet has promised to the unworthy. The exasperation of being there, of having eyes, yet almost seeing not, went far toward quelling any deep emotions and dissipating the spell of the place, the somnolent calm, the soothing peace, the atmosphere almost as of Nirvana which brooded there, as we sat on the ancient stones and looked down upon the Place of Great Intelligence, the Veranda of and the veritable Tree of Knowledge. . . .

The broad stone staircase which leads down to the court from the north commands the view of the temple and tree which uncounted thousands have drunk in with ecstasy, a place which has resounded for centuries with prayers and chants. . . .

E. M. Forster, 1920 C.E.

The glory is . . . gone from Boddh-Gaya, where Buddha obtained enlightenment, but a small temple exists, where he is adored by favour of the British Government in a half-hearted fashion. Boddh-Gaya is a sunken area; standing on its edge, one looks down on a tangle of paths and votive bells. No Indians worship there, for Buddhism has died out in India, in accordance with its own law. But pilgrims from Thibet sometimes light lamps so that the floor of the temple looks like a lake of fire and streams of hot air agitate the dirty banners above the image. Behind the temple is a neglected tree, descendant of the Bo Tree where Buddha sat and struggled with evil until "the different regions of the sky grew clear, the moon shone forth, showers of flowers fell down from the sky upon the earth, and the night gleamed like a spotless maiden."

In a letter to Alice Clara Forster
Gya, Behar 29 January 1913
Enclosed is a leaf from the sacred Pipul Tree at Boddh Gaya. I have two & send you the best one — !

Dearest Mother

. . . Masood has again arranged for me and I am now sponging on Nawab Syed Zafar Nawab Saleh, in whose carriage I went to Boddh Gya. Boddh Gya — not to be confused with the Vishnu temple at Gya about which I wrote to Ruth & Agnes — is the place where Sakya muni (as he was then called) obtained enlightenment — i.e. became Buddha; and it is the most sacred place in the Buddhist religion. Buddhism, though it started in India, has not died out from it, and so the pilgrims to the Boddh Gaya temple are all from distant countries e.g. Burma and Tibet. Tibetans were there this afternoon, squat people with rough hair, filling the ante chamber of the temple and crouching between the barbaric pillars. Beyond them the shrine was a pool of fire. They had lighted hundreds and hundreds of tallow lamps, and above the radiance sat the giant statue of Buddha, pointing to the earth to bear him witness that he had gained enlightenment, and covered, like the pillars, with gold

leaf. Over his head, dimly visible, swung canopies and
streamers, waving in the hot air that rose from the
floor —Meanwhile the Tibetans chanted or turned
their prayer wheels or clashed cymbals, blew on horns
of shell and beat gongs; or there were strange rituals
— e.g. each looked into a bowl of water intently and
at a signal drank a little. — I fancy the water reflects
the universe and that by drinking it they draw up
knowledge, but I must find out. At the back of the
shrine outside the temple, grows the sacred tree under
which, or rather under the ancestor of which, Buddha
sat. Squares of gold leaf have been stuck on to the
trunk and boughs. The temple, together with several
acres of garden full of trees and flowers and votive
stones, chapels, bells, and statues, lies in a deep court-
yard below the level of the surrounding country. The
view when one drives up and sees everything suddenly
from the edge of the embankment, is, as books say,
"not easily forgotten." There can't be anything like it
in the world.

Rabindranath Tagore, 1935 C.E.

I had once gone on a visit to Buddha-Gaya, and
it had thrilled me to think that he who had hallowed the
earth by the touch of his feet had once come to that very
place in the flesh. Why, I had thought with a pang, had
I not been born in his day, that I might have received his
holy influence directly with all my mind and all my
body!

At the same time, it had occurred to me that the
immediate present is extremely limited in its compass,
and hazy with the dust raised by the whirlwind of contemporary events. History has proved again and again
that nearness in time clouds our vision, so that we fail to
realize fully the greatness of the supremely great among
us. How often in his lifetime Buddhadeva was hurt and

wronged by the spite and antagonism of petty minds; how often they spread false calumny about him to belittle his transcendent greatness! Hundreds of men who were near to him in the physical sense could never feel the immense distance that separated him from them in spirit; in the common haunts of men his uncommon sublimity went unrecognized. It was just as well, therefore, that it had not been given to me to see him amid the dust and haze of current events.

John Blofeld, 1956 C.E.

In Bodhgaya, from ten in the morning till five in the afternoon, a burning, dust-laden wind like a blast from the desert made it impossible to go out of doors. I used to lie almost naked against the stone flags in the shaded courtyard of the *Dharmasala*, reading or sleeping, and gasping with open mouth like a newly landed fish. But in the early mornings and during the last two hours of daylight, that scorching, dust-blighted place offered the keenest spiritual delights. Behind the five-towered *Vihara* can be found two objects which, for those Buddhists who like myself do not scorn the idea of mere things possessing a sanctity of their own, are so sacred as to command the deepest possible veneration. One of these is a young tree marking the exact sight of its lineal ancestor, the original Bodhi Tree, beneath whose boughs the Lord Buddha attained Enlightenment. The other is a large marble slab covering the original *Vajrasana*, the Bodhi-shaded place where the Lord Buddha seated himself to attain Enlightenment, resolutely determined to die on that spot or obtain a complete victory there over primordial ignorance, the source of all suffering and all evil. . . .

I [believe] that the power which certain places have of evoking a mood of intense spirituality stems chiefly from the atmosphere created by the pious

Monks at the Mahabohdi Temple

thoughts, high aspirations and ardent prayers of generations of pilgrims who have come to those places century
after century with deep faith in their hearts. If I am right
in so believing, then whether or not a sacred place is
really the exact site of the event said to have taken place
there does not much affect the spiritual stimulus it provides.

John Huntington, 1985 C.E.
    Perhaps the old Tibetan woman this author saw
during a 1969 visit to Bodhgaya, who was starting her
second million full body prostrations in front of the
shrine, best characterizes the importance of the shrine
— to her and to all Buddhists everywhere, Bodhgaya is
the *vajrasana*, the indestructible seat that has become

the sacred point from which all else in the Buddhist faith emanates. Above all else it is worthy of the reverence and offerings from the faithful. It is a Buddhist axiom that each person should practise according to his own ability, and it is here at Bodhgaya that practice, from the most profound discourses on the Dharma to the simplest acts of faith, is most appropriate. Even for the non-Buddhist, to go there is to gain a real sense of the history, the pres-ent vitality and the future of Buddhism.

Kate Wheeler, 1990 C.E.

Inside the stupa, peace and reverence prevail over the desperate competition outside. Though there is sound and movement, a stillness permeates the atmosphere. Under the trees, athletic Tibetan men in singlets, stout old grannies, fresh faced German devotees fling themselves on boards, completing a hundred thousand prostrations. Hidden among dozens of smaller stupas, a handsome old man with a ponytail chants a ritual of ultimate compassion, offering his body to unhappy ghosts, hungry demons and the spirits of disease. Thai women in gauzy white pensively walk around the stupa's marble perimeter. They carry thermoses of tea for a number of Thai men who have chosen to ordain as monks here, in this most meritorious place: next to the golden fence surrounding the Diamond Seat. The new monks squat awkwardly in their new robes, as they speak promises to older monks who hide their faces behind palm fans.

Marvels and horrors alike have been seen around the stupa: a crazy Indian man who thinks he's Krishna, posing eerily as he plays an invisible flute. A Tibetan monk wraps his ring finger in buttered cloth and sets it afire, sacrificing his flesh for world peace. A tapeworm crawls from the mouth of a sleeping pilgrim. On a full moon night, a young European woman feels an evil spirit wants to possess her mind — she is so profoundly terrified that she must return home.

Bodh Gaya is a magician's bag of tricks, where compassion and corruption, desperation and devotion coexist. The local Hindu temple is said to hold land in the names of dead people and ephemeral Hindu gods, thus making it impossible for indentured peasants to own their own land. Meanwhile, donations flow from overseas to build more lovely temples, filled with intricate carvings that represent the beauty of enlightenment.

Still, many of the Buddhist institutes, as well as individual pilgrims, make efforts to benefit the local people. There are free meals for children as well as outreach programs, at several temples. On a typical Bodh Gaya evening, while I was watching the sun set behind a huge Buddha statue, a German passerby dosed me with sacred ashes that had been spontaneously generated by a South Indian saint, supposedly. Meanwhile, at the next table, a Western nun who was temporarily flush with money offered dinner to a dozen village kids.

No miracle occurred on that first visit to Bodh Gaya. On the full moon night, for example, I vowed to stay awake meditating under the Bodhi tree, like the Buddha, and get enlightened, like the Buddha. Instead I got sleepy, like myself, and by three a.m. I was out cold, on my straw pallet at the Thai temple.

Still, in Bodh Gaya, my intuition began to connect with the unmiraculous astonishment of ordinary life. One morning, so early on a cloudless day that the golden sunlight still left long blue morning shadows, I walked alone across the temple gardens. Suddenly I encountered an elderly, elfin Bhutanese man, who seemed to pop from the ground between the redleafed croton bushes. He barely reached my shoulders; I felt exceedingly large and pink, in my sweatshirt and long cotton skirt. The Bhutanese man wore a knee length tunic of tightly woven wool, no socks over his knotty brown calves.

Both of us had glasses: his were round, carved from rock crystal; mine were discount plastic, imitation tortoise shell.

Through these lenses, our eyes met; some incomprehending recognition flashed between us. This is what I think we would have said, if our communication had taken form in words: "Whoever you are, you're here, too, and I understand why you came."

Allen Ginsberg, 1963 C.E.
Bodh Gaya April 14? ('63)

Death is not a single thing.

—— —— ——

Morning — woke in Mahabodhi Society Bldg — fan turning high ceilings — a cough — mosquitoes rare last nite — itch, Scabies returned — a cold, in lungs phlegm — my toe sore, second toe nicked constantly — slight sore throat — eyes blurred & smarting from acromyacin from conjunctivitis — smoking cough & lungs retched — hack — agh —

Dream — a tall man in the dream skating to Australia or chasing around on Dodgems from Cony Island playland — eitherway, a mirrorlike surface for the ground, sea or tin — something happened I don't remember — a tall figure in a suit like at Rockerfeller (*sic*) Center the Radioannouncer — Nowhere.

Worrying about drugs, lsd. Should I take or not.

— — — — — —

Last nite under the Bo tree, Stars, the square pointy temple.

Anne Waldman, 1973 C.E.

I BOW AT BODHGAYA
I bow at Bodhgaya
Prostrate all around Mahabodhi Temple
Circumambulate on my knees
One prostration is worth a thousand!
(— what young Ingie student said in
Darjeeling — seeing my greed for enlightenment)
I've just embraced a guru who said Do these
100,000 times-various practices,
then come back
I'll show you the secrets of the universe!

I say it dutifully:
I take refuge in the precious Buddha,
Dharma, Sangha
Give up personal history, imagination,
hope, fear
parents, relatives, lovers, friends,
worldly goods, ambition, my quirky poetry
all grandiose megalomaniacal plots to save the world
& do these prostrations for numberless sentient beings
who for countless suffering lifetimes
were once, each one of them,
or will be,
my very own mother
AH

I inch around the temple with light of Asia in my eyes
irritated, knees bloody, aspiring to what crazy
wisdom?
Old Tibetan lady in Darjeeling said
this would be good for my figure —
Was she Buddha in guise of hag,
or Mara tempting me to future vanities?

A sweaty "hairy bag of water"
I rest under the Bodhi Tree
descendant of one Tathagata
sat under — upon his inscrutable
diamond throne —
his Vajra daughter.

The Enlightenment
Under the Bodhi Tree

Thich Nhat Hanh, 1991 C.E.

Beneath the pippala tree, the hermit Gautama focused all of his formidable powers of concentration to look deeply at his body. He saw that each cell of his body was like a drop of water in an endlessly flowing river of birth, existence, and death, and he could not find anything in the body that remained unchanged or that could be said to contain a separate self. Intermingled with the river of his body was the river of feelings in which every feeling was a drop of water. These drops also jostled with one another in a process of birth, existence, and death. Some feelings were pleasant, some unpleasant, and some neutral, but all of his feelings were impermanent: they appeared and disappeared just like the cells of his body.

With great concentration, Gautama next explored the river of perceptions which flowed alongside the rivers of body and feelings. The drops in the river of perceptions intermingled and influenced each other in their process of birth, existence, and death. If one's perceptions were accurate, reality revealed itself with ease; but if one's perceptions were erroneous, reality was veiled. People were caught in endless suffering because of their erroneous perceptions: they believed that which is impermanent is permanent, that which is without self contains self, that which has no birth and death has birth and death, and they divided that which is inseparable into parts.

Gautama next shone his awareness on the mental states which were the sources of suffering — fear, anger, hatred, arrogance, jealousy, greed, and ignorance. Mindful awareness blazed in him like a bright sun, and he used that sun of awareness to illuminate the nature of all these negative mental states. He saw that they all arose due to ignorance. They were the opposite of mindfulness. They were darkness — the absence of light. He saw that the key to liberation would be to break through ignorance and to enter deeply into the heart of reality and attain a direct experience of it. Such knowledge would not be the knowledge of the intellect, but of direct experience.

In the past, Siddhartha had looked for ways to vanquish fear, anger, and greed, but the methods he had used had not borne fruit because they were only attempts to suppress such feelings and emotions. Siddhartha now understood that their cause was ignorance, and that when one was liberated from ignorance, mental obstructions would vanish on their own, like shadows fleeing before the rising sun. Siddhartha's insight was the fruit of his deep concentration.

He smiled, and looked up at a pippala leaf imprinted against the blue sky, its tail blowing back and forth as if calling him. Looking deeply at the leaf, he saw clearly the presence of the sun and stars — without the sun, without light and warmth, the leaf could not exist. This was like this, because that was like that. He also saw in the leaf the presence of clouds — without clouds there could be no rain, and without rain the leaf could not be. He saw the earth, time, space, and mind — all were present in the leaf. In fact, at that very moment, the entire universe existed in that leaf. The reality of that leaf was a wondrous miracle.

Though we ordinarily think that a leaf is born in the springtime, Gautama could see that it had been there for a long, long time in the sunlight, the clouds, the tree, and in himself. Seeing that the leaf had never been born, he could see that he too had never been born. Both the leaf and he himself had simply manifested — they had never been born and were incapable of ever dying. With this insight, ideas of birth and death, appearance and disappearance dissolved, and the true face of the leaf and his own true face revealed themselves. He could see that the presence of any one phenomenon made possible the existence of all other phenomena. One included all, and all were contained in one.

The leaf and his body were one. Neither possessed a separate, permanent self. Neither could exist independently from the rest of the universe. Seeing the interdependent nature of all phenomena, Siddhartha saw the empty nature of all phenomena — that all things are empty of a separate, isolated self. He realized that the key to liberation lay in these two principles of interdependence and non-self. Clouds drifted across the sky, forming a white background to the translucent pippala leaf. Perhaps that evening the clouds would encounter a cold front and transform into rain. Clouds were one manifestation; rain was another. Clouds also were not born and would not die. If the clouds understood that, Gautama thought, surely they would sing joyfully as they fell down as rain onto the mountains, forests, and rice fields.

Illuminating the rivers of his body, feelings, perceptions, mental formations, and consciousness, Siddhartha now understood that impermanence and emptiness of self are the very conditions necessary for life. Without impermanence and emptiness of self, nothing could grow or develop. If a grain of rice did not have the nature of impermanence and emptiness of self, it could not grow into a rice plant. If clouds were not

empty of self and impermanent, they could not transform into rain. Without an impermanent, non-self
nature, a child could never grow into an adult. "Thus,"
he thought, "to accept life means to accept impermanence and emptiness of self. The source of suffering is a
false belief in permanence and the existence of separate
selves. Seeing this, one understands that there is neither
birth nor death, production nor destruction, one nor
many, inner nor outer, large nor small, impure nor pure.
All such concepts are false distinctions created by the
intellect. If one penetrates into the empty nature of all
things, one will transcend all mental barriers, and be liberated from the cycle of suffering."

From Asvagosha, The Buddha-Karita, *1st century* C.E.
Then bursting the shell of ignorance, having
gained all the various kinds of perfect intuition, he
attained all the partial knowledge of alternatives which
is included in perfect knowledge.

He became the perfectly wise, the Bhagavat, the
Arhat, the king of the Law, the Tathagata, He who has
attained the knowledge of all forms, the Lord of all science. . . .

When the Bodhisattva had thus attained perfect
knowledge, all beings became full of great happiness; and
all the different universes were illumined by a great light.

The happy earth shook in six different ways like
an overjoyed woman, and the Bodhisattvas, each dwelling
in his own special abode, assembled and praised him.

Voices of Destruction
and Renovation

*The Ghaznavid and Ghurid armies from Turkey
did considerable damage at Bodh Gaya. Despite Burmese*

attempts to renovate the area in the thirteenth century, Bodh Gaya fell into desolation. In the sixteenth century, a Saivite priest moved into the temple complex and established a small monastery. The monastery expanded, and by the time Buddhist attention turned again on Bodh Gaya, the monastery's leaders, the Mahantas, had no intention of quitting the spot. During the Mahantas' tenure, the Mahabodhi Temple slipped into ruin and the Burmese again stepped in. Between 1819 and 1837, the king of Burma, Bagyidaw, funded the area's restoration. Soon thereafter, the British initiated further restoration and excavation. However, tensions started to rise when the Saivite Mahanta began aggressively Hinduizing the area, converting the statue of Buddha in the Mahabodhi Temple into a Hindu icon and obstructing Buddhist worship at the temple. By this time, two more people had joined the restoration efforts: Sir Edwin Arnold, author of Light of Asia, *and the Sri Lankan Buddhist Angarika Dharmapala, who, to consolidate support for the cause, had in 1891 founded the Mahabodhi Society. Dharmapala ran into trouble when he tried to install a Gupta image of the Buddha, donated by the Japanese, first in the Mahabodhi Temple, then in the nearby Burmese rest house leased from the Mahanta. The Mahanta was Bihar's second largest landholder and a formidable opponent. Dharmapala lost a first suit for Buddhist rights to the area. A subsequent suit lodged by the Mahanta against the monk in charge of the Gupta image's care was decided against the defendant. Dharmapala died in 1933, vowing to continue the fight for the Temple in his next rebirth. Ultimately, the publicity generated by his efforts led to a compromise. In 1953, the Bodh Gaya Temple Act went into effect, turning the management of the temple complex over to a managing committee run by Hindus and Buddhists. Under this new management, Bodh Gaya became fully accessible to the international Buddhist community.*

Siridhammasoka, Burmese ruler, 1298 C.E.

The Burmese king recorded his donations for restoration of the temple complex in the following inscription:

When 218 years of the era of the Religion of the Lord Buddha had passed away, Siridhammasoka, the Ruler of Jambudvipa, built 84,000 chaityas, one of which was situated on the site, where the Buddha took a meal (of rice porridge offered by Sujata before attaining Enlightenment). This shrine, owing to the effluxion of time, fell into ruin, and was repaired by the Mahathera Pinthagugyi. Subsequently, it was repaired by Thadomin. It again fell into disrepair, and King Sinbyuthikhin deputed the Royal Preceptor, Siridhammarajaguru, to undertake the work of repair. Sirikassapa, the disciple of the Preceptor, had sufficient funds, but could not take the work in hand (owing, probably, to the absence of skilled artisans) — He, therefore, sent Varavasi, a junior Thera, to King Pyutathin Min, who complied with the solicitation for assistance. The work of repair was begun on Friday, the 10th, waxing of Pyatho 657 B.E. (January 1295 C.E.). The following offerings were dedicated to the shrine: flags and streamers, 1,000 bowls of rice and 1,000 lamps (for several times), 2 boys in the place of the donor's own children, and gold and silver flowers and cloth hung on bamboo framework. In order to provide for the daily offering of rice at the shrine, at all times, land, slaves, and cattle were purchased and likewise dedicated. May this meritorious deed of mine lead me on to Nibbana! May I become a disciple of Metteyya, the coming Buddha!

The Dharmasvamin, 1234–36 C.E.

The Dharmasvamin visited Bodh Gaya during the time of the Ghurid onslaughts. These were largely responsible for Bodh Gaya's subsequent dilapidation.

At the time of the Dharmasvamin's visit to

Vajrasana, the place was deserted and only four monks were found staying [in the Vihara]. One [of them] said, "It is not good! All have fled from fear of the Turushka soldiery." They blocked up the door in front of the Mahabodhi image with bricks and plastered it. Near it they placed another image as a substitute. They also plastered the outside door [of the temple]. In its surface they drew the image of Mahesvara in order to protect it from non-Buddhists. The monks said, "We five do not dare to remain here and shall have to flee." As the day's stage was long and the heat great, said the Dharmasvamin, they felt tired, and as it became dark, they remained there and fell asleep. Had the Turushkas come, they would not have known it.

At daybreak they fled towards the North following the rut of a cart, and for seventeen days the Dharmasvamin did not see the face of the image [i.e. the Mahabodhi image]. At that time also a woman appeared, who brought the welcome news that the Turushka soldiery had gone far away.

Then the Dharmasvamin returned to Vajrasana, and stayed there worshipping and circumambulating the image of Mahabodhi.

From a description in the Englishmen, *a journal published in Calcutta.*

Published in the nineteenth century, the article is an example of the growing interest in the site that was developing during the period.

The whole of the plinth and lower mouldings buried under accumulation of rubbish; the floor of the sanctum and of the great hall in front 4 feet lower than the level of a rough stone-floor laid by the Burmese, who had partially cleared away the heaps of rubbish in front, — the great hall roofless; the half-hall, or porch of the second storey, roofless; the whole of the front of the temple above the level of the third chamber fallen, disclosing a great triangular gap, about 20 feet high and 12 feet wide at best; the stairs leading up from lowest floor or ground floor or terrace, from which the towers spring, roofless; the whole of the facade of the platform to the east a mound of ruins; the whole south facade of platform ruinous, but retaining here and there portions of original work; the entire west face of the platform of the temple buried under rubbish, which itself was held up by a rivetment wall, 32 feet high, of plain brick and mortar, unplastered, and looking for all the world like a dilapidated jail wall.

Sir Edwin Arnold, 1893 C.E.

In 1879, Sir Edwin Arnold helped popularize Buddhism in the West with his verse biography of the Buddha, Light of Asia. *Just over a decade later, his article* "East and West — A Splendid Opportunity," *published in the* Daily Telegraph, *threw the situation at Bodh Gaya into the public light and helped to awaken concern among English speakers about the area's restoration. At the beginning of the article, he invited his readers on an imaginary pilgrimage:*

I would today, in these columns . . . respectfully invite the vast and intelligent British public to forget, for a little while, home weather and home politics, and to accompany me, in fancy, to a sunny corner of their empire, where there centres a far more important question, for the future of religion and civilisation, than any relating to parish councils or parish pumps. I will by their leave, tell them of beautiful scenes under warm skies; of a temple fairer and more stately as well more ancient, than almost any existing fane; and will also show them how the Indian Government of Her Majesty, supported by their own enlightened opinion, might, through an easy and blameless act of administrative sympathy, render four hundred millions of Asiatics for ever the friends and grateful admirers of England.

We will spread the magic carpet of Kamar-az-zaman, told of in the *Arabian Nights* and pass at once upon it to Patna, the busy city beside the Ganges, some 350 miles by rail from Calcutta. The closing days of March are hot there, and the river glitters as if it were molten gold under the fiery sun. We will not stay accordingly to inspect the indigo factories; or to visit the wonderful Golah, where 140,000 tons of rice can be laid up; nor the government opium factory where enough of that most useful and benign drug is stored to put the whole world to sleep. We will take train from Bankipore for Gaya, only fifty-seven miles away, and having rested in that town for the night, we shall have ordered carriages to be ready at break of day to convey us four koss further — some seven or eight miles — into the hills which are hereabout just across the valley of the Ganges.

I said you should see beautiful scenery, and surely this is such. The road, broad and well made, runs between the Gay Hills on the right and the bright slow-stealing stream of the ancient Nilajan on the left. The mountain flanks are covered with cactus, wild indigo, and korinda bushes, showing a little temple perched upon almost every peak; while down on the flat, and especially along the sandy levels bordering the river, green stretches of palm groves are interspersed with sal and tamarind trees, the undergrowth being long tiger grass and the common but ever-lovely ground palmetto, *chamoreops humilis*. The air, deliciously cool before the sun rises, is full of birds abroad for food — crows, parakeets, mynas, the blue-winged rollers, the green and scarlet "hammer-smiths," black and white kingfishers, bee birds, bronze and emerald, with graceful silvery egrets stalking among the cattle. Later on, when the sky grows warmer, you will see clouds of lovely butterflies among the flowers of the orchids and poisonous datura, with sun-birds and dragon-flies skimming along the blue and pink lotuses in the pools. The people whom we meet upon the road are dark-skinned patient peasants going with their products to Gaya and Bankipur, while those whom we shall overtake will be mainly pilgrims of the day wending their way to the immeasurably holy place towards which we also are bound. For, see! they also at the fifty miles quit the main track, and turning to the left by a less excellent but still carriageable road, which winds under the now welcome shade of the jak-trees and mangoes, are making for that most sacred spot of all hallowed places in Asia, towards which our own feet and thoughts are bound.

It is here! Beyond the little village of mud huts and the open space where dogs and children and cattle bask together in the dust, beyond the Mahunt's College, and yonder great fig tree which has split with its roots that wall, twelve feet thick, built before England had ever been discovered, nestles an abrupt hollow in the surface, symmetrical and well-kept, and full of stone images, terraces, balustrades, and shrines. It is oblong — as big, perhaps, altogether as Russel Square, and surrounded on its edges by small houses and buildings. From one extremity of the hallowed area rises with great beauty and majesty a temple of very special style and design. The plinth of the temple is square, with a projecting porch, and on the top of this soars to the sky a pyramidical tower of nine storeys, profusely embellished with niches, string courses, and mouldings, while from the truncated summit of this an upper pinnacle rears itself, of graceful form, topped by a gold finial, representing the amlaka fruit. A smaller pyramidical tower stands at each corner of the roof of the lower structure, and there is a broad walk round the base of the Great Tower. Over the richly worked porch which fronts the east a triangular aperture is pierced, whereby the morning glory of the sun may fall through upon the gilded image seated in the sanctuary with in. That image, you will preceive, is — or was — of Buddha, and this temple is the holiest and most famous, as well as nearly the sole surviving shrine of all those eighty-four thousand fanes erected to the Great Teacher by King Asoka, two hundred and eighteen years after the Lord Buddha's Nirvana.

Yet more sacred even than the cool, dark sanctuary into which we look, to see the sunbeams kissing the mild countenance of the Golden Buddha inside; more intensely moving to the Buddhists who come hither, and richer with associations of unspeakable interest and honour than King Asoka's stately temple, or even those stone railings carved with mermaids, crocodiles, elephants, and lotus flower, which the king himself commanded, and which still surround the shrine, is yonder square platform of stone, about a yard high from the ground, out of which a tree is growing. That is the Maha Bodhi tree — in the opinion of superstitious votaries the very original Bodhi tree, miraculously preserved — but more rationally that which replaces and represents the ever memorable shade under which the inspired Siddhartha sat at the moment when he attained Sambodhi, the supreme light of his gentle wisdom. It is a fig tree — of the ficus Indica species — with the well known long glossy leaves. Its stem is covered with patches of gold leaf, and its boughs are hung with streamers of white and coloured cloth, while at its root — frequently watered by the pious with sandal oil and attar of roses — will probably be seen sitting a Brahman priest of the Saivite sect [a sect of Shiva devotees] intoning mantras. You will hear him say, "Gaya! Gaya Sirsa, Bodhi Gaya," for though he is praying on behalf of Maharatta pilgrims, and does not know or care for Buddha, yet ancient formulas cling to the spot and to his lips. And, beyond all doubt, this is the spot most dear and divine, and precious beyond every other place on earth, to all the four hundred million Buddhists in China, Japan, Mongolia, Assam, Cambodia, Siam, Burma, Arakan, Nepal, Tibet and Ceylon. This is the authentic site, and this the successor-tree. . . .

Why, then, is it today in the hands of Brahman priests, who do not care about the temple, except for the credit of owning it, and for the fees which they draw? The facts are these. Until the thirteenth century — that is, for more than 1,400 years — it was exclusively used and guardianed by Buddhists, but fell into decay and neglect, like other Buddhist temples, on the expulsion of Buddhism from India. Three hundred years ago a wandering Saivite ascetic visited the spot, and settled down, drawing round him gradually the beginning of what is now the College of Priests established there. So strong have they since become in ownership, that when the Bengal Government in 1880 was repairing the temple and its grounds, and begged for its embellishment from the Mahunt a portion of Asoka's stone railing which he had built into his own house, the old Brahman would not give it up, and Sir Ashley Eden could not, or did not, compel the restoration.

The Buddhist world had indeed, well-nigh forgotten this hallowed and most interesting centre of their faith the Mecca, the Jerusalem, of a million Oriental congregations. When I sojourned in Buddha-Gaya a few years ago, I was grieved to see Maharatta peasants performing "Shraddh" in such a place, and thousands of precious ancient relics of carved stone inscribed with Sanskrit lying in piles around. I asked the priest if I might have a leaf from the sacred tree.

"Pluck as many as ever you like, sahib," was his reply, "it is nought to us."

Ashamed of his indifference, I took silently the

three or four dark shining leaves which he pulled from the bough over his head, and carried them with me to Ceylon, having written upon each the holy Sanskrit formula. There I found them prized by the Sinhalese Buddhists with eager and passionate emotion. The leaf presented by me to the temple at Kandy, for example, was placed in a casket of precious metal and made the centre of a weekly service, and there and then it befell that, talking to the gentle and learned priests at Panadure — particularly to my dear and wise friend, Sri Weligama — I gave utterance to the suggestion that the temple and its appurtenances ought to be, and might be by amicable arrangements with the Hindoo College and by the favour of the Queen's Government, placed in the hands of a representative committee of the Buddhist nations.

I think there never was an idea which took root and spread so far and fast as that thrown out thus to the sunny temple-court at Panadure, amid the waving taliputs. Like those tropical plants which can almost be seen to grow, the suggestion quickly became an universal aspiration, first in Ceylon and next in other Buddhist countries. I was entreated to lay the plan before the Oriental authorities, which I did. . . .

Angarika Dharmapala, 1891 C.E.

Twentieth-century Bodh Gaya owes more to Angarika Dharmapala than to any other contributor. Below, the Angarika describes the history of his long relationship with Bodh Gaya.

I visited the place in company with a Japanese priest, the would-be successor of the High Priest of the Shingonsu sect on the 24th January last. The imperishable associations of the place influenced me so much that a strange impelling force came over me and made me to stay there and do all that was in my power for the restoration of the place to its legitimage custodians — the members of the holy Sangha. I held communication with my co-religionists in Japan, Burma, Siam, India and with my countrymen in Ceylon. It was most painful for me to witness the vandalism that was taking place there constantly, unobserved doubtless by those who would shudder at the sight. The most beautiful statues of the teacher of the Nirvana and the Law, — some in the attitude of meditation, some in the attitude of exhortation, some in the attitude of Nirodha Samapatti, some in the attitude of unrevelling philosophical disquisitions, some in the attitude of preaching, — are still cared for and quietly allowed to perish by exposure. Wandering alone in the bamboo groves to the east of Lilajam I came across statues plastered to the walls of an irrigating well near about the village Mucharin identified with the "Muchalinda" tank. Stones carved with Buddha's images are to be found used as weights to the levers for drawing water. I have seen ryots in the villages surrounding the temple using admirably carved stones as steps to their huts. I have seen 3 feet high statues in an excellent state of preservation buried under rubbish, to the east of the Mahant's Baradari. A few are plastered to the eastern outer wall of the garden along the bank of the Lilajan; and the Asoka pillars, the most ancient relic of the site — indeed, "the most antique memorials of all India" which graced the temple pavement, are now used as posts of the Mahant's Kitchen! The best and the most elaborately carved statues and girdlings are now in the Samadhi to the east of the temple. . . .

In January, 1891, I visited Bodh Gaya, the holy spot in India where the Buddha received enlightenment. From the mountains behind Bodh Gaya, Gautama came, worn out by six years of the fasting and self-torture practised by Indian ascetics. He had learned that mortification of the flesh did not enfranchise the spirit. Alone, deserted by his disciples, he came down to a beautiful grove of trees, always a haven in burning India. He sat under a delicate, wide-spreading fig-tree — the sacred *bo*-tree — determined to remain until he had achieved knowledge and freedom. And that very night, under the brilliant full Indian moon, he attained to Buddhahood.

Bodh Gaya is six miles south of the city of Gaya, in Bihar. My heart swelled with emotion as I rode along the bank of the river, through groves of screw-pines and palmyra-palms, and passed pilgrims journeying afoot to this holiest shrine of Buddhism. Bodh Gaya is to the Buddhist what the Holy Sepulcher is to the Christians, Zion to the Jews and Mecca to the Mahommedans. Perhaps no other place in the world has been so venerated for so long a period by so many people. For twenty-five hundred centuries Buddhist pilgrims have come — from Ceylon, Burma and Siam, from China, Japan and Korea from Turkistan and Tibet, to see the holy tree and the place where the Buddha sat.

For nearly seventeen hundred years Bodh Gaya was in the hands of the yellow-robed Buddhist monks. The original temple was built by command of the great Indian Emperor Asoka, after his conversion to Buddhism. During the great Buddhist period in India, Bodh Gaya was the abode of as many as ten thousand student-monks. At the end of the twelfth century, the Mahommedan invaders destroyed the holy places and massacred the resident monks. The Brahmans, by their persecutions, had already brought about a decline of Buddhism in India; the Moslem conquerors completed the work of destruction. Bodh Gaya languished into decay. Finally, some wandering Hindu fakirs of the Sivaite persuasion squatted on the grounds adjacent to the site of Asoka's temple and in the course of time became masters of the place. The temple was rebuilt by the Government of India in 1884. Six years later, the officials, not finding at the spot any representative Buddhist with whom to deal, handed over the inner management of the temple to the Sivaite fakirs but retained external jurisdiction.

In Bodh Gaya, when I beheld the *bo*-tree, an off-shoot of the original tree under which the Buddha sat, I had the same winged peace of soul as the humblest pilgrim from Burma. Reverently I visited the brick temple, built in the form of a pyramid, and examined the carvings on the ancient stone railing. But I was filled with dismay at the neglect and desecration about me. The *mahant* — the head of the Hindu fakir establishment — had disfigured the beautiful images. At the end of a long pilgrimage, the devout Buddhist was confronted with monstrous figures of Hindu deities. It seemed an outrage that this holiest temple of the Buddhists should be under the management of a man whose ancestors had always been hostile to Buddhism.

I had intended to stay a few weeks and then return to Ceylon; so I had only a few *rupees* with me. But, when I saw the condition of the shrine, I began an agitation to restore it to Buddhist control. I communicated with the leading Buddhists of the world and urged them to rescue Bodhi Gaya from the Siva-worshipping Hindu fakirs. On May 31, 1891, I started the Maha Bodhi Society, to rescue the holy Buddhist places and to revive Buddhism in India, which for seven hundred years had forgotten its greatest teacher. In 1892 I started the journal of the society, *The Maha Bodhi Society*, which is still in existence and well known among the Buddhists of Great Britain and the United States. . . .

I returned to Bodh Gaya. Actively as I had identified myself with the Buddhist cause, I still wore only the white robe of a student. But in October, 1895, I put on the yellow robe; I became an anagarika. . . .

I worked night and day when I was in India. I

paid no heed to my health — a bowl of rice and a few vegetables for daily food and four hours' sleep were sufficient, as they are now. After ten years of perseverance, I succeeded in obtaining the consent of the Government to the erection of a comfortable rest-house for Buddhist pilgrims at Bodh Gaya. It consisted of ten rooms, an assembly-hall that would hold five hundred persons and a big corridor built like a cloister. There were baths, where weary pilgrims who had come from afar could refresh themselves, and a kitchen, where poor travellers could cook the food they had brought with them. The two or three resident monks and I were happy to minister to the material and spiritual needs of the five or six hundred annual pilgrims from all parts of Asia. We never felt solitary; nor did we miss the activities of the outside world in that quiet grove that had witnessed the spiritual triumph of Gautama.

The Dalai Lama, 1959 C.E.

Since China's invasion of Tibet in 1949–50 and the Dalai Lama's departure from his homeland in 1959, Tibetans have come in ever greater numbers to Bodh Gaya. There, the Dalai Lama has met with Tibetan pilgrims and Buddhists from around the world on numerous occasions.

I reached Bodh Gaya. I was deeply moved to be at the very place where the Lord Buddha had attained Enlightenment. . . . Whilst there, I received a deputation of sixty or more Tibetan refugees who were also making a pilgrimage. A very moving moment followed when their leaders came to me and pledged their lives in the continuing struggle for a free Tibet. After that, for the first time in this life, I ordained a group of 162 young Tibetan novices as *bhikshus*. I felt greatly privileged to be able to do this at the Tibetan monastery which stands within sight of the Mahabodhi temple, next to the Bodhi Tree under which the Buddha finally attained Enlightenment.

Monuments

The Buddha's seat under the Bodhi tree (the Diamond Throne or Vajrasana), the place where he walked up and down after his enlightenment (the Cankramana Shrine), the place where he sat and gazed upon the Bodhi tree (the Animescalocana Stupa), the place where he sat emanating rays from his body (the Ratnagraha Shrine): each of the Buddha's movements at Bodh Gaya has been marked over the centuries with a monument — merit for its donor and a signpost for pilgrims.

THE BODHI TREE

The Bodhi tree which now stands at Bodh Gaya is said to be an ancestor of the original. A pipal or fig tree, the Bodhi tree was first attacked, according to legend, by King Asoka's wife. Disturbed by rumors that "Bodhi" was the object of her husband's most passionate devotion, she ordered her "rival" killed. Her servant attempted to destroy the tree. Stories differ as to whether or not her mistake was discovered in time to reverse the inflicted damage. Grown from a sapling which had sprung from its parent tree, today's tree, dating from the nineteenth century, is generally believed to derive from the famous Ceylonese offshoot of the original, believed to have been planted by King Asoka's daughter.

Peter Matthiessen, 1978 C.E.

In what is now known as Bodh-Gaya — still a pastoral land of cattle savanna, shimmering water, rice paddies, palms, and red-clay hamlets without paved roads or wires — a Buddhist temple stands beside an ancient pipal, descended from that *bodhi* tree, or "Enlightenment Tree," beneath which this man sat. Here

107

in a warm dawn, ten days ago, with three Tibetan monks in maroon robes, I watched the rising of the Morning Star and came away no wiser than before. But later I wondered if the Tibetans were aware that the *bodhi* tree was murmuring with gusts of birds, while another large pipal, so close by that it touched the holy tree with many branches, was without life. I make no claim for this event: I simply declare what I saw there at Bodh Gaya.

From the Asokavadana, *second century* C.E.

Now although King Asoka had given a hundred thousand pieces of gold to the places marking the Buddha's birth, his enlightenment, his setting in motion the Wheel of the Dharma, and his parinirvana, his faith was particularly roused by the Bodhi tree, since that was where the Blessed One had realized complete unsurpassed enlightenment. He therefore sent to the place of Bodhi an offering of the most precious jewels.

Now Asoka's chief queen was named Tisyaraksita. [She was a very jealous woman] and she thought: "Although the king pursues his pleasure with me, he sends all the best jewels to Bodhi's place!" She therefore asked a Matanga woman to bring about the destruction of "Bodhi, her rival." The sorceress said she would do it, but first demanded some money. When she had been paid, she muttered some mantras and tied a thread around the Bodhi tree; soon it began to wither.

The king's men quickly informed Asoka of this fact. "Your majesty," one of them said, "the Bodhi tree is drying up."

And he added:

> "The place where the seated Tathagata
> obtained omniscience and understood
> the whole world just as it is —
> the Bodhi tree, O chief of men, is dying!"

The news made Asoka collapse on the ground in a faint. His attendants splashed some water in his face, and when he had somewhat regained consciousness, he said, sobbing:

"When I looked at the king of trees, I knew
that even now I was looking at the Self-Existent
Master.
If the tree of the Lord comes to die,
I too shall surely expire!"

Now Tisyaraksita saw the king afflicted with sorrow and said: "My lord, if Bodhi should happen to die, I will bring about your pleasure!"

"Bodhi is not a woman," said the king, "but a tree; it is where the Blessed One attained complete unsurpassed enlightenment."

Tisyaraksita [now realized her mistake]. She summoned the Matanga woman and asked whether it was possible to restore the Bodhi tree to its previous healthy condition.

"If there is still some life left in it," said the sorceress, "I shall be able to revive it." She then untied the thread, dug up the ground all around the tree, and watered it with a thousand pitchers of milk a day. After some time, it grew to be as it was before.

The king's men quickly told Asoka: "Rejoice, your majesty, the tree has returned to its previous state!"

The king was so overjoyed that, gazing at the Bodhi tree, he proclaimed:

"I will do something that Bimbisara
and all the other resplendent royal lords never did.
I will twice perform the highest honors;
I will bathe the Bodhi tree
with jars full of fragrant waters,

*and I will undertake to honor the sangha
with a great quiquennial festival."*

The king then had a thousand jars of gold, silver,
cat's eye, and crystal filled with fragrant water. He had
much food and drink prepared, and collected a pile of
perfumes, garlands, and flowers. He bathed, put on clean
clothes that had never been worn and still had long
fringes on them, and he observed the fast day by main-
taining the eight precepts. Then, holding a small spoon
of incense, he went up to the roof of his dwelling, turned
in all four directions, and began to implore the disciples
of the Buddha to assemble, as a favor to him.

Elizabeth Ruhamah Scidmore, 1903 C.E.

Aside from the historic and religious associa-
tions of this particular bo- or pipul-tree, the *Ficus religiosa*
has a character and interest quite its own, the effect of its
symmetrical growth and well-balanced foliage masses,
heightened by the continual agitation of its brilliant,
dark-green leaves. Even on that still afternoon each
individual, heart-shaped leaf, with its long-drawn, tapering tendril tip, was trembling and spinning on its slen-
der foot-stalk, until the whole tree mass was in agitation
— every one of the myriad glossy, green leaves with a
separate light as these thousands of perpetually moving
mirrors caught the sun. The restlessness and activity of
these bo-leaves, vibrating and striking together with a
tinkling noise like the patter of soft raindrops on still
nights, make the pipul the most grateful shade-tree, and
the reflections of its glossy leaves suggest always the first
stir of a rising breeze. This flashing, sparkling, flickering
play of light all over the tree gives the pipul its unique
and individual character — something like the dazzling,
glittering trees that one sees in pictures by imperfect
vitascope. The pipul trembles to this day in reverence for

the one who became Buddha beneath its branches, and as symbol of continual change and motion, the impermanency of the world. The pipul whispers to Rishaba, the Hindus say, every word it hears, for which reason it is never planted in the bazaar where trade must employ the lie. Brahmans claim that Brahma planted the pipul-tree, and that Vishnu, who in his ninth avatar became Buddha, was born beneath a pipul-tree. The Hindu pilgrims, who come in such thousands every year to offer unleavened cakes and repeat mantras to this tree at Buddha-Gaya, before worshiping the print of Vishnu's footsteps at Brahm-Gaya, believe that a service beneath its branches will relieve their ancestors for one hundred generations back. . . .

Buddhists regard the Bo-tree as too sacred to be touched or robbed of a leaf, and devout Burmese pilgrims kneel, fix their eyes upon it, and in a trance of prayer wait until a miraculous leaf detaches itself and flutters down. It seemed sacrilege when the Brahman snapped off a leaf and offered it to me with the universal Indian gesture of the begging palm, and, at a request for more, snatched off a whole handful of trembling green hearts, as ruthlessly and brainlessly as the troop of monkeys in the bo-tree at Anuradhpura had done a few weeks before.

Despite the reverently worded mantra with which his own people address the tree, this Brahman butcher, responsive to a single rupee, continued to snatch off and break away twig after twig until I had a great green bouquet of nearly one hundred living, quivering leaves of Buddhist prayer. With no seeming appreciation of the sacrilege, he said: "Some people are satisfied with just one leaf. They bow to it, pray to it, and carry it away in a gold box." Then he set himself down on the Vajrasana, the Diamond Throne, to yawn and scratch his lean arms as he adjusted his drapery.

Eric Lerner, 1972–73 C.E.

He pointed to a tree surrounded by a heavy, carved stone railing and a curious mixture of reverent pilgrims and gawking sightseers. We stood off to the side. I wondered if I was supposed to say anything. Nice tree. Big deal. Its bark was dry and blotchy, its limbs kind of droopy. Like an old, retired man whiling away his empty time on a park bench. I was ready to leave. Instead, we sat down on a flat stone surface in a corner of the courtyard. I noticed after a moment that Bill's eyes were closed and his hands folded loosely in his lap. I did the same.

Almost immediately, that new-found sensor, which for lack of better understanding I referred to as my "body," came alive. I felt a surge of power flowing through me. My back straightened up and my head and shoulders pulled into line. I felt my chest drawn forward in the direction of that tree. An enormous calm enveloped me. All the noise and humming and activity receded to a faint background whisper. I intuitively felt some inkling, some tiny hint of what had transpired in this spot twenty-five centuries ago. Was still going on. Right now. My mind rushed first for explanation, then for phrases of description like "vibrations" and "sanctified ground." But the words were babbling. I relaxed into awe. Place and time lost their meaning. *Where* I was experiencing this and *when* had no relevance.

My body told me it was so. It told me that the world can whir and hum and crank on with its noisy business, and yet the stillness is there. The peace is within. Prostrations and chanting and supplication and prayer clogged the air and yet that cool, empty space beneath that tree remained untouched. The Buddha still sat there, as he did twenty-five hundred years ago, with eyes closed and attention turned inward. And even though he was alone then, in silence, still the outside world confronted him. His own desires for that world, his senses, and the machinery of his mind assaulted him with a thousand prostrations and supplications and prayers for his attention. And he continued to turn inward, deeper and deeper within.

I was just on the edge, the most distant approach to that space within, standing before an unknown universe of infinite possibility. To go further I could carry nothing with me, no baggage of the outer world. These past weeks had been a reluctant, painful process of giving up that baggage. But I'd done it. And so forfeited my right to travel out there. I would be blown out if I tried. That kind of tourism was dead for me.

We seemed to open our eyes together. I shook my head slowly in amazement. Few words came out. As my mind started rolling again, though, it wanted to know . . . how, what had I felt? Where had I been?

Sandy Boucher, 1991 C.E.

Bodh Gaya: November 18, 1991

Last night Crystal and I took turns listening to piano music on the Walkman. We've been gone from the United States for over a month now, in Thailand and then trekking in the Nepalese Himalayas; we thought we might want to tune in to something familiar. At first the music was soothing, then it touched into my sadness for the poverty and suffering we see all around us, and I cried.

In the morning we visit the temple here at the Bhutanese complex, entering a wonderland of color. Scenes from the Buddha's life are beautifully modeled in relief on the walls and painted in rich hues. A majestic gold-skinned, gorgeously draped Buddha sits flanked by two other regal male figures. Every inch of wall and beam and corner has been elaborately modeled and painted and adorned.

In the temple we meet a Tibetan-born pilgrim who lives in Canada, is visiting here with husband and son. Like most Tibetans we have met, she radiates friendliness. She offers to take us to the Tibetan tent-restaurant, leading us into the middle of town and down a side lane. We enter a long canvas khaki tent with kitchen at one end, and earthen platforms on either side where people pay two rupees a night to sleep. In the middle of the dirt floor stand a few plank tables and benches. A Tibetan woman waits on us. A tall brown-robed lama cooks our breakfast. The food is good and very cheap — 22 rupees (less than a dollar) for two omelets, two Tibetan breads with butter, and tea!

On our way to the Bodhi Tree, we follow a group of white-clothed pilgrims under the dusty trees that line the street. The pilgrims hold their hands together in a prayerful position before them and chant as they walk. Ahead of us we see the great complex of temples and stupa, gardens, walks and stone balustrades that has been built around the ancient tree. We wander among them, and make our way to the gigantic lotus pond. Out in the middle, as if floating on the wide flat leaves, sits an orange-robed buddha in meditation posture, and above him rises the great cobra head of the naga (serpent + human being) king, who the story says rose up to protect him from the rain as he sat in deep absorption.

Finally we come to the Bodhi Tree itself, surrounded by a high stone fence hung with brightly colored prayer flags. We step inside the enclosure to see an enormous ancient tree, its heavy limbs propped with sticks. A four-foot-high saffron cloth wraps the base of the tree. Prayer flags are strung between its branches.

In this enclosure the pilgrims in their white clothes sit among shaven headed monks in orange robes, nuns draped in white or orange cloth. A large flat surface

Meditating under the Bodhi Tree

holds food offerings — plates of rice, plates of fruit.

Most of the seated pilgrims are women, their eyes closed in meditation. They hold a stillness. Indeed, here among all these people, all this color, there exists a deep silence. It's what I recognize in Buddhism. A gentle, open feeling, an allowing of all of us here.

I find a place among the meditating women, sit and look up at the gnarled heavy branches of the tree. The ancestor of this tree shaded Siddhartha as he sat day after day inviting "bodhi," perfect knowledge. It witnessed his moment of enlightenment, an event so deeply embedded in time, two thousand five hundred years ago. I close my eyes, and feel the profound silence of this place holding me.

After a while I begin to have something of that feeling of enclosure and stillness that I experienced on the Nuns Island in Sri Lanka. It was there that one day I slipped through a fold in time to find myself in the forests of ancient India, seeing a slim young man in an orange robe whom I knew to be the Buddha, talking with his monks and the enlightened women who surrounded him. That same energy holds me, here, a feeling of a presence, some echo of the particular human being who awoke to the light of perfect understanding so long ago.

Now a female voice begins to chant. I open my eyes to see an Indian or Sri Lankan nun holding a bull horn. In a nasal voice, she chants the Pali syllables, and some of the pilgrims join her in the chant. Her crudely amplified voice does not shatter the silence, but rides it, weaves with it. I look at the faces of the women meditating near me, absolutely motionless in their pure white robes. These are the literal descendants of the women and men who listened to the Buddha give his lectures. It is said that during the Buddha's lifetime, many people needed only to hear him speak to reach enlightenment. I have read the verses in the *Therigatha* in which the theris or female elders, the enlightened ones, who must have looked a great deal like the women around me, sing of the moment at which they "woke up."

I listen to the chanting, surrendering to the deep silence that underlies it. I am so grateful to be here, for I understand that no matter how different we may appear, in skin colour and size and costume, all of that falls away before the flame of shared humanity that burns in us, our potential for enlightened mind.

I feel at home here, as if who I am has been welcomed and given space to flower. I feel the ancient tree, so alive in its garments of prayer flags and shiny leaves, speaking to me. I want never to leave this place.

Later, back at the Bhutanese guest house I sink into sleep, overcome mostly, I think, by the air pollution here — feeling very heavy and almost dizzy.

Finally Crystal wakes me, saying she is hungry and feeling ill with swollen glands. I wish there were a way to bring her soup, here to the room, as she did for me in the lodge in the Himalayas when I was sick — but there doesn't seem any way to carry it back. So I help Crystal get up and get dressed, and we take a rickshaw to the Tibetan restaurant, where we eat hot and sour soup and vegetable momos. Three young Tibetan monks lie propped up together on the bed-platform. Eating, we look across at their wide flat-nosed buddhalike faces smiling at us.

Now we're back at the Bhutanese guest house, hearing someone play a fiddle in a room down the hall. It sounds like Appalachian mountain music!

Crystal and I talk about what we're learning about each other on this journey. After all, we have only known each other three months. We're learning to soften to each other. Particularly because of my own having been sick and incapacitated twice on this trip, I am able to be kind and compassionate with her illness now.

I go to sleep feeling the deep silence of the Bodhi Tree.

Rick Fields, 1990 C.E.

A few years ago I spent a week doing a retreat next to a stream at the foothills of the Sangre de Cristo mountains in southern Colorado. The ground rules were fairly simple: retreatants were to live as close to "nature" as possible. Instead of sleeping in a tent, I slept either under the stars or under a tarp. I didn't build a fire, but ate bread, cheese, dried fruits, nuts. I drank water from the stream, and steeped tea in a bottle warmed by the sun. I never used a flashlight and left books, paper, and pen behind.

Like any other heat-seeking mammal, I followed the sun as it climbed the hillside and by sunset I could look out across the broad valley which, millions of years ago, was the floor of a vast sea. During the mornings, I stayed in my sleeping bag until the sun reached the stream, and then, I sat under one of the great pines, and practiced, watching my breath come and go like a gentle wind. It was during one of these morning sessions that it suddenly occurred to me that the Buddha got enlightened under a tree.

This may seem obvious, at least to people familiar with the story of the Buddha's life, but it nevertheless struck me as something of a revelation. All the Buddhist retreats I had attended in America had taken place inside — in polished black-and-white Japanese-style zendos, or rough-hewn reconverted "barndos," in luminously colored Tibetan temples, or in city lofts or generic Holiday Inn conference rooms, or in cabins and maybe tents. Of course, I had walked, sat, and lay down under trees, in various states of contemplative ease, but I had never — nor had any of my fellow Buddhists, so far as I knew — meditated under a tree for a sustained length of time, as the Buddha had done.

Of course, there were good reasons for this. Sitting under a tree or beneath an overhanging rocky ledge exposes us to the weather as well as to animals and insects. In the Buddha's own time, the forests of India contained tigers, rhinos, elephants, cobras, and scorpions. Nowadays, we seem to have reduced the dangerous to the merely distracting. We stay inside to avoid mosquitoes, flies, ants, spiders, stray dogs, and inquisitive neighbors.

Yet there is another perspective. The person who meditates outside for a few days may come to see dangers and distractions as messengers. Such messengers may arrive in surprising shapes. Midway through my retreat I found myself unable to crawl out of a particularly slippery and muddy hole of self-pity — until one morning a yellow jacket landed on my bare stomach, took a good bite, and flew off. Stung into awareness, self-pity and indulgence vanished. A small but crucial turning point, it worked just as well — if not better — than the "encouragement stick" wielded by watchful zendo monitors.

A little later, crossing the stream which divided our wilderness from the civilized amenities of base camp, I noticed a snake. Like the bee that had bitten me, it too was black with a yellowish stripe: a common Western garter snake, the field-guides say. But there was something a little uncommon, even strange about this particular snake. Poised upright in an elegant S-shaped curve, it didn't move at all, save for the flickering forked tongue, black as coal with two flame-red tips. We stared at each other. A field-guide might have attributed its unwavering gaze to the fact that snakes have two sets of transparent scales covering their eyes, but the intensity of its perfect stillness and the S-shaped pose made me think of the mythical *nagas*, the serpentine Indian water spirits reputed to guard treasures hidden beneath the surface of lakes and rivers. So I bowed slowly, three times, forehead to the ground, and inhaled the pine resin of the earth. Still the snake did not move. The snake just looked not so much at me as through me, as if to say, "This is how to be, this is how to keep your meditation, in the world you are returning to."

These outdoor encounters — with the yellow jacket and snake — made me wonder about the Bodhi tree under which the Buddha had attained enlightenment. . . .

With time my curiosity grew into an obsession, and three years after my retreat in the Colorado mountains I boarded an Air India jet for the two-day flight to Delhi; then took an overnight train to the market town of Gaya, in Bihar; and hired a *tempo* — a three-wheeled motor-scooter — for the final journey to Bodhgaya.

The trip had taken three or four days, depending on whether you counted the day lost crossing the international dateline. The setting sun cast a dreamy orange glow over the open fields at the edge of town. I left my bag at the Burmese Vihar, showered, and walked through the market, past the open-air stalls selling incense, candles, and red and yellow flowers floating in shallow clay bowls, in through the outer gate past the ragged line of squatting beggars and urchins, and on through the inner gate to the temple complex itself. There were many trees, at least for this part of India, and a series of stone walkways and broad worn steps descending to the entrance of the Maha Bodhi Temple itself — 180 feet tall, with buddhas and bodhisattvas carved into every niche.

The tree I was looking for was, in fact, totally obscured by the temple. I came upon it, in the course of my circumambulation, behind the temple in a sanctuary surrounded by a stone fence, six or seven feet high, which could be entered through an iron gate that was now padlocked shut for the night. The tree was shapely and well-proportioned, with four limbs branching out from a smooth trunk which was wrapped, on that first evening, in gold and white brocade. As soon as I saw it, the temple itself seemed reduced to the status of the merely ornamental — nice enough, perhaps, but hardly necessary.

I returned as early as I could the next morning. I was not the first one there. Tibetan monks in their rough red robes were doing prostrations on shiny well-worn wooden boards pointed in the direction of the temple and tree, along with a scattering of Westerners dressed in sweatpants and T-shirts. Tibetans, Bhutanese and Ladakhis wearing dusty *chubas* spun prayer-wheels and fingered beads; Thais, Sinhalese, and Burmese laymen and women walked in silent contemplation or animated conversation. Japanese in white shirts and dark trousers walked briskly and snapped photos.

The iron gate to the tree was open this time. Inside were twenty or so Burmese, men and women, wearing the white of pilgrimage. Three saffron-robed monks led the kneeling group in chanting the three refuges in Pali: *"Buddhanam saranam gochammi . . ."* The oblong stone marking the diamond seat where the Buddha had sat facing east, his back to the tree, was strewn with flower petals, and shaded by delicate rice-paper parasols.

Over the next few days, I often joined pilgrims from around the world as they entered the little enclosure to pay homage and perform ceremonies. The Japanese, immaculate in black robes over snow-white kimonos, their freshly shaven heads glistening in the sun, chanted the *Heart Sutra*. Burmese, Thai, and Sinhalese chanted in Pali, Taiwanese in Chinese. Tibetans lit butterlamps and hung prayer flags.

One evening I sat next to a gray-clad Korean nun who sat on her knees, back straight, eyes downcast in rapt concentration. She stayed immobile all day and maybe all night too. The Indian caretaker locked and unlocked the gate to let various groups of pilgrims in as we went on sitting on the far side of the tree. The roots had broken through the circular concrete support, and were raising and breaking out of the confinement of the stone floor. The pale green long-stemmed heart-shaped leaves trembled in the slightest breeze. . . .

Bodhi trees were planted all over India and Nepal. There is one now in the Deerpark in Sarnath, where Buddha first taught, transplanted from the tree the Emperor Ashoka first sent to Ceylon. There is another in Lumbini, the birthplace of the Buddha — a gnarled, twisty, old tree set against the stark sky. When I saw it in that desolate place I felt heartened as if I had come across an old friend who was making the same pilgrimage as myself.

But we cannot be too literal, either about buddhas or trees. As the Indian scholar Dipak K. Barua tells us, "The bo tree was not Ashvata in all cases, the different buddhas having different trees." And since — according to the Buddha — we are all potential buddhas, any tree can be a bodhi tree. Which means, I think, that if we want to become buddhas we have to find our own trees. Buddhas and trees come together after all.

THE DIAMOND THRONE OR VAJRASANA: SEAT OF ENLIGHTENMENT

Over the centuries, the Bodhi tree has been shifted from its original site. That site is part of the main temple. The sandstone slab of the diamond throne now lying under the Bodhi tree, though not the first, is the oldest object to be seen at Bodh Gaya.

Hiuen Tsiang, mid-seventh century C.E.

In the middle of the enclosure surrounding the *Bodhi* tree is the diamond throne *(Vajrasana)*. In former days, when the Bhadra-kalpa was arriving at the period of perfection *(vivartta)*, when the great earth arose, this *[throne]* also appeared. It is in the middle of the great *chiliocosm*; it goes down to the limits of the golden wheel *[the golden circle]*, and upwards it is flush with the ground. It is composed of diamond. In circuit it is 100 paces or so. On this the thousand Buddha of the Bhadra-kalpa have sat and entered the diamond *Samadhi*; hence the name of the diamond throne. It is the place where the Buddhas attain the holy path *[the sacred way of Buddhahood]*. It is also called the *Bodhimanda*. When the great earth is shaken, this place alone is unmoved. Therefore when Tathagata was about to reach the condition of enlightenment, and he went successively to the four angles of this enclosure, the earth shook and quaked; but afterwards coming to this spot, all was still and at rest. From the time of entering on the concluding portion of the kalp, when the true law dies out and disappears, the earth and dust begin to cover over this spot, and it will be no longer visible. . . .

The old people say that "as soon as the figures of this Bodhisattva sink in the ground and disappear, the law of Buddha will come to an end." The figure at the south angle is now buried up to its breast.

Ekai Kawaguchi, January 1899 C.E.

The night of that day I spent meditating on the "Diamond Seat" under the Bodhi-tree — the very tree under which, and the very stone on which, about two thousand five hundred years ago, the holy Buddha sat and reached Buddhahood. The feeling I then experienced is indescribable: all I can say is that I sat the night out in the most serene and peaceful ecstasy. I saw the tell-tale moon lodged, as it were, among the branches of the Bodhi-tree, shedding its pale light on the "Diamond Seat," and the scene was superbly picturesque, and also hallowing, when I thought of the days and nights the Buddha spent in holy meditating at that very spot.

> *While seated on the Diamond Seat, absorbed*
> *In thoughtful meditation full and deep*
> *The lunar orb, suspended o'er the tree —*
> *The Sacred Bodhi tree — shines in the sky.*

I wait with longing for the morning star
To rise, the witness of that moment high
When His Illumination gained the Lord
The Perfect Buddha, Perfect Teacher Great.

RATANACANKAMA CAITYA

The Ratanacankama Caitya honors the place
where the Buddha walked up and down three weeks after
his enlightenment. It was originally flanked by a row of
pillars which supported a roof. Of these pillars, only a few
bases and one pillar remain. The promenade at Bodh
Gaya is only the most important of several memorials to
the places where the Buddha walked in North India.

I-Tsing, 671–95 C.E.

In India both priests and laymen are generally in
the habit of taking walks, going backwards and forwards
along a path, at suitable hours, and at their pleasure:
they avoid noisy places. . . . If any one . . . adopts this
habit of walking he will keep his body well, and thereby
improve his religious merit. Therefore there are cloisters
. . . where the World-honoured [Buddha] used to walk,
on the Vulture Peak, under the Bo-tree, in the Deer Park,
at Ragagriha, and in other holy places. They are about
two cubits wide, fourteen or fifteen cubits long, and two
cubits high, built with bricks; and on the surface of each
are placed fourteen or fifteen figures of an open lotus-
flower, made of lime, about two cubits (= three feet) in
height, one foot in diameter, and marked (on the surface
of each figure) with the footprint of the Sage. At each
end of these walks stands a small Kaitya, equal to a man's
height, in which the holy image, i.e. the erect statue of
Sakyamuni, is sometimes placed. When any one walks
towards the right round a temple or a Kaitya, he does it
for the sake of religious merit; therefore he must perform

it with special reverence. But the exercise [I am now speaking of] is for the sake of taking air, and its object is to keep oneself in good health or to cure diseases.

THE MAHABODHI TEMPLE

No one knows who built the Mahabodhi Temple. While many pilgrims attribute its construction to King Asoka, archaeologists currently date the oldest parts of the structure to the Kushana period (50 B.C.E.–200 C.E.). The temple has been restored many times over the centuries.

The Dharmasvamin, 1234–36 C.E.

The Gandhola of Vajrasana is called in Tibetan either *Gandhakuti*, or the Pinnacle. It was erected by the Dharmaraja Asoka and is 35 cubits in height. It can clearly be seen from a distance of two stages. The Dharmasvamin said that its pinnacle of glittering white looked like a flame and that it shone like a shield placed flat on the ground in sunshine. In front of the eastern door of the Gandhola there were three [covered] passages.
. . .

The face of the Mahabodhi image inside the Gandhola is two cubits, i.e. 36 inches, in height. One is never satiated to behold such an image, and has no desire to go and behold another. The Dharmasvamin said that even people with little faith when standing in front of the image felt it impossible not to shed tears.

I-Tsing, 671–95 C.E.

[W]e came to the Mahabodhi Vihara, and worshipped the image of the real face [of the Buddha]. I took stuffs of thick and fine silk, which were presented by the priests and laymen of Shan-tung, made a kashaya (yellow robe) of them of the size of the Tathagata, and myself offered this robe to the Image. Many myriads of [small]

Offerings of candles at the Mahabohdi Temple

canopies [also], which were entrusted to me by the Vinaya-master Hiuen of Pu, I presented on his behalf. The Dhyana-master An-tao of Ts'ao charged me to worship the image of Bodhi, and I discharged the duty in his name.

Then I prostrated myself entirely on the ground with an undivided mind, sincere and respectful. First I wished for China that the four kinds of benefits should widely prevail among all sentient beings . . . in the region of the Law . . . and I expressed my desire for a general reunion under the Naga-tree to meet the honoured [Buddha] Maitreya and to conform to the true doctrine, and then to obtain the knowledge that is not subject to births.

126

C. H. Forbes-Lindsay, 1903 C.E.

The temple lies in a depression of the ground, which detracts somewhat from its appearance. It is, nevertheless, an imposing building, rising to a height of one hundred and seventy feet from the ground. It is a nine-storied pyramid, embellished in the usual manner with crowded forms and figures. The structure is in a remarkable state of preservation, considering that it probably dates from the third or fourth century of the present era. In fact, it is difficult to associate its appearance with the thought of such extreme old age.

Lillian Luker Ashby, 1907 C.E.

Mrs. Ashby married a British officer and together they lived for a short time in Gaya, near Bodh Gaya. Ashby watched Hindu and Buddhist pilgrims pass by her house every day and often visited the temple complex.

The colossal Temple of Buddh Gaya, twenty-three centuries old, with its beautiful, well-preserved frieze of lotus leaves, the architectural motif throughout, like every spot hallowed by tradition and sanctified by the devotion of generations, is permeated by a mystic air of worship. For nearly a thousand years, this ancient mass was completely buried by the silt from flood waters of the Ganges. . . .

The central part of the Temple is occupied by a gigantic black marble figure of the Buddha, seated in meditation, before which burns an everlasting flame from a black stone cauldron full of pure *ghi*, constantly replenished by women votaries of Mongolian origin. The image of Gautama's mother stands in another large hall. Small idols and carvings, depicting incidents in the life of the great teacher, fill every available niche. In the foyer is hung a monstrous brass bell with a clapper the thickness of a man's body. This is rung each morning as a call to worship. The sonorous, deep-throated sound

127

penetrates the pall-like atmosphere of Gaya, and is audible for miles around.

Elizabeth Ruhamah Scidmore, 1903 C.E.

All about the Bo-tree, the Diamond Throne, the Cloister, and the temple doorway, the stones were daubed with gold-leaf and ocher. The Brahman guide was just able to tell that these yellow smears were the offerings of pious Burmese, but to any further questions concerning the Burmese and their intermittent gilding the Brahman returned a dumb stare. He led us into the temple, through an archway in a wall twenty feet thick, to a square whitewashed cell, and up to a second chilly, white vault where the light fell through a triangular east window full upon the image on the carved basalt altar. It was a tawdry, gilded image, more asleep than serenely meditating, with a Hindu caste-mark on its brow — "Buddha's mother!" said the Brahman. For further shock and disillusionment, it was only necessary to note that the image was attired in a red merino petticoat and a tinsel-bordered cape — "to keep the image warm," said the Brahman, winding his grimy sheet more closely around him in that chill sanctuary. There was a litter of food and flower, incense and candle offerings on the altar in true Burmese fashion, scores of Tibetan flags and streamers in the corners of the room, while old Buddhist bas-reliefs built into the wall were buttered and garlanded in the Hindu manner — a medley of religions in the one shrine. It was hard to believe that this untidy vault, this religious lumber-room, was the supreme shrine, the ark, the tabernacle, the holy of holies. It was harder to realize that the stone image, the shabby old "Buddha's mother," all daubed with gold-leaf, successor to innumerable images of gold, perfumed paste, basalt, sandstone, and stucco — this clumsy image, with its solid, vacant face, was intended for the same beautiful, passionless Teacher who meditates, steeped in the peace of eternal Nirvana, in the gilded temples of Japan or beneath Kamakura's pine-trees.

Walter Del Mare, 1905 C.E.

The shrine in the temple contains a gilt figure of The Buddha Renouncing the World, having the trisul or trident mark painted on his forehead. Around him are coloured marble Buddhas from Burma, and above is a nude standing image of gilt stone with the wheel of life in one hand. On the stairs stands a black stone, with some traces of gilding left, bearing an inscription in Pali. From the top of the basement story can be seen the Maher Hills, which rise to a height of over 1,600 feet above the sea. Over the entrance to the shrine is the following inscription: "This ancient temple of Mahabodhi, erected on the holy spot where Prince Sakya Sinha became a Buddha, was repaired by the British Government under the order of Sir Ashley Eden, Lt. Gov. of Bengal, Anno Domini 1880." How far any English inscription would be appropriate here is questionable; but surely the date is, to say the least of it, of doubtful taste. As well might the Turks put an inscription over the Church of the Sepulchre to the effect that it had been rebuilt "in the year of the Hegira 1225."

Eric Lerner, 1972–73 C.E.

The next day the streets were quieter. It was early morning. Bill, a friend from Benares, seemed to know just what was going on with my mind and body, so he held my hand, as it were, with a soothing string of not too meaningful conversation that had the effect of lulling me into a sense of familiarity.

The Bodhi Temple lay down a hill beneath the road. As we walked toward it, the hum of energy in the air increased in pitch. I could feel it. Bill explained that

129

a few years before he had been deeply involved with Tibetan practice. At that time it was the only form of Buddhism in India. To me, its external trappings, visual symbolism, and ritual activity were entirely antithetical to the Buddha's simple teaching of the end of suffering through knowing reality. I looked at the elaborately carved medieval prismatic shape of the temple. I saw only a pile of rock. Everywhere devotees were bowing down full length on the ground over and over and over, as if doing calisthenics for football practice.

"Do they see Buddha as some sort of God?" I asked Bill.

"I suppose that on the popular level they do, and that's where most people's practice is. But, you know, it's no different in Burma or any of the other countries where Theravada, the supposedly pure teaching of Buddha, is practiced. The real Tibetan teaching isn't worship at all, though. Even though they do the same prostrations and mantras, to those who are serious it means something very different. Just another way of confronting the ego."

I would have argued the point but we were at the temple now and the swirl of activity forced me to watch each step I made. I stopped and stared at a very old Tibetan man rhythmically bowing, kneeling, then fully prostrating before a statue of the Buddha. What did he want? What did he expect? It was confusing to me. It confronted some growing inner sense of mine of what this end of suffering was really all about. Not statues, not chanting. There's nothing out there! I felt like shouting it. Inside, inside. I wanted to turn around and head back to the peace of the *vihara*. Instead Bill led me by the arm around the temple, under strings of colored cloth prayer flags, through the whirring of the little prayer wheels, the revolving metal drums on sticks that the Tibetans carry.

Encounters

S. R. Wijayatilake, 1963 C.E.

It was interesting to see pilgrims from various parts of the world, particularly the Tibetans. One could see from their rites and ceremonies and their manner of worship their devotion to the Master. It was most elevating to see them lost in meditation and prayer. They are undoubtedly a people who have dedicated themselves to the Buddha. Their rituals may seem strange but their precision, quiet discipline and patience were an object lesson to us.

Walter Del Mare, 1905 C.E.

While our driver was getting ready to go back we visited the convent of Sanyasis. The priests at the temple had given us permission to pluck a couple of leaves from the Bo-tree, and on comparing them with those gathered at Anuradhapura they were found to be broader leaves with relatively shorter tendrils. The priests also gave us a nosegay, which we afterwards handed to the leader of a party of Tibetan pilgrims, and it was a great pleasure to watch their childish delight over the gift.

Anne Cushman, 1993 C.E.

What touches me most, though, is not the statuary, but the practitioners. Since the Mahabodhi temple's rediscovery, Buddhists from all over the world have founded branch temples in Bodh Gaya, and the Mahabodhi grounds are aswirl with the maroon robes of Tibetans, the black of Japanese, the saffron of Sri Lankans, the amber of Burmese. In shaded alcoves, monks doing prostrations repeatedly hurl themselves face down onto polished boards, their hands and elbows protected by pads against the force of their devotion. A Korean woman in a plain grey pantsuit circumambulates the temple with the slow, almost imperceptible steps of walking meditation. Bright-eyed young Tibetan monks — judging from their faces, they can't be more than ten or eleven years old — cluster under a feathery neem tree, laughing and playing with marbles and toy cars. One of them takes off his sandals and runs and slides, runs and slides, down the Bejewelled Walk, his robes flapping around him.

Kate Wheeler, 1990 C.E.

Our destination was the Thai temple past the far end of town, its delicate, fanciful gilt architecture bespeaking the never-ending elegance, the perfect gestures, of spiritual attainment. There, we would meditate for three weeks, awakened each morning by thighbone trumpets as Himalayan monks performed meditative rituals; watching the parade of life from the safety of the high, iron gates. Beggars, dogs, cattle, and prancing little boys. Stunted ponies the size of Great Danes, pulling carts stuffed with whole families. Hindu holy men. Fresh faced Tibetans. Local folk on foot or bicycle. Despite their poverty, some visiting teachers claim that many local people have strong merits from the past. Former students of the Buddha, they have been reborn in this significant place; as soon as they begin to meditate, they reach purity of mind.

Every so often, a busload of skinny Indian women in saris debouched at the Thai temple, and the women would go inside to admire the golden effigy of Buddha, who is considered to be one of Vishnu's avatars.

In the brief interval before our retreat began, we haggled for meditation shawls with sharp-trading Tibetan ladies; and visited some of the spectacular temples and monasteries built by Bhutanese, Japanese, Tibetans. And of course, we went to revere the stupa.

Just outside it, we learned the Indian system for

dealing with beggars. A line of ancient women crouched against the wall. At the head was another crone, sitting in front of a table piled with stacks of small change. We broke down one rupee into paisa, minute increments of value; now we had enough weightless, fluted coins to distribute one by one. When the change ran out, we understood why we had been followed by a strong man with a rattan club. He menaced those ladies whose clutching hands were empty of coin, until they sat down again. Next were the post card vendors, who understand the world's financial markets sufficiently to fix three prices for their folding strips of images: one price for Indians, a higher one for Westerners, the highest for Japanese.

John Blofeld, 1956 C.E.

Much of my leisure time at Bodhgaya I spent with an unhappy Chinese monk who had lived for two years in the Tibetan temple (the Chinese temple being occupied by a nun) and who suffered from the terrible disability of knowing no language which anybody around him could understand. His joy on hearing me address him in Chinese was unbounded; he seemed to want to laugh and cry at the same time. On the day following my arrival, he prepared with his own hands a splendid vegetarian banquet, to which I was bidden to bring any of my new acquaintances at Bodhgaya whom I chose. After months of uninterrupted silence — for some reason, he did not seem to be intimate with the Chinese nun — he talked and talked and talked, reveling in the sound of his voice like a castaway mariner lately delivered from a desert island. Poor, unhappy man that he is, he seems to be doomed to spend the rest of his life in that place, being afraid to go back to China and having no money and no papers to enable him to live in Burma or Thailand where so many of his compatriots are living. Even the Calcutta Chinatown would afford no shelter to a monk with no money and no friends there.

Lillian Luker Ashby, 1907 C.E.

Surya and I often took the children in their double gocart for an afternoon picnic in the Temple Gardens, where this famous tree held a strong fascination for us. The pipal, like the aspen, has a constant vibration in its heart-shaped leaves, quite independent of any breeze. On even the stillest day it possesses a rustling animation.

One afternoon, while we were near by, a wrinkled old Tibetan, leaning heavily on his staff, turned in from the highway. He hobbled up the long terrace toward the Bo Tree and us. He looked a hundred years old, and might have been more. He was one of that legion who, over a period of years, have made the thousand-mile journey on foot, begging their way, in order to reverence the Bo Tree and to adore the Buddha in the Temple, by these acts to lessen the number of incarnations between them and the perfect rest, Nirvana.

When the dim and almost sightless eyes viewed his long-sought objective, he stopped and gazed in wonderment. A far-away expression of beatific happiness overspread the wrinkled face. The old eyes glowed with new luster. He could see the gates of paradise. For a long time he merely stood there, drinking in the marvelous sight, listening to the other-worldly voices of its whispering leaves.

He began to tell his beads, possibly blessed for him by some lama in a far, crag-surmounting Tibetan monastery. Then he fell prostrate before the tree. He lay motionless, spent with age, fatigue, and emotion. Once he raised his head to gaze again upon his arboreal Buddha.

A little later we passed that way again. The pilgrim had not moved. A Temple mali was attempting to arouse him, but his soul had gone on its way to Nirvana. He had died beneath the Bo Tree in the full flush of happiness, at the moment of accomplishing the great desire of his life. He would not have asked for more. . . .

Ruins of monasteries in front of the Dhamekh stupa

SARNATH
(Isipattana)

Where the Buddha First Taught

Better than a thousand verses
that are senseless and unconnected
with the realization of Nibbana
is a single verse of sense, if on hearing it
one is calmed.

— *The Dhammapada*,
5th–1st c. B.C.E.,
translated from the Pali by Daw Mya Tin

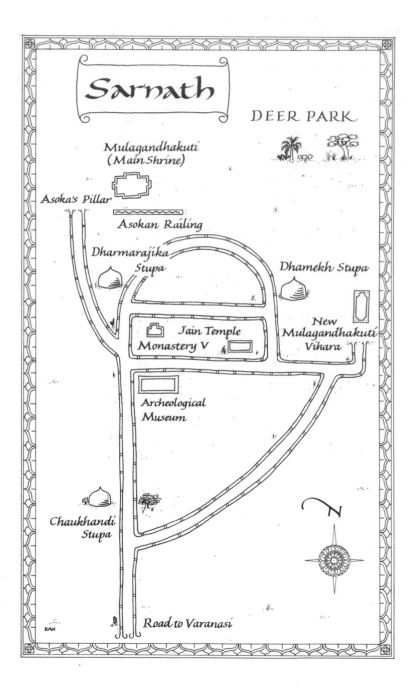

Sarnath

DEER PARK

Mulagandhakuti
(Main Shrine)

Asoka's Pillar

Asokan Railing

Dharmarajika
Stupa

Dhamekh Stupa

Jain Temple
Monastery V

New
Mulagandhakuti
Vihara

Archeological
Museum

Chaukhandi
Stupa

N

Road to Varanasi

EAH

hen the Buddha delivered his first sermon in Sarnath, he was faced with the problem of putting ineffable mysteries into words. He knew how much his ideas could be altered by language. He knew that some ears would hear and understand differently from other ears, and he tailored his teachings, we are told, to suit both more and less prepared listeners. Travel writers face the challenge of rendering experience into words. Pilgrim accounts confront us with a multiplicity of perspectives. Visitors' accounts, one after another, form and reform our image of Sarnath. Yet, they scarcely prepare visitors for what they will see.

Buddhist sites in India have decayed so much over the centuries that travelers must reconstruct them in their minds to recover a sense of what the Buddha and his disciples once saw. Sarnath's landscape is fairly flat, dotted with beautiful trees and with monuments that poke out abruptly from green, groomed earth. From the foundations of ancient monasteries lying in the grass, travelers must mentally erect walls and buildings, an exercise akin to raising a living landscape from the contour lines on a map.

Some travelers prove more adept at this than others, and responses to the site range from delight to disgust. The Sri Lankan pilgrim Justice Wijayatilake lauds Sarnath's "ennobling influence." Mr. Blofeld compares it to a "tourist resort." One traveler expresses relief that Sarnath is not Benares, the "capital of heathendom," while another visitor is moved by the whisperings of its trees in the summer wind: "The rustling seemed like voices."

After his enlightenment, the Buddha journeyed to Sarnath, outside Varanasi, to deliver his first sermon. It was in this sermon that he presented the essential tenets of

Buddhism: the Middle Way, the Four Noble Truths, and the Eightfold Path. According to the most common version of the story, he delivered his sermon to the five ascetics with whom for six years he had practiced austerities in the forest. Though the five had lost faith in the Buddha when he broke his fast, they could sense when they met him in Sarnath that something in him had changed, that he had surpassed them in wisdom and grace. Even before he opened his mouth to speak, they leapt up from the ground to pay him homage. The five became Buddha's first converts to Buddhism.

Sarnath was among the first Buddhist pilgrimage sites to be explored by the British. Attention was drawn to the site in 1798 when the British resident in Benares, Jonathan Duncan, published a short article noting the loss of precious relics, cast into the Ganges by agents of the Maharaja during a reckless hunt for building materials. Archaeological work began at the site soon after Duncan's article appeared. These archaeological activities inspired a number of British people in India to visit Sarnath. However, it was not until Angarika Dharmapala, in the early part of this century, began raising money for the restoration of Sarnath's monuments, that the site became, after Bodh Gaya, a second hub of Buddhist activity in India.

Where the Buddha
First Taught

Hiuen Tsiang, mid-seventh century C.E.

This country is about 4,000 li in circuit. The capital borders [on its western side] the Ganges river. . . . The families are very rich, and in the dwellings are objects of rare value. The disposition of the people is soft and humane, and they are earnestly given to study. They are mostly unbelievers, a few reverence the law of Buddha. The climate is soft, the crops abundant, the trees [fruit trees] flourishing, and the underwood thick in every place.

From *Asvagosha*, The Buddha-Karita, *first century* C.E.
At Bodh Gaya, the Buddha was asked,
"Where, O teacher of the world, will the holy one turn the wheel of the Law?"

"In Varanasi, in the Deer Park will I turn the wheel of the Law; seated in the fourth posture, O deities, I will deliver the world."

There the holy one, the bull of the Sakya race, pondered, "For whom shall I first turn the wheel of the Law?"

The glorious one reflected that Rudraka and Arada were dead, and then he remembered those others, the five men united in a worthy society, who dwelt at Kasi.

Then Buddha set out to go joyfully to Kasi. . . .

In Vanara in a householder's dwelling he was lodged for the night; in the morning he partook of some milk and departed, having given his blessing.

. . . Thence he came to the Ganges, and he bade the ferryman cross.

"Good man, convey me across the Ganges, may the seven blessings be thine." "I carry no one across unless he pays the fee."

"I have nothing, what shall I give?" So saying he went through the sky like the king of birds; and from that time Bimbisara abolished the ferry-fee for all ascetics.

Then having entered Varanasi, the Gina, illumining the city with his light, filled the minds of all the inhabitants of Kasi with excessive interest.

The next day at the end of the second watch, having gone his begging round collecting alms, he, the unequalled one, like Hari, proceeded to the Deer Park.

On the Road to Sarnath

John Huntington, 1985 C.E.

One can follow the old route [to Sarnath] north along the west bank of the Nairanjana River where, with the exceptions of some power lines and the ubiquitous trucks of the Indian highways, some sights must closely resemble those that greeted Sakyamuni on his first post-Enlightenment trip. The countryside exhibits lush growth during the rainy season and usually abundant grain production. The cultivation methods have changed little over the centuries and although there is a modern railway bridge and elevated right-of-way . . . a ploughman, very possibly [the present-day plough-man's] own ancestors, would have been among the views that greeted the newly enlightened Buddha on his journey north to the Rsipatana Mrgadava [Deer Park].

Michael Shoemaker, 1912 C.E.

So careful were the Brahmins to destroy every vestige of Buddhism, to efface all traces, that his very name has vanished from monuments, legends, and traditions, and scarce a man from end to end of the land of his birth and former splendor knows that he ever existed. . . . In Benares there is nothing. One must go to Sarnath to find a trace of the great teacher. It is not far distant, therefore let us leave these Hindus and their city and turn to at least a cleaner faith — if it can be considered a "faith" at all.

Leaving the Hindu city, one draws deep breaths of pure air as the carriage rolls off into the country under trees and through green fields. The recollection of the horrors of Benares are not easily overcome, but if anything can do that, the journey to Buddha's ancient seat of learning will accomplish it. One seems to have left the body behind with Hinduism — this is all of the mind. . . .

Evidently this is a rich section, as the plains over which one passes are clothed with fruit trees and rich with grain. On approaching the site of Sarnath, the first building to attract the eye is the remains of the towers built to commemorate the visit of the Emperor Humayun [on the Chaukambhi Stupa]. The road beyond leads through a wood whose trees are evidently of great age, and under whose boughs Gautama, so the legend runs, took the form of an antelope and offered himself to the King of Benares in place of one which was to have been sacrificed for the royal table.

John Blofeld, 1956 C.E.

I reached Banaras . . . by train and went on to Sarnath by pedicab — a more humane development of the rickshaw which takes the form of a tricycle with a saddle in front for the man who propels it and a rickshaw-like "armchair" behind for one or two passengers. The road is still picturesque, its traffic consisting of modern vehicles interspersed with bullock-carts and an occasional camel or elephant. Many of the houses along the way are topped by realistic sculptured peacocks among which real peacocks perch and fly, so that it is sometimes amusing to speculate upon which of the birds are statues and which are not.

Anne Cushman, 1993 C.E.

Two days later, we leave Bodh Gaya well before dawn, to avoid a statewide political protest that threatens to close down all the roads. We're heading for the Deer Park at Sarnath — just outside the 5,000-year-old city of Varanasi — where the Buddha gave his first teachings. But a few hours from Bodh Gaya, we find ourselves snarled in a spectacular traffic jam. Rumor has it that the backup started the night before when a coal truck overturned and spilled its cargo across the highway; now traffic is at a standstill for close to 100 kilometers.

Most of the vehicles are huge rust-colored trucks (there's only one truck manufacturer in India), their prows gaily decorated with the icons of various gods and goddesses — Durga, Shiva, Kali, Krishna — and wreathed with tinsel, streamers, and strings of withered vegetables. The drivers honk their horns convivially, lie down for naps under their vehicles, cook meals over roadside fires. Vendors appear, selling peanuts and bananas. One man passes with a frying pan and a basket of eggs on his head; for 15 rupees, he says, he'll make us breakfast. Sometime midmorning, someone in our group remembers it is the day before Christmas.

"The more suffering you go through on a pilgrimage, the more merit you get," Larry reminds us. But actually, the group remains quite blithe. In the late afternoon, we disembark from our foundered vehicle and walk into the nearby village, where we check into a grimy truckstop motel that, as my roommate remarks, is "quite lovely, really, if you don't look at the mattresses too closely." We eat curried potatoes and cauliflower, chapati, rice, and dal in a railway restaurant; then rattle back to the motel in bicycle rickshaws, through a smoky, crowded marketplace lit by wood fires and oil lamps. Jan says, "This is the first Christmas I've ever had that really felt like Christmas."

That night I dream that the Buddha is coming to give a Dharma talk in the street outside our motel. I lean out the window and crane my neck to see him; but all I can glimpse is the back of his shaven head as he disappears into the crowd.

The next morning the traffic jam has melted away — for once, impermanence is on our side — and we drive unimpeded to the luxurious Hotel Varanasi Ashoka. The marble lobby is presided over by a stunned-looking Santa Claus enshrined in silver and magenta tinsel like a Hindu deity. After blissfully hot showers, we head to the ruins of the Deer Park at Sarnath, where the brick foundations of long-abandoned temples mark the spot where the Buddha first proclaimed the Four Noble Truths: the existence of suffering; its origin; the possibility of ending it; and the way to do so.

The Five Ascetics

Not all the Buddha's biographers agree on the identity of the five men to whom the Buddha preached his first sermon. Some describe them as the group of men sent out by the Buddha's anxious father to find his wayward son. The view which has prevailed, however, sees them as the five ascetics with whom the Buddha fasted and meditated during the six years before his enlightenment. Though the men lost faith in Gautama's sincerity when they saw him break his fast, the Buddha chose them to be the first audience to hear his teachings and journeyed to Sarnath expressly to find them.

Fa-hsien, 400 C.E.

[P]roceeding west along the Ganges for twelve *yojanas,* [Fa-hsien] reached the city of Varanasi in the country of Kasi. About ten *li* northeast of the city is the Deer Park Retreat of the Rishis. Originally a Pratyeka Buddha lived in this park, and wild deer often came here for shelter. When the Blessed One was about to become a Buddha, devas announced from the sky:

"The son of King Suddhodana, who renounced his home to acquire supreme truth, will attain to Buddhahood after seven days."

On hearing this the Pratyeka Buddha entered Nirvana. Therefore his place is called the Deer Park of the

A pilgrim circles the Dhamekh stupa

Rishis. After the Blessed One's accession to Buddhahood, men of later ages built a retreat here. Buddha wished to convert Kaundinya and his four companions, but these five men said to each other:

"For six years this monk Gautama lived as an ascetic on one grain of sesame and one of rice a day, yet he did not obtain the truth. Now that he is living among men, having thrown off all mental and physical restraints, what truth can he have obtained? If he comes today, let us be sure not to speak to him."

When Buddha arrived, however, the five men felt impelled to rise and salute him. Sixty paces further north is the place where Buddha sat facing east when he preached his first sermon and converted Kaundinya and his companions. Twenty paces north of this is the place where Buddha predicted the future of Maitreya. Fifty paces to the south is the spot where the dragon Elapatra asked Buddha when he could be freed from his dragon form. Stupas built at all these spots are standing to this day. There are also two monasteries, both of which are occupied by monks.

From Asvagosha, The Buddha-Karita, second century C.E.

When the five ascetics saw the Buddha approaching them, they conspired amongst themselves to ignore him, saying:

"This is Gautama who has come hither, the ascetic who has abandoned his self-control.

"He wanders about now, greedy, of impure soul, unstable and with his sense under no firm control, devoted to inquiries regarding the frying-pan.

"We will not ask after his health, nor rise to meet him, nor address him, nor offer him a welcome, nor a seat, nor bid him enter into our dwelling."

Having understood their agreement, with a smiling countenance, spreading light all around, Buddha

advanced gradually nearer, holding his staff and his beg-
ging-pot.

Forgetful of their agreement, the five friends,
under his constraining majesty, rose up like birds in their
cages when scorched by fire.

Having taken his begging-bowl and staff, they
gave him . . . water for washing his feet and rinsing his
mouth; and bowing reverentially, they said to him,
"Honoured Sir, health to thee."

"Health in every respect is ours, — that wisdom
has been attained which is so hard to be won," so saying,
the holy one thus spoke to the five worthy associates:

"But address me not as 'worthy Sir,'— know that
I am Gina, — I have come to give the first wheel of the
Law to you. Receive initiation from me, — ye shall
obtain the place of Nirvana." . . .

Then at the mendicants' respectful request the
chief of saints bathed in the tank, and after eating
ambrosia he reflected on the field of the Law. . . .

Brahman and the other gods came surrounded
by their attendants, summoned each from his own
world; and Maitriya with the deities of the Tushita heav-
en came for the turning of the wheel of the Law.

The omniscient lion of the Sakya then caused
all the assembly, headed by those who belonged to the
company of Maitriya, to turn the wheel of the Law.

"Listen, O company belonging to Maitriya, ye
who form one vast congregation, — as it was proclaimed by those past arch-saints, so is it now proclaimed by Me."

The First Sermon

*The First Sermon lays out some of the most basic
precepts of Buddhism. In his sermon, the Buddha first*

describes what is called the Middle Way, the way of life which the monk seeking the path to enlightenment should follow.

THE MIDDLE PATH

From Asvagosha, The Buddha-Karita,
second century *C.E.*

There are the two extremes, O mendicants, in the self-control of the religious ascetic, — the one which is devoted to the joys of desire, vulgar and common,

And the other which is tormented by the excessive pursuit of self-inflicted pain in the mortification of the soul's corruptions, — these are the two extremes of the religious ascetic, each devoted to that which is unworthy and useless.

These have nothing to do with true asceticism, renunciation of the world, or self-control, with true indifference or suppression of pain, or with any of the means of attaining deliverance.

They do not tend to the spiritual forms of knowledge, to wisdom, nor to Nirvana; let him who is acquainted with the uselessness of inflicting pain and weariness on the body,

Who has lost his interest in any pleasure or pain of a visible nature, or in the future, and who follows this middle Path for the good of the world, —

Let him, the Tathagata, the teacher of the world, proclaim the good Law, beginning with that manifestation of the good Law which consists of the (four) noble truths.

FOUR NOBLE TRUTHS

Thich Nhat Hanh, 1991 *C.E.*

"Brothers, there are four truths: the existence of

suffering, the cause of suffering, the cessation of suffering, and the path which leads to the cessation of suffering. I call these the Four Noble Truths."

NOBLE EIGHTFOLD PATH

From **The Digha Nikaya,** *Sutta 22:*
The Mahasatipatthana Sutta, 5th–1st c. B.C.E.
"And what, monks, is the Noble Truth of the Way of Practice Leading to the Cessation of Suffering? It is just this Noble Eightfold Path, namely: — Right View, Right Thought; Right Speech, Right Action, Right Livelihood; Right Effort, Right Mindfulness, Right Concentration.

"And what, monks, is Right View? It is, monks, the knowledge of suffering, the knowledge of the origin of suffering, the knowledge of the cessation of suffering, and the knowledge of the way of practice leading to the cessation of suffering. This is called Right View.

"And what, monks, is Right Thought? The thought of renunciation, the thought of non-ill-will, the thought of harmlessness. This, monks, is called Right Thought.

"And what, monks, is Right Speech? Refraining from lying, refraining from slander, refraining from harsh speech, refraining from frivolous speech. This is called Right Speech.

"And what, monks, is Right Action? Refraining from taking life, refraining from taking what is not given, refraining from sexual misconduct. This is called Right Action.

"And what, monks, is Right Livelihood? Here, monks, the Ariyan disciple, having given up wrong livelihood, keeps himself by right livelihood.

"And what, monks, is Right Effort? Here, monks, a monk rouses his will, makes an effort, stirs up energy, exerts his mind and strives to prevent the arising of unarisen evil unwholesome mental states. He rouses his will . . . and strives to overcome evil unwholesome mental states that have arisen. He rouses his will . . . and strives to produce unarisen wholesome mental states. He rouses his will, makes an effort, stirs up energy, exerts his mind and strives to maintain wholesome mental states that have arisen, not to let them fade away, to bring them to greater growth, to the full perfection of development. This is called Right Effort.

"And what, monks, is Right Mindfulness? Here, monks, a monk abides contemplating body as body, ardent, clearly aware and mindful, having put aside hankering and fretting for the world; he abides contemplating feelings as feelings . . . he abides contemplating mind as mind . . . he abides contemplating mind-objects, ardent, clearly aware and mindful, having put aside hankering and fretting for the world. This is called Right Mindfulness.

"And what, monks, is Right Concentration? Here, a monk, detached from sense-desires, detached from unwholesome mental states, enters and remains in the first jhana, which is with thinking and pondering, born of detachment, filled with delight and joy. And with the subsiding of thinking and pondering, by gaining inner tranquility and oneness of mind, he enters and remains in the second jhana, which is without thinking and pondering, born of concentration, filled with delight and joy. And with the fading away of delight, remaining imperturbable, mindful and clearly aware, he experiences in himself the joy of which the Noble Ones say: 'Happy is he who dwells with equanimity and mindfulness,' he enters the third jhana. And, having given up pleasure and pain, and with the disappearance of former gladness and sadness, he enters and remains in the fourth jhana, which is beyond pleasure and pain, and purified by equanimity and mindfulness. This is called Right Concentration. And that, monks, is called the way of practice leading to the cessation of suffering."

KONDANNA

After hearing the Buddha's first sermon, the five ascetics became the Buddha's first converts. Their leader, Kondanna, is said to have described in verse the moment of his realization. The verse is included in a collection of verses composed by the early Buddhist monks. Written in Pali, the collection is called the Theragatha *and is a companion volume to the* Therigatha, *containing the verses of the early Buddhist nuns.*

From the Theragatha, fifth century B.C.E.

[R]eborn before our Exalted One, in the village of Donavattu, not far from Kapilavatthu, in a very wealthy Brahmin family, he came to be called by his family name, Kondanna. When grown up he knew the three Vedas, and excelled in runes concerning marks. Now when our Bodhisat was born, he was among the eight brahmins sent for to prognosticate. And though he was quite a novice, he saw the marks of the Great Man on the infant, and said: "Verily this one will be a Buddha!" So he lived, awaiting the Great Being's renunciation. When this happened in the Bodhisat's twenty-ninth year, Kondanna heard of it, and left the world with four other sons of mark-interpreting brahmins, Vappa and others, and for six years dwelt at Uruvela, near the Bodhisat, during the latter's great struggle. Then when the Bodhisat ceased to fast, they were disgusted and went to Isipatana. There the Buddha followed them, and preached his Wheel sermon, whereby Kondanna and myriads of Brahma angels won the fruition of the first path. And on the fifth day, through the sermon on

"No sign of my Soul," Kondanna realized arahantship
[and spoke these words:]

> Brother Kondanna, wakened by the Wake: —
> Lo! he hath passed with vigour out and on;
> Sloughed off hath he the dyings and the births,
> Wholly accomplishing the life sublime.
> And be it "flood" or "snare" or "stumbling-stone,"
> Or be it "mountain" hard to rive in twain,
> The net, the stumbling-stone I've hacked away,
> And cloven is the rock so hard to break,
> And crossed the flood. Rapt in ecstatic thought
> I dwell, from bondage unto evil freed.

Chaukhandi Stupa

*On the way to the Deer Park in Sarnath, the trav-
eler passes a stupa on the road said to mark the spot where
the Buddha first met the five ascetics. The stupa is topped
by an octagonal tower built in 1588 by the Mughal gover-
nor under Emperor Akbar, Govardan, to commemorate
Humayun's visit to the area. While no relics have been
found in the stupa, Guptan sculptures suggest that the
monument dates from the fifth century or earlier.*

S. R. Wijayatilake, 1963 C.E.

As we approached [Sarnath] in the distance was
the imposing monument known as *Choukandi*. It is an
ancient stupa built about the 2nd or 3rd century A.C. It
would appear that in the 7th century Emperor Akbar had
constructed a tower on the top of this stupa to commemorate the visit of his father Humayun who was a
refugee from his enemies who were out for his blood.
This tower is quite conspicuous and it stands above the
stupa quite out of proportion and style to the rest of the

The Deer Park

monument. It is noteworthy that this stupa stands on
the very spot where the Buddha after he attained
Enlightenment at Gaya met the five ascetics who were
his associates but had gone away disgusted when the
Buddha abandoned self-mortification and other
penances which were the order of the day among the
priests and the ascetics of the time. . . .

[The First Sermon] conveying the unassailable
Truth which ultimately revolutionized the religious
and social structure in India [was] a revelation to the
ascetics who had given themselves to all kinds of pri-
vations in search of a solution to the problem of suffering. We could see a few of them with their eyes closed

154

lost in contemplation and the rest with a smile of understanding nodding their heads in assent. One or two of them would be feeling their matted hair or their limbs bereft of all fat and muscle. They were perhaps thinking of all the pain they subjected themselves to, all in vain. Here was a simple solution to a problem which had worried them from the time they took to the road in search of inner happiness. As the five ascetics realised the Truth one could see a change in the scene. The gathering clouds were wafted away by a breath of wind and there was a fragrance in the air which was so ethereal that man and beast paid their obeisance to the Master.

The Deer Park

Not far down the road from the stupa marking the site of the five ascetics' encounter with the Buddha, the traveler arrives in Sarnath. Though there are a number of twentieth-century Buddhist temples in Sarnath, built and maintained by monks from Tibet, China, and Japan, the principal attraction of Sarnath is the Deer Park where the Buddha preached his first sermons and accepted the first monks into the Buddhist order.

Hiuen Tsiang, mid-seventh century C.E.

To the north-east of the river Varana about 10 li or so, we come to the sangharama of Lu-ye . . . [Deer Park]. Its precincts are divided into eight portions [sections], connected by a surrounding wall. The storeyed towers with projecting eaves and the balconies are of very superior work. There are fifteen hundred priests in this convent who study the Little Vehicle according to the Sammatiya school. . . .

Within the precincts of the enclosure [of the

sangharama] there are many sacred vestiges, with viharas and stupas several hundred in number.

S. R. Wijayatilake, 1963 *C.E.*
It was so fascinating to see deer roaming about
quite unafraid of man. Truly Sarnath is a haven of peace.
Although the stupas and monasteries lay fallen there is a
majestic serenity about this place. We could picture to
ourselves the Buddha in a previous birth straining himself to save a deer at the risk of his own life. [See below.]
This place is sanctified by this act of gallant chivalry of
the Bodhisattva, who sacrificed his own life to save the
deer. The deer roaming about this shangrila symbolize
this supreme act of sacrifice

THE DEER JATAKA

*While the early Chinese pilgrim Fa-hsien under-
stood the park's name, Deer Park, to derive from the deer
who had sought a safe haven in the company of an earlier Buddha, the Pratyeka Buddha, the most common narrative traces the park's origins to a previous birth of the
Buddha as the golden-skinned lord of a herd of deer.*

From The "Nigrodha-Miga Jataka," fifth century B.C.E.
to first century C.E.
Long ago, when Brahma-datta was reigning in
Benares, the Bodisat came to life as a deer. When he was
born he was of a golden colour; his eyes were like round
jewels, his horns were white as silver, his mouth was red
as a cluster of kamala flowers, his hoofs were bright and
hard as lacquer-work, his tail as fine as the tail of a
Tibetan ox, and his body as large in size as a foal's.
He lived in the forest with an attendant herd of
five hundred deer, under the name of the King of the
Banyan Deer; and not far from him there dwelt another

156

deer, golden as he, under the name of the Monkey Deer, with a like attendant herd.

The king of Benares at that time was devoted to hunting, never ate without meat, and used to summon all the townspeople to go hunting every day, to the destruction of their ordinary work.

The people thought, "This king puts an end to all our work. Suppose now in the park we were to sow food and provide water for the deer, and drive a number of deer into it, and close the entrance, and deliver them over to the king."

So they planted in the park grass for the deer to eat, and provided water, and tied up the gate; and calling the citizens, they entered the forest, with clubs and all kinds of weapons in their hands, to look for the deer. And thinking, "We shall best catch the deer by surrounding them," they encircled a part of the forest about a league across. And in so doing they surrounded the very place where the Banyan Deer and the Monkey Deer were living.

Then striking the trees and bushes, and beating on the ground, with their clubs, they drove the herd of deer out of the place where they were; and making a great noise by rattling their swords and javelins and bows, they made the herd enter the park, and shut the gate. And then they went to the king, and said to him:

"O king! by your constant going to the chase, you put a stop to our work. We have now brought deer from the forest, and filled your park with them. Henceforth feed on *them!*" And so saying, they took their leave and departed.

When the king heard that, he went to the park; and seeing there two golden-coloured deer, he granted them their lives. But thenceforth he would sometimes go himself to shoot a deer, and bring it home; sometimes his cook would go and shoot one. The deer, as soon as they saw the bow, would quake with the fear of death, and take to their heels; but when they had been hit once or twice, they became weary or wounded, and were killed.

And the herd of deer told all this to the Bodisat. He sent for the Monkey Deer, and said:

"Friend, almost all the deer are being destroyed. Now, though they certainly must die, yet henceforth let them not be wounded with the arrows. Let the deer take it by turns to go to the place of execution. One day let the lot fall upon my herd, and the next day on yours. Let the deer whose turn it is go to the place of execution, put his head on the block, and lie down. If this is done, the deer will at least escape laceration."

He agreed: and thenceforth the deer whose turn it was used to go and lie down, after placing his neck on the block of execution. And the cook used to come and carry off the one he found lying there.

But one day the lot fell upon a roe in the herd of the Monkey Deer who was with young. She went to the Monkey Deer, and said, "Lord! I am with young. When I have brought forth my son, we will both take our turn. Order the turn to pass by."

"I cannot make your lot," said he, "fall upon the others. You know well enough it has fallen upon you. Go away!"

Receiving no help from him, she went to the Bodisat, and told him the matter. He listened to her, and said, "Be it so! Do you go back. I will relieve you of your turn." And he went *himself,* and he put his neck upon the block of execution, and lay down.

The cook, seeing him, exclaimed, "The King of the Deer, whose life was promised to him, is lying in the place of execution. What does this mean?" And he went hastily, and told the king.

The king no sooner heard it than he mounted his chariot, and proceeded with a great retinue to the place, and beholding the Bodisat, said, "My friend the King of the Deer! did I not grant you your life? Why are you lying here?"

"O great king! a roe with young came and told me that the lot had fallen upon her. Now it was impossible for me to transfer her miserable lot to any one else. So I, giving my life to her, and accepting death in her place, have lain down. Harbour no further suspicion, O great king!"

"My Lord the golden-coloured King of the Deer! I never yet saw, even among men, one so full of forbearance, kindness, and compassion. I am pleased with thee in this matter. Rise up! I grant your lives, both to you and to her!"

"But though two be safe, what shall the rest do, O king of men?"

"Then I grant their lives to the rest, my Lord."

"Thus, then, great king, the deer in the park will have gained security, but what will the others do?"

"They also shall not be molested."

"Great king! even though the deer dwell secure, what shall the rest of the four-footed creatures do?"

"They also shall be free from fear."

"Great king! even though the quadrupeds are in safety, what shall the flocks of birds do?"

"Well, I grant the same boon to them."

"Great king! the birds then will obtain peace, but what of the fish who dwell in the water?"

"They shall have peace as well."

And so the Great Being, having interceded with the king for all creatures, rose up and established the king in the Five Precepts, and said, "Walk in righteousness, O great king! Doing justice and mercy to fathers and mothers, to sons and daughters, to townsmen and landsmen, you shall enter, when your body is dissolved, the happy world of heaven!"

Thus, with the grace of a Buddha, he preached

the Truth to the king; and when he had dwelt a few days in the park to exhort the king, he went away to the forest with his attendant herd.

And the doe gave birth to a son as beautiful as buds of flowers; and he went playing about with the Monkey Deer's herd. But when its mother saw that, she said, "My son, henceforth go not in his company; you may keep to the Banyan Deer's herd!" And thus exhorting him, she uttered the verse —

Following the Banyan Deer:
Dwell not with the Monkey Deer.
Better death with the Banyan Deer
Than life with the Monkey Deer.

Now after that the deer, secure of their lives, began to eat men's crops. And the men dared not strike them or drive them away, recollecting how it had been granted to them that they should dwell secure. So they met together in front of the king's palace, and told the matter to the king.

"When I was well pleased, I granted to the leader of the Banyan Deer a boon," said he. "I may give up my kingdom, but not my oath! Begone with you! Not a man in my kingdom shall be allowed to hurt the deer."

When the Banyan Deer heard that, he assembled the herds, and said, "Henceforth you are not allowed to eat other people's crops." And so forbidding them, he sent a message to the men: "Henceforth let the husbandmen put up no fence to guard their crops; but let them tie leaves round the edge of the field as a sign."

From that time, they say, the sign of the tying of the leaves was seen in the fields, and from that time not a single deer trespassed beyond it; for such was the instruction they received from the Bodisat.

And the Bodisat continued thus his life long to instruct the deer, and passed away with his herd according to his deeds.

IMPORTANT MONUMENTS
IN THE DEER PARK

DHARMEKHA STUPA

The British archaeologist believed the Dharmekha stupa marked the spot where the Buddha delivered his First Sermon. The original stupa was expanded several times. The inside, now exposed at the top, is composed of Mauryan brick (from Asoka's times), while the outer and lower area is decorated in fifth-century Guptan reliefs. As a form of offering, many pilgrims rub gold leaf onto the sides of the stupa.

Michael Shoemaker, 1912 C.E.
The village of Sarnath near by is insignificant and of no worth, but beyond it rises the still stately remains of the great tower marking the spot where Buddha for the first time exposed his doctrines — [to four beggars]. It is a ruin, of course, but rises over one hundred feet, the lower section of large stones and the upper of brick which was once encased in stucco, and probably gilded, and surmounted by the T or umbrella. . . . Around it stood a great monastery whose foundations are plainly traceable to-day. Ruins cover the earth in all directions; evidently the town was of extent, but this tower is the only building rising above the foundations. The whole was finally destroyed in the tenth century during a public insurrection when the insurgents burnt both monks and monastery and the place was given over to the jackals.

Walter Crane, 1907 C.E.
[W]e saw the great Tope (called the Dhamek).

161

This stood on rather higher ground, and was apparently built of rubble, which was exposed at the top, but the
sides were covered with fine bands of carved ornament
in stone, carried to a considerable height, and consisting of a frieze of bold scroll work of a Greek character,
alternating with bands of a kind of Chinese-like diagonal diaper, divided by plain belts of stone. At intervals
these bands were intersected by flat dome-shaped
forms slightly projecting beyond the bands, and in
these were recesses intended, no doubt, originally to
contain seated figures of Buddha. These flat dome-
shaped forms, connected by bands, suggested a pal-
isade, which may have been the original way of enclosing and protecting these topes or tombs; and they may
also have been the early form or prototype of the curious clustered dome-shaped pinnacles which are multi-
plied to form the spires of Jain temples so often seen in
India.

DHARMARAJIKA STUPA OF ASOKA

*The Dharmarajika Stupa was pulled apart in the
eighteenth century when Jagat Singh, the Dewan of Raja
Chet Singh of Banaras, began to plunder Sarnath for
building materials. Finding a green marble casket, the
Dewan dumped its contents — reliquary ashes — into the
Ganges. The original stupa was built by Asoka and
enlarged five times, first in the Kushan period, then in the
fifth or sixth century, in the seventh century, in the ninth
to the eleventh centuries and in the twelfth century.
Today, thanks to Jagat Singh, it lies in complete ruins.*

Jonathan Duncan, Esq., 1808 C.E.

I herewith beg leave to deliver to the Society a
Stone, and a Marble Vessel, found the one within the
other, in the month of January, 1794, by the people
employed by Baboo Juggut Sing in digging for stones

from the subterraneous materials of some extensive and ancient buildings in the vicinity of a temple called *Sarnauth*, at the distance of about four miles to the northward of the present city of *Benares*.

In the innermost of these cases (which were discovered after digging to the depth of eighteen *hauts*, or cubits, under the surface) were found a few human bones, that were committed to the *Ganges*, and some decayed pearly, gold leaves, and other jewels of no value, which cannot be better disposed of than by continuing in the receptacle in which they must have so long remained, and been placed upon an occasion on which there are several opinions among the natives in that district. The first, that the bones found along with them, may be those of the consort of some former Rajah or Prince, who having devoted herself to the flames on the death of her husband, or on some other emergency, her relations may have made (as is said not to be unprecedented) this deposit of her remains as a permanent place of lodgment; whilst others have suggested that the remains of the deceased may have probably been thus temporarily disposed of, till a proper time or opportunity should arrive of committing them to the Ganges, as is usually observed in respect to these *pushpa*, or flowers; a term by which the *Hindus* affect to distinguish those residuary vestiges of their friends dying natural deaths, that are not consumed by the fire, to which their corpses are generally exposed, according to the tenets of their religion.

But I am myself inclined to give the preference to a conclusion differing from either of the two former, viz. that the bones found in these urns must belong to one of the worshippers of BUDDHA, a set of *Indian* heretics, who, having no reverence for the *Ganges*, used to deposit their remains in the earth, instead of committing them to that river; a surmise that seems strongly corroborated by the circumstance of a statue or idol

163

of BUDDHA having been found in the same place under ground, and on the same occasion with the discovery of the urns in question, on which was an inscription, as per the accompanying copy of the original, ascertaining that a temple had between 700 or 800 years ago been constructed there for the worship of that deity.

THE MAIN SHRINE

The Main Shrine marks the place of the hut, called the Mulagandakuti, where the Buddha stayed during his visits to Sarnath. The Shrine dates from the sixth century C.E., but has been added to since that time. A railing, hewn from a single block of Chunar sandstone, stands inside. Carved around 200 B.C.E., the railing was probably designed to stand on top of the nearby Dharmarajika Stupa.

Hiuen Tsiang, mid-seventh century C.E.

In the great enclosure is a *vihara* about 200 feet high; above the roof is a golden-covered figure of the Amra fruit. The foundations of the building are of stone, and the stairs also, but the towers and niches are of brick. The niches are arranged on the four sides in a hundred successive lines, and in each niche is a golden figure of Buddha. In the middle of the *vihara* is a figure of Buddha made of *teou-shih (native copper)*. It is the size of life, and he is represented as turning the wheel of the law *(preaching)*.

Walter Crane, 1907 C.E.

There were the remains of an ancient Buddhist temple near. In what was probably the inner shrine was a sculptured standing figure of Buddha, about two-thirds life size, in *alto relievo*. The figure was represented in a long robe, the limbs being boldly expressed through the drapery, which hung broadly and smoothly over them, without folds, except at the sides, which were treated in the rather formal spiral manner of early Greek work.

The American lady remarked on seeing this figure that, "The gentleman seems to have put his legs through his clothes."

The figure was framed in a border of astralagus, cut in low relief, having a running escalloped border outside it and stepped mouldings. The doorway to this shrine, too, had a richly carved bordering.

There were many most interesting fragments collected together in and around a building near. In the court was a large circular carved stone. This was called Buddha's umbrella, and its original position was over the head of a large figure of the saint, sculptured in the round, close by. The design of the umbrella, was a lotus flower, the flower of life, the petals radiating from the centre, and enclosing this were a series of concentric rings of pattern; the first consisted of rosettes, or smaller lotus flowers, alternating with grotesque lions, winged horses, elephants, camels, and bulls; the next showed the anthemion, doubled or reversed, alternating with the fylfot or gammadion (drawing of a swastika), and another form frequent in early Greek pattern (as well as Chinese) the geometric four-petalled flower. There were numerous small figures of Buddha here, treated in a similar way to the one first mentioned, as well as other sculptures of a Hindu type, resembling those at Ellora.

THE ASOKAN PILLAR

The Asokan Pillar, unearthed at Sarnath by F. O. Oertel in 1904–5, was topped by a lion capital, now housed in the Sarnath Museum. A warning against the splitting of the Buddhist sangha is inscribed in the Brahmi script on its face.

The Asokan Pillar

From Asoka, Sarnath Pillar Edict, 274–232 B.C.E.

. . . No one shall disrupt the Samgha.

If a monk or nun disrupts the Samgha, he or she shall be required to put on a white robe and to live in non-residence.

This edict should be published both in the Samgha of the monks and in the Samgha of the nuns.

King Priyadarsi [Asoka] says:

Place one copy of this edict in the cloister of the vihara; give another copy to the lay disciples. The lay disciples shall assemble every fast day to study this edict. Every official shall regularly attend services on every fast day in order to familiarize himself with the edict and understand it fully.

Moreover you [i.e. Asoka's officials at Pataliputra] shall send orders throughout the district under your administration putting this edict into effect. Your subordinate shall do the same in all fortified towns and the districts surrounding them.

Hiuen Tsiang, mid-seventh century C.E.

To the south-west of the *vihara* is a stone *stupa* built by Asoka-raja. Although the foundations have given way, there are still 100 feet or more of the wall remaining. In front of the building is a stone pillar about 70 feet high. The stone is altogether as bright as jade. It is glistening, and sparkles like light; and all those who pray fervently before it see from time to time, according to their petitions, figures with good or bad signs. It was here that Tathagatha . . . having arrived at enlightenment, began to turn the wheel of the law (*to preach*).

Walter Crane, 1907 C.E.

At Sarnath we saw the results of recent excavations. There was a wonderful pillar made out of a single piece of marble, but fractured in digging it out. One part stood upright in the earth, the other lay horizontally. The top or cap was placed under an awning near by. It was formed of four lions facing outwards, their heads, chests, and fore limbs being alone visible, their claws resting on the rim of a circular fillet, on which was sculptured in low relief a horse, an elephant, a lion, and a bull, each animal being placed between a wheel of a solar character, each wheel having twenty-four spokes. Below this fillet was a curved drooping fringe of leaves such as are characteristic in Persian columns as well as Hindu. The marble of which the column and the sculptures were made was of a peculiar greyish almost of a flesh colour, with small spots. Both the column and the sculptures were very highly polished, and the treatment of the lions was remarkably Greek in character with perhaps a touch of Persian or even Assyrian formalism in the treatment of the heads and manes of the lions. The animals in relief, between the wheels, too, were remarkably free, spirited, and well modelled.

BUDDHA WALK
Hiuen Tsiang, mid-seventh century C.E.

Not far to the south of this spot are traces where the four Buddhas of a bygone age walked for exercise. The length *(of the promenade)* is about fifty paces and the height of the steps *(stepping spots)* about seven feet. It is composed of blue stones piled together. Above it is a figure of Tathagata in the attitude of walking. It is of a singular dignity and beauty. From the flesh-knot on the top of the head there flows wonderfully a braid of hair. Spiritual signs are plainly manifested and divine prodigies wrought with power.

THE LAKE
On the edge of a park is a small, placid lake, now

bordered by a zoo, which has attracted a few comments from visitors.

Hiuen Tsiang, mid-seventh century C.E.

To the west of the *sangharama* enclosure is a clear lake of water about 200 paces in circuit; here Tathagatha occasionally bathed himself. To the west of this is a great tank about 180 paces round; here the Tathagatha used to wash his begging-dish.

To the north of this is a lake about 150 paces round. Here Tathagatha used to wash his robes. In each of these pools is a dragon who dwells within it. The water is deep and its taste sweet; it is pure and resplendent in appearance, and neither increases nor decreases. When men of a bad character bathe here, the crocodiles . . . come forth and kill many of them; but in case of the reverential who wash here, they need fear nothing.

By the side of the pool where Tathagatha washed his garments is a great square stone, on which are yet to be seen the trace-marks of his kashaya *(kia-sha)* robe. The bright lines of the tissue are of a minute and distinct character, as if carved on the stone. The faithful and pure frequently come to make their offerings here; but when the heretics and men of evil mind speak lightly of or insult the stone, the dragon-king inhabiting the pool causes the winds to rise and rain to fall.

Major Rowland Raven-Hart, 1956 C.E.

But what has happened to [Hiuen Tsiang's] three lakes? — "in each of which dwells a dragon. When men of bad character bathe there the crocodiles come forth and kill them, but the reverential need fear nothing." I could find one only, down towards the Burmese monastery, with boys fishing and swimming in it, which speaks well for the good character of Sarnath kids; or the mellowing influence of time on the crocodiles. I wonder if Hiuen Tsiang risked a swim: I did, borrowing a wet loincloth from an amused lad, and escorted by naked urchins. The water was pleasantly lukewarm, but rarely deep enough for swimming, and the bottom was mud. I saw no crocodiles.

THE HISTORY OF DEER PARK AND THE MODERN MULAGANDHAKUTI VIHARA

While Hiuen Tsiang and Fa-hsien found a number of monks assiduously studying in the monasteries which remained in their times at Sarnath, the site was virtually deserted for almost a thousand years. Early archaeologists at the site reported evidence of a period of massive and sudden destruction. One archaeologist in the 1800s wrote:

It will have been observed that every excavation made near Sarnath revealed traces of fire. I myself found charred timber and half-burnt grain. The same things were also found by Major Kittoe, besides the evident traces of fire on the stone pillars, umbrellas and statues. So vivid was the impression of a great final catastrophe by fire fixed in Major Kittoe's mind, by the discoveries made during his excavations, that he thus summed up his conclusions to me in a few words: "All has been sacked and burnt, priests, temples, idols, all together. In some places, bones, iron, timber, idols, &c., are all fused into huge heaps; and this has happened more than once." The destruction of this large monastery would appear to have been both sudden and unexpected, for Mr. Thomas records that Major Kittoe found the remains of ready-made wheaten cakes in a small recess in the chamber towards the north east angle of the square. Mr. Thomas himself also found portions of wheat and other grain spread out in one of the cells. These discoveries would seem to show that the conflagration had been so sudden and rapid as to force the monks to abandon their very food. In short, all existing indications lead to a necessary inference that the destruction of the building by whomsoever caused, was effected by fire applied by the hand of an exterminating adversary rather than by any ordinary accidental conflagration.

Anagarika Dharmapala, 1931 C.E.

Finding the site in a state of utter dilapidation and neglect, the Anagarika Dharmapala, a prominent Buddhist at the turn of the nineteenth century who was instrumental in bringing about the restoration of the Buddhist monuments at Bodh Gaya, organized Sarnath's rehabilitation. He petitioned wealthy Indians and Westerners for money to restore the site and, in an essay published in the *Maha Bodhi Journal,* made a plea for Buddhism and for the restoration and promotion of the important Buddhist sites in India, in particular, of the Deer Park in Sarnath. The essay was entitled "Holy Isipatana, Sarnath, Benares."

The external portion of the Buddha religion was destroyed by the Moslem fanatics, while the literary portion of the religion was destroyed by the theologians of the Brahmanical cult. They also distorted the teachings of the Compassionate Teacher by misrepresenting him a Nastika and a reviler of the Vedas. The Moslems forgot the past history of the religion they extirpated, while the Brahmin theologians painted the Lord as an enemy of the Brahmanical faith. The social harm done to India by the alien vandals and the priestly theologians have brought the teeming millions to a state of asinine ignorance. Untouchability, the institution of virgin widows, caste oppression, bacchanalian orgies and ceremonial superstitions are keeping them in ignorance and indescribable impoverishment. For a thousand years the compassionate democratic teachings of the Devatideva Sakyamuni Buddha have been crushed out of existence by hostile forces. The Indian masses can only be saved by the dissemination of the progressive teachings of the Sammasambuddha. The Lord Buddha appeared as the Great Physician to treat all classes alike. He was the embodiment of universal pity. He made no distinction between man and woman — for the first time in the history of the world women became preachers and missionaries. Art, industries, agriculture, commerce, reached their zenith. A Greater India came into existence with Buddhagaya, Isipatana, Sankassa, Kusinara, Rajgir, and Nalanda as centres of learning. For a thousand years India has continued to decline, and the time is ripe to disseminate the democratic teachings of the All-merciful Lord.

THE MULAGANDHAKUTI VIHARA

Through his speeches and writings, Dharmapala succeeded in raising money for not only Sarnath's restoration but the construction of a new Buddhist temple on the grounds of the Deer Park. This is the Mulagandhakuti Vihara. When the Vihara opened, in 1931, a number of prominent Indian nationalists spoke, evoking the teachings of the Buddha to reiterate their own message of freedom and brotherhood.

Rabindranath Tagore, 1931 C.E.

The spiritual illumination in India, which ages ago shed its radiance over the continent of Asia, raised its memorial on the sacred spot near Benares where Lord Buddha had proclaimed to his disciples his message of love's supreme fulfillment. Though this monument representing the final hour of liberation for all people was buried under dust and forgotten in India, the voice of her greatest son still waits in the heart of silent centuries for a new awakenment to hearken to his call.

Today when in spite of a physical closeness of all nations a universal moral alienation between races has become a fateful menace to all humanity, let us, in this threatening gloom of a militant savagery, before the widening jaws of an organized greed, still rejoice in the fact that the reopening of the ancient monastery of Sarnath is being celebrated by pilgrims from the West and the East.

Numerous are the triumphal towers built to perpetuate the memories of injuries and indignities inflicted by one murdering race upon another, but let us once for all, for the sake of humanity restore to its full signficance this great memorial of a generous past to remind us of an ancient meeting of nations in India for the exchange of love, for the establishment of spiritual comradeship among races separated by distance and historical traditions, for the offering of the treasure of immortal wisdom left to the world by the blessed One to whom we dedicate our united homage.

Dr. Surendranath Das Gupta, 1931 C.E.

Presiding over the meeting, Das Gupta's words were summarized in newspaper accounts of the opening celebration.

[T]he president said that nowhere in the history of the world before Lord Buddha did they hear of any teacher of religion who was ever filled with such an all-absorbing sympathy and love for the suffering humanity. He wished that in these days of communal and minority dissensions Lord Buddha had once more appeared and had shown them the way how a man could meet his fellow brother and embrace him with love.

In conclusion, the president said that only one man in India seemed to have been convinced of the truth of Buddhism that violence would not be stopped by violence. All would have seen what power such a conviction had given to this great man. He in his loin cloth had brought about the unification of the masses of India and was trying to dictate his terms to the greatest military power of the world. In no other country was such an experiment conducted and with so much success.

Since its opening, the Vihara has become one of the principal sights at Sarnath and one of the favorite subjects of Sarnath's travel writers. It seems to have moved Major Raven-Hart, Justice Wijayatilake, and Professor Naravane more than any other monument at Sarnath.

S. R. Wijayatilake, 1963 C.E.

[W]e proceeded to the *Mulagandhakuti Vihara* built by the Anagrika Dharmapala and his disciples in 1931. It is a magnificent structure of great architectural beauty with its 110 foot high tower reminiscent of the Maha-Bodhi vihara at Buddha Gaya. As we entered the vihara what impressed us most was the quiet dignity of the place. There is only one image and that is of the Buddha. It radiates the message of Love and Peace. The frescoes on the walls have been painted by a famous Japanese artist — Kosetsu Nosu. The colour scheme and the style adopted by the artists add to the serenity of the atmosphere. Buddha relics discovered at Taxila are enshrined in this vihara. Close to this vihara are a Chinese temple, a Jain temple and a Burmese temple. The characteristic features of their art and architecture create an atmosphere all their own, but a common feature is the spirit of devotion and dedication which is quite evident. Fortunately, the evils of commercialism which sometimes follow tourist propaganda have not marred the tranquillity of the scene.

V. S. Naravane, 1965 C.E.

Inside the temple, everything is pure and spotlessly clean. Incense fills the air. And, from behind a curtain of embroidered silk, the familiar countenance of the Enlightened One peeps out — calm, compassionate, delicately chiselled, reassuring and yet not without a trace of sadness. So enchanting does this spot appear that on the morrow we return here; and this time we start at dawn, as all good travellers ought to. We see the temple silhouetted against the eastern horizon. Gradually the outlines become clearer. And as the early sun "catches the turret in a noose of light," we murmur to ourselves the words which Sir Edwin Arnold chose as the title of his poem, *The Light of Asia.*

Major Rowland Raven-Hart, 1956 C.E.

I attended "evensong" there repeatedly, a very simple service: like all Buddhist services in principle it was a service of praise, not of prayer, and directed not to the Buddha "up there" (as we think of Heaven), nor — and far less — to the Buddha-statue on the altar, but to the Buddha-germ (if one may use the phrase) within the worshipper.

It began with a recitation, intoned and not sung, kneeling on little mats provided to temper the marble floor, but sitting-kneeling and not upright, the legs either below the trunk or beside it, the feet to the rear. This part is unvarying, a salutation to the "Three Gems," the Buddha, the Dharma, the Order. . . .

After the invocation, there was a shift to a sitting position, the legs crossed, and another long chant. This part varies: as a rule it is taken from the shorter discourses of the Lord — when there was an epidemic at Besarh, for instance, or when a monk was bitten by a snake, an expression of love and good-will to all living things, the "metta" just mentioned. Everything is from memory: there was of course no accompaniment to the chant, no organ or instrument, and the only "harmony" came when one of the seven monks present got momentarily out of phase with the rest: there was a huge drum in one corner, but I never heard it, and forgot to ask when, if ever, it was used. A big bell hung in the porch, with a slung bamboo as striker, but had no part in the service: it was sounded by visitors on entering and leaving, Hindus and Moslems as well as Buddhists, since no Buddhist temple has any restriction on shoeless entry. . . . A bell or gong is often rung before an act of reverence so that others may hear, rejoice with you in your good action, and share in it. . . . I doubt if one out of twenty of those who rang it had any idea why they did so, except that it made a nice noise.

And after the chants came a long silence: the two minutes of Armistice Day seem long, but this was interminable. It seems to me a pity that there are not more ritual silences in Christian worship.

That was all; but I shall not easily forget those services, with the few candles throwing an almost theatrical light up onto the face of the image, and a broad river of moonlight streaming right across the temple-floor between the line of monks and myself.

Encounters

Maha Sthavira Sangharakshita (D. P. E. Lingwood), 1949 C.E.

Sangharakshita arrived in Sarnath with his friend Buddharakshita, hoping to find admission to the Buddhist sangha. They were met with suspicion and their request refused.

Rarely in the history of Buddhism can two candidates for admission to the Sangha have been more quickly or more cruelly disappointed. Though we were allowed, rather grudgingly, to stay in the vast, empty Rest House, from the first the attitude of the five or six

176

resident monks towards us was clearly one of incompre-
hension, suspicion, and hostility. Our going barefoot
might have been overlooked, and even our interest in
meditation excused, but to be altogether without money
was, we were made to feel, the unforgivable offence.
Indeed, when we confessed that we had been trying to
practise the precept of not handling gold and silver, the
observance of which was of course incumbent on sra-
maneras and bhikshus alike, and that for the past few
months we had not possessed as much as a single anna
between us, they reacted rather as though we had told
them we had leprosy. From that moment our fate was
sealed. In the eyes of these representatives of "Pure
Buddhism" we were no better than beggars, and it was
clear they wanted nothing to do with us. They were even
unwilling to give us a little food. When, in response to
the bell, we turned up at the dining-hall, we heard one
of them murmur angrily, "Why do they come without
being asked?" After the open-handed hospitality of the
Hindu ashrams we had visited, such an attitude came as
a shock indeed.

Nevertheless, we decided not to be discouraged.
In the case of a step so important as the one we now
wanted to take, difficulties were bound to rise, and the
best thing we could do was to treat them as tests.
Accordingly, at the first opportunity, we acquainted the
monks with our religious history and made the formal
request for ordination. After listening to our account in
silence, they said they would consult among themselves
and let us know their decision. It was not long in coming. They were all members of the Maha Bodhi Society,
they explained, and in view of the fact that the Society
would be responsible for the maintenance of monks
ordained under its auspices, they were not permitted to
ordain anyone without the consent of the General
Secretary. Since the Society was at present very short of

funds, they were sure that in our case this consent would not be forthcoming.

Though we had known what the verdict would be, the shock when it came was none the less acute. All our plans were laid in ruins, all our hopes destroyed. Bitterly disappointed, we returned to Benares.

Gary Snyder, 1962 C.E.

The Mahabodhi Society has a modern Buddhist temple near the stupa with murals on the inside painted in the 1930s by a Japanese artist. It also has a huge two-floored pilgrim's resthouse across the street, where we proceeded. I hunted up the Bhikku-in-charge, a Ceylonese man, and we were given a room immediately. On the first floor, all the rooms had been semipermanently taken over by Tibetan Lamas, and the courtyard in back was a campground of almost a hundred Tibetans, men, women and children. Cooking on little campfires, sprawled out on sheepskins napping, taking their clothes off and looking for lice — some even bathing at a faucet — with their big packboards and loads set up in piles here and there. And how different from the average Indians — who are often sullen and argumentative — laughing and horseplaying constantly. (Sign at bus stop: "2:30 to 1:30. Just time. No bus will come and start.")

There was an English Lama living nearby I heard, so next day, after paying our respects to the temple and stupa, and the Deer Park which is fenced and has four or five species of deer playing around in it, we went to visit him. He had been an M.D. and Oxford Graduate; became a Hinayana Bhikku, and then changed to the dark red Tibetan robes "as his understanding of Buddhism deepened." The turning point had come, he says, when the Dalai Lama paid an official visit to Sarnath a few years previously. As he came into the *vihara* (temple), the Tibetan Lamas were lined on one side of the hall, the Bhikkus on the other—and the Lamas all bowed as the Dalai passed, but the yellow-robed Bhikkus just stood there. After the Dalai had finished his prostrations before the Buddha-image, and was starting back out the hall, our English friend suddenly crossed over from the Bhikku side where he'd been standing and stood with the Lamas, and bowed. Later he got a real Tibetan ordination, and was able to spend a summer in a monastery *(gompa)* in Ladakh, then was chased back to India proper by the government, which has closed Ladakh to outsiders on account the Chinese are trying to take it over. His name is Lobzang (equals "novice") Jivaka. Never heard his English name. He was sincere enough, but I felt making too much of being a Westerner. Athough he still hadn't had much actual Tibetan meditation training or philosophical study, he was already preparing to publish a book about his experiences.

Every third Tibetan will try and sell you a coin, a dagger, some jade earrings, or an old *tanka*.

Walking around the stupa, I had noticed an elderly and dignified Lama also doing circumambulation. After a while he approached me, with serene and sagelike countenance, his wispy white beard blowing in the breeze. My heart beat faster as I thought of secret initiations and hidden gurus — he came up to me, smiled benignly, and slipped a handful of Tibetan coins from his robe, inviting me to buy.

> *At Sarnath*
> *a Rongbuk, and a*
> *twisty-horned white-bellied*
> *antelope, some*
> *elk and deer*
> *behind barbed wire.*

a Lama tries
to sell Tibetan coin
the Grove where Buddha spoke.

The Dalai Lama, 1959 C.E.

I . . . travelled to Sarnath and the Deer Park, where the Buddha had preached his first sermon. With me I had a small retinue of staff, including Ling Rinpoché, Trihang Rinpoché and, of course, my Masters of the Robes, the Ritual and the Kitchen. On arrival, I found that something like two thousand Tibetan refugees, newly arrived through Nepal, had assembled, knowing that I planned to give a teaching. They were in very poor condition, but I could see that they were facing their hardship with great spirit. Tibetans are indefatigable traders and already they had set up stalls. Some were selling a few valuables they had managed to bring with them, others were selling old clothes. Many sold just tea. I was much encouraged by their vigour in the face of such suffering. Each person could have told a tale of desperate hardship and cruelty, yet here they were making the best of what little life had to offer them.

This first week-long teaching in the Deer Park was a wonderful event for me. It meant a great deal to be able to give it in the very place where the Buddha himself had taught 2,500 years before. During the course of it, I concentrated on the positive aspects of our ordeal. I reminded everyone of the Buddha's own words when he said that suffering is the first step towards liberation. There is an old saying, too, that "pain is what you measure pleasure by."

Marie Beuzeville Byles, 1953 C.E.

The Venerable Sangharatana Thera, the bhikkhu in charge, extended a warm welcome and I was given a room in the monster pink wedding-cake dharmasala erected by Birla, the religious millionaire of India. The life of the competent hard-working bhikkhu in charge at Sarnath bore no resemblance to that of the yellow-robed ones of the Buddha's day, whose work was solely to learn the art of quieting their minds in meditation and living so as to be no trouble to the laity; mundane work was forbidden, except in so far as it was necessary to cater for their simple needs, such as repairing their monasteries, making, dyeing and patching their robes, keeping their lodgings clean, tidy and sanitary. But at Sarnath, what with the pilgrims at the dharmasala, the schools and dispensary run by the Maha Bodhi Society, the tourists from Banaras, and the VIP . . . who came to worship at the Deer Park, the Ven. Sangharatana had scarcely a minute to call his own from dawn to dusk, when he led the chanting at the temple. . . .

The pilgrims who came to Sarnath dharmasala usually stayed only a couple of days, long enough to worship at the temple and the stupa and to visit the places of interest. A few of them cooked their food on Primuses in their rooms, and a few like me, ate with the resident bhikkhus in the little dining-room, for doing which a fixed charge was made (otherwise lodging at dharmasalas is free; you merely give such donation towards expenses as you can afford). Most had servants to cook for them. Some of the Tibetans cooked on little fires under the spreading mango tree in the quadrangle. The very poorest of these Tibetans walked all the way from Sarnath with packs on their backs and slept out under the bamboos in the park near the temple, spreading their voluminous gowns over them by way of covering at night. Once again it was the Tibetans who won the heart with their ready smiles. There was a lass from Lhasa, who went to a convent school in Kalimpong and spoke a little English. She had to attend mass every morning; when the teacher prayed to Christ, she prayed to Buddha. For what did she pray? "The happiness of all beings, animals and insects as well as humans. If you have an enemy, you do good things for him. A Buddhist cannot have an enemy. You pray that everyone may be reborn among the angels, for all is suffering here, but among the angels, all is happiness." It was not exactly a form of Buddhism my friends would consider orthodox. But it produced a people who seemed to show forth the teaching of the Buddha, more than a very great many of the orthodox. She introduced me to her lame uncle, a lama, or monk, and the light that shone from his eyes surely revealed the Deathless.

Perspectives

Eliza Ruhamah Scidmore, 1903 C.E.

It was ten o'clock, and after four hours in the headquarters of heathendom [Benares] we were glad to return to the quiet, empty spaces of the cantonment, realizing more than before what an appalling task confronts the missionaries, and what generations of such blindly bigoted Ganges worshipers must pass away before any change can be hoped for. A century of British law, order, cleanliness, and sanitary improvement avails nothing against the superstitions and practices of twenty-five centuries. Yet in this same center of bigotry and superstition Gautama Buddha won the people from their idolatry, their superstitions and caste creed, and for eight hundred years his doctrines prevailed. With this precedent, the ultimate conversion of the Hindus need not be despaired of. We drove that afternoon by a dusty, tamarind-shaded road to Sarnath, the Deer Park of Benares, where the Buddha preached, defied the Brahmans, and built up his great following. Only a few ruins remain of the great group of buildings, the crumbling tope in a deserted common the only object above ground described by Fahien and Hiuen Tsiang. "Did Sarnath pay?" asked my table d'hote neighbor that night, and I stammered for an answer. "Because," she said, "they told us there was nothing to see, that it wouldn't pay us to drive out there just to see some rubbishy old stones and brick heaps."

Marie Beuzeville Byles, 1953 C.E.

The most distressing feature of Sarnath were the mangy dogs with their ribs sticking out like skeletons. With the avidity of the starved they snatched for and fought over the scraps that were thrown to them. And there was an aged cow which lay sick and dying for many days. Before we Westerners condemn the Buddhist refusal to take life to save pain, let us remember that we condemn the aged and diseased men and women to the same misery that Buddhists condemn animals. They at least are consistent. We are not.

Major Rowland Raven-Hart, 1956 C.E.

I was very happy at Sarnath. All the monks showed me true Buddhist hospitality, from the very busy Secretary-in-charge downwards. The Librarian was especially helpful, searching out passages in the Texts for me, and translating them into English as I wrote. . . .

The whole place is charming, full of birds and bird-songs: the area for a mile around is a sanctuary for birds and beasts. Swallows abounded, dipping in their broken flight; and their cousins with the ridiculously long and thin tails, especially down by the pool; and lots of the bright green Bee-eaters, unable to go to bed without fuss enough for a flock of eagles. And once I saw King Solomon's bird, the hoopoe, a strutting pair of them: once only, though the call which gives them their name was not uncommon. I spent much of the time in the open,

A monk meditating near the Dhamekh stupa

lying on the grass under trees, watching with sleepy supe-
riority the unquiet little white cloud-wisps hurrying across
the shallow sky. As so often in Indian Autumns that sky
seemed very close at hand, so close that it surprised me
when the boughnets did not catch those cloudlets as they
passed. I could imagine myself in a well-kept park with
smooth grass-sward now at its best just after the Rains,
and distant clumps of trees to close the spacious view.

I know how easy it is to read mental conceptions
into landscapes; but I could not help contrasting Sarnath
with Bodh-Gaya. There the temple is in a hollow, closely set about with crowded votive stupas, densely walled
with trees whose leaves rustle peace: here everything is

open to the four winds and the world. There it was con-templation, withdrawal into self-knowledge: here the sending-forth of the new message, the revelation to mankind.

"Go ye now, monks, and wander for the gain of the many, for the welfare of the many, out of compassion for the world. Preach, monks, the Dharma which is lovely in the beginning, in the middle, in the ending, in the spirit and in the letter." Thus the Lord, here in Sarnath; and "the welfare of the many" is, I think, the message of Sarnath itself.

Vulture Peak, Rajagriha

RAJAGRIHA
(*Rajagrha; Rajgir
Kusagara-pura*)

Where the Buddha Tamed the Elephant Nalagiri

*Here is the beginning in this world
for an insightful mendicant:
guarding the senses, contentment,
discipline conducive to liberation,
association with virtuous, pure living,
and diligent friends.*

— *The Dhammapada,*
5th-1st c. B.C.E.,
translated from the Pali by Thomas Cleary

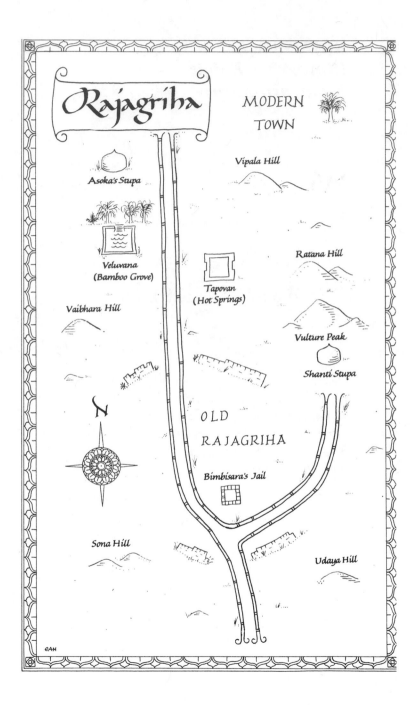

*T*he Buddha and his disciples meditated alone on Vulture Peak, outside of Rajagriha. Depending on the traveler's point of view, Vulture Peak appears to be a small mountain or a large hill. In the eyes of the Tibetan pilgrim, the Dharmasvamin, it was even less than that. "In Tibet," the Dharmasvamin suggested, "the Vulture Peak would be considered a hill of middling height." Vulture Peak's less hardened travelers find its "middling height" high enough. Fa-hsien called Vulture Peak "imposing," while Allen Ginsberg complained on the slopes of a dry mouth and the burning sun. Though not Himalayan, Vulture Peak raises travelers high above the surrounding landscape, offering them a pleasant contrast between the grit of ground level and the lonely silence of the skies, a contrast which would have been particularly striking during the Buddha's lifetime when Rajagriha was a busy metropolis, crammed with shops and houses and bartering merchants. It was not an easy place to live at that time. The Buddha survived two assassination attempts in Rajagriha and witnessed his loyal patron, King Bimbisara, suffer imprisonment at the hands of the king's own son and successor Ajatasatru. Vulture Peak must have been a pleasant haven in the Buddha's day from the noises and fuss of the metropolis. Today, though its commanding height lifts travelers above an emptier landscape, and though its slopes are dotted with monuments, the mountain continues to offer visitors the age-old invitation to meditate and to escape from the world below.

The image of the holy man on the mountain is familiar in most religions. Equally familiar is the image of the mountain as an abode of the gods: Mt. Kailasa is home to the divine Hindu couple Siva and Parvati; Mt. Olympus harbors the marble palaces of the Greek gods; Mt. Wu T'ai is sacred to the bodhisattva Manjusri. The place of mountains in religion may reflect the strange

189

pull they exert on our imaginations. We are most of us drawn to beaches and mountains, intrigued by their liminality: beaches fold into the inaccessible darkness of the ocean, mountains rise into the elusive sky. From the slope of a mountain, the world below appears small, far away and surprisingly ordered. Looking down from Vulture Peak, the Buddha's disciples may well have sensed the possibility of victory over the lusts and strife and turmoil of the earthly realm below.

In the Buddha's time, Rajagriha was the capital of the North Indian kingdom Magadha. Rajagriha's king Bimbisara, who was sympathetic to the Buddha's teachings, provided the sangha with its first grant of land. Known as the Bamboo Grove, the land became a haven for the Buddha and his disciples during the rainy seasons. When the rain stopped and members of the order took to the road, many went to meditate in the caves of Rajagriha's Vulture Peak. The Buddha spent years of his life and gave many of his sermons in Rajagriha, including the principal Mahayana sutras — the "Perfection of Wisdom" or Prajnaparmita *sutras — which he delivered to a select audience of elder disciples and enlightened beings on Vulture Peak.*

In Asoka's day (274–232 B.C.E.), pilgrims associated Rajagriha with the story of Devadatta and the elephant Nalagiri. Devadatta, the malefactor in countless Buddhist stories, incited Nalagiri to charge the Buddha. Succumbing to the Buddha's calming influence, the wild beast broke his charge. Devadatta then threw a rock upon the Buddha from a promontory on Vulture Peak. The rock only grazed the Buddha's foot and Devadatta was foiled again.

Soon after the Buddha's death, the capital of Magadha was moved to Pataliputra and Rajagriha began to fall into decline. By the nineteenth century, according to one British report, Rajagriha was no more than a small town. Since then the ruins of the ancient city, lying only a few miles from the ancient Buddhist university of Nalanda, have regained importance on the pilgrim's map.

On the road to Rajagriha

On the Road to Rajagriha

S. R. Wijayatilake, 1963 *C.E.*

It was a long drive [from Gaya] as there was little variety in the scene. We went through fields of paddy, millet and other grains with sugarcane and groves of neem and mango. Perhaps the only thing of any significance was a Jain temple with its pure white domes. Unlike in Ceylon where there are so many residential houses alongside the road we hardly saw any and we were all the time wondering where the rural folk live. There were hardly any boutiques or shops either. Perhaps they prefer to avoid the main highways. When we had done about half the journey, in the distance we could see the hills of Rajagaha Nuwara. As we came closer they appeared to be a natural fortification to this ancient Kingdom, now a desolate waste.

Major Rowland Raven-Hart, 1956 C.E.
We arrived late at Rajgir, the terminus, and I had a three-quarter mile walk to the Dak Bungalow in the dark, stumbling after a sure footed boy who had piled the two remaining items of my luggage on his head. . . . In compensation for our lateness I had enjoyed from the train a wonderful hour when the landscape draped itself in low, horizontal smoke-wreaths, and the Rajgir hills leapt up to greet us; and after sunset I had been granted something which I had seen only once before in my life, a "pseudo-sun" in the East, the rays from the real sun below the horizon seen on their way past the earth to infinity, and therefore seeming to converge to a point which rose slowly as the real sun sank.

The Buddha's First Visit to Rajagriha

Siddhartha came to Rajagriha once during the six years before his enlightenment. He was curious, perhaps to meet with the ascetics and wise people known to live in the caves and hills outside the city. Even then, Siddhartha was a magnetic figure. As he entered Rajagriha, the city's citizens, taken with his splendid serenity and incandescent grace, fell over one another trying to catch a glimpse of the stranger in their crowded streets. Hearing rumors about the beautiful beggar, the king, Bimbisara, went to meet him. Impressed by Siddhartha's speech, the king invited the young man to return to Rajagriha — after he had found the knowledge he was seeking.

The capital of the Magadha empire, Rajagriha's streets, shops, houses, and people bustled with activity and color. Yet it is the hills, not the city, which visitors see first on the road to Rajagriha.

From Sir Edwin Arnold, Light of Asia, 1879 C.E.

> Round Rajagriha five fair hills arose,
> Guarding King Bimbisara's sylvan town;
> Baibhara, green with lemon-grass and palms;
> Bipulla, at whose foot thin Sarsuti
> Steals with warm ripple; shadowy Tapovan,
> Whose steaming pools mirror black rocks, which ooze
> Sovereign earth-butter from their rugged roofs;
> South-east the vulture-peak Sailagiri;
> And eastward Ratnagiri, hill of gems.

From the Mongolian Lalitavistara, 1323–28 C.E.

When day broke, [Sakya Muni] put on . . . the yellow robe, took his bowl, went out through the Hot Water gate, and entered the great city of Rajagriha, moving with a walk so graceful that one could not look at him enough, [who was] gentle and at peace, his organs relaxed. When he went there, begging alms, the inhabitants of the city of Rajagriha saw this one who had a body that was the color of polished gold and was so beautiful that one could not look at it enough. And they wondered very much: "Who is this? Is this the lord of the world, Brahma? Is this the lord of gods, Indra? Is this the lord of Atakavati, Vaisravana?

"Or is this a god who dwells in a pure region, in hermitage?" While they were wondering, they were

193

looking from the roofs of the houses, unable to find enough space in the shops and in the market. Those who were too much concerned with their noble origin were watching him over the tops of the door-frames inside their houses. The merchants, fond of trading, left their trade and admired [him]. The drinkers, fond of wine, left their wine and did the same. More and more did King Bimbisara hear that all of those who came from every direction were admiring [the Bodhisattva], their hands folded, and he looked from the top of his palace, marvelled very much, and spoke: "Let us worship this great saint and show him our respect! Watch where he goes!" And when he set them to watch, he, King Bimbisara, learned that (the Bodhisattva) had gone to the king of mountains, a mountain called Pandava, and he [King Bimbisara] went there, and followed him. When [King Bimbisara] looked at him, he saw that [the Bodhisattva] was sitting in resplendent brilliance on a grass mattress, and he hastily alighted from his chariot and bowed to [the Bodhisattva's] feet.

In a happy mood, they spoke cheerful words to each other. Then King Bimbisara spoke thus to the Bodhisattva: "Whose son are you, supreme saint who creates happiness beyond comparison? Why, at such a young age, are you living in a deserted forest? What [do you think] of taking half of my whole realm under your rule, and enjoying the pleasures of desire?" When he had said this, the Bodhisattva spoke in a voice pleasant to the hearing:

> "I am the son, O great king, of Suddhodana.
> All these pleasures of the world
> confront [us] with emptiness, just like illusions.
> They burn up, like a great fire.

> "At first, when one seeks [them] they cause suffering.
> Unable to find them, one is burnt still more.

Even if one finds them, one cannot restrain oneself,
and they cause many [more] sufferings.

"They [men] are likely to become still more thirsty
after drinking something bitter.
Even if one single person collects
all the possessions of all the gods and men, and dis-
poses of them [all by himself]
no feeling of satisfaction and moderation is born.

"Being in their power, oh great king,
one suffers, unable to reach that edge of samsara,
revolving like the wheel of a vehicle,
four times immemorial until now!

"I do not wish any pleasure of desire.
I have come into a deserted forest,
leaving the pleasures of a Cakravartin [universal
king],
because ultimately [pleasures] throw one into evil,
even if I had [such] desires."

When he had spoken so in detail, King Bimbisara
said:

"I beg forgiveness for my asking
what I have spoken in my ignorance of you,
who were born in the family of a great king,
and who have given up the pleasures of the world.
Deign to forgive me! . . .

"Deign [to bestow upon] us a portion of it,
when you obtain the supreme sanctity!"
And bowing his head to [the Bodhisattva's] feet,
he made a circumambulation, and went back.

The Old and New Cities of Rajagriha

There are at Rajagriha the remains of two cities next to one another. In the Buddha's time, the "old city" was heavily fortified and nestled in the hills: Its ruined fortifications still stand. The "new city" sits farther away from the hills' protection. Built during or just after the Buddha's time, the "new" city is thought to owe its existence to a period of strength and stability when fortifications and embracing hills were deemed unneccessary. At least, that is the current theory: Hiuen Tsiang and Dharmasvamin have their own stories about Rajagriha's name and the "new" city's origins.

Thanks to nineteenth-century excavations, modern visitors know which city is which and what they are seeing. However, the first visitors to describe Rajagriha in the nineteenth century had little information to go on — only local, inaccurate rumor. Knowing nothing about the site's early association with Buddhism, Mr. Buchanan, excerpted below, was hard put to understand the city's historic remnants.

IN THE BUDDHA'S DAY

From Asvagosha, The Buddha-Karita, *first century* C.E.
A picture of Rajagriha in the Buddha's day:
Rajagriha with its beautiful palaces [is] distinguished by the five hills, well guarded and adorned with mountains, and supported and hallowed by auspicious sacred places. . . .

FOURTH TO THIRTEENTH CENTURIES

Early descriptions of Rajagriha make a clear distinction between the sites of the old and the new cities of Rajagriha.

Old City

Fa-hsien, 400 C.E.

[They] entered a valley surrounded by five hills as if by a city wall. This is the site of the old city of King Bimbisara, which is five or six *li* from east to west, and seven or eight *li* from north to south. This is where . . . King Ajatasatru gave wine to a black elephant in order to injure Buddha. In the garden of Ambapali in the northeast corner of this city Jivaka built a monastery to invite Buddha and his 1,250 disciples to receive his offerings. The ruins still remain. But the city is desolate, without inhabitants.

Hiuen Tsiang, mid-seventh century C.E.

[W]e arrive at the city Kusagara-pura . . . or "the royal city of best grass (*lucky grass*)." This is the central point of the kingdom of Magadha. Here the former kings of the country fixed their capital. It produces much of the most excellent, scented, fortunate grass, and therefore it is called "the city of superior grass." High mountains surround it on each side, and form as it were its external walls. On the west it is approached through a narrow pass, on the north there is a passage through the mountains. The town is extended from east to west and narrow from north to south. It is about 150 *li* in circuit. The remaining foundations of the wall of the inner city are about 30 *li* in circuit. The trees called *Kie-ni-kia* (*Kanakas*) border all the roads, their flowers exhale a delicious perfume, and their colour is of a bright golden hue. In the spring months the forests are all of a golden colour.

The Dharmasvamin, 1234–36 C.E.

In ancient times the town had eight hundred houses. Nowadays it has only six hundred. Some four hundred houses were built of bricks. To the North of Rajagriha there was a hot spring. To the South lay a

mountain stretching from East to West. Below the town
of Rajagriha, on the fringe of a marshy ground, lay the
Veluvana grove whose trees had a more vivid green
colour than those [of other groves]. On the western slope
of the summit of the mountain there was a path which
followed an unaccentuated stretch of the slope. By following it, one reached the Vulture Peak, which lay to the
south of a small hill.

New City

Hiuen Tsiang, mid-seventh century C.E.
[W]e come to the town of Rajagriha. . . . The
outer walls of this city have been destroyed, and there
are no remnants of them left; the inner city (*walls*),
although in a ruined state, still have some elevation
from the ground, and are about 20 li in circuit. In the
first case, Bimisara-raja established his residence in
Kusagara; in this place the houses of the people, being
close together, were frequently burned with fire and
destroyed. When one house was in flames, it was impossible to prevent the whole neighbourhood sharing in the
calamity, and consequently the whole was burned up.
Then the people made loud complaints, and were unable
to rest quietly in their dwellings. The king said, "By my
demerit the lower people are afflicted; what deed of
goodness can I do in order to be exempt from such
calamities?" His ministers said, "Maharaja, your virtuous
government spreads peace and harmony, your righteous
rule causes light and progress. It is by want of due attention on the part of the people that these calamities of fire
occur. It is necessary to make a severe law to prevent
such occurrences hereafter. If a fire breaks out, the origin
must be diligently sought for, and to punish the principal guilty person, let him be driven into the cold forest.

Now this cold forest (*sitavana*) is the place of corpses abandoned (*cast out*) there. Every one esteems it an unlucky place, and the people of the land avoid going there and passing through it. Let him be banished there as a cast-out corpse. From dread of this fate, the people will become careful and guard (*against the outbreak of fire*)." The king said, "It is well; let this announcement be made, and let the people attend to it."

And now it happened that the king's palace was the first to be burned with fire. Then he said to his ministers, "I myself must be banished"; and he gave up the government to his eldest son in his own place. "I wish to maintain the laws of the country (*he said*); I therefore myself am going into exile."

At this time the king of Vaisali hearing that Bimbisara-raja was dwelling alone in the "cold forest," raised an army and put it in movement to invade . . . when nothing was ready (*to resist them*). The lords of the marches . . . hearing of it, built a town, and as the king was the first to inhabit it, it was called "the royal city" (Rajagriha). Then the ministers and the people all flocked there with their families.

It is also said that Ajatasatru-raja first founded this city, and the heir-apparent of Ajatasatru having come to the throne, he also appointed it to be the capital, and so it continued till the time of Asoka-raja, who changed the capital to Pataliputra, and gave the city of Rajagriha to the Brahmans, so that now in the city there are no common folk to be seen, but only Brahmans to the number of a thousand families.

1900S TO THE PRESENT

Francis Buchanan, 1838 C.E.

The immediate vicinity of Behar is remarkably

beautiful. Being supplied with numerous canals, a large extent is continually irrigated with machinery, and under a constant succession of luxuriant crops, while the rugged hills, brick buildings, and ruins give a pleasing variety to the scenery.

By far the most celebrated place of Hindu worship in this division is Rajagriha or the King's house; and for many ages it has no doubt been one of the principal seats of superstition in the country, and in all probability has been long the seat of empire. The small town still named Rajagriha clearly in my opinion marks out the original seat of empire, as is implied by its name, and is situated on the north side of the ridge of mountains, to which it has communicated its name, towards its east end, about seven or eight miles northwest from Giriyak, which I have described as a palace of Jarasandha, who is by all acknowledged to have been king of India, and several monuments attributed to him are shown near Rajagriha; but, although the town stands on the massy rampart of an old fortress, the natives to my great surprise have no tradition of this having belonged to Jarasandha, on the contrary they in general attribute the fortification to Sher Shah.

Major Rowland Raven-Hart, 1956 C.E.

[T]o-day all [of the area around Rajagriha] is thick leopard-jungle, and the official guidebook suggests that you get clear of it before dark. I could not identify one tree in ten: mango, mahua, pipal, wild jackfruit, neem, siris were among them. Dragonflies were in swarms so dense that I had to flap a handkerchief in front of my face to clear my way; and there were dozens of butterflies, coloured like Hollywood ties and more. Birds abounded, more heard than seen.

Maha Sthavira Sangharakshita
(D. P. E. Lingwood), 1949 C.E.

Taking advantage of a sudden change in the weather, which since our arrival in Rajgir had been cold, windy, and rainy, we set out one Sunday afternoon for the Gridhyakuta or Vulture Peak. Our way led through the hill-encircled valley where the old city of Rajagriha, capital of the kingdom of Magadha, had once stood. As we entered the opening known as the North Gate we at once became aware of the pin-drop silence of the place. The road, which must have existed in the time of the Buddha and King Bimbisara, ran southward through a dense jungle of huge white-flowered cactus trees that were branched like candelabra, ragged thorn brushes, and clumps of slim yellow bamboo. After walking for about half an hour in the hot sunshine we passed the ruins of the Manniyar Math, a Jain temple which had originally been a seat of snake-worship. Soon after this we came to the site of Bimbisara's Jail. Here it was that the aged king had been imprisoned by his son Ajatasatru. Only the foundations of the building remained.

Allen Ginsberg, 1963 C.E.
Rajgir: Dream

Taxicab with Peter going up modern street as in a previous dream existence — the place is a big park on the left trees and grass for blocks on the right a band of greenery & fields leading to the river, as perhaps Chicago —

In the taxi — we have just eaten in the Ordona restaurant or the Miro Cardona restaurant — or we have an old apartment in the Miro Cardona Apts or we live on Ordona Circus — We are in a taxi speeding up Broadway to the hotel — It's just an accident we're living there, I think to myself — only I wish Leroi Jones didn't know about that in the dream — I'm not sure what my sin is — but it's numbered by Ordona —

Now that we're in familiar territory up on Broadway it seems, I want to stop the cab & get a maybe trolley or subway — we're just coming home from a ship or airplane — but Peter, with whom I am not talking that afternoon, says "Ordona" to the Taximan so that we speed all the way uptown into the Two Dollar taxi-meter zone — But time is money, so we'll get home faster — he has work to do, several letters to send off immediately, that has to be taken care of, I envisage his four air letters all prepared to be signed —

The new apartment we live in is very polished & modern and suave — mahogany sideboards and window frames & a folding bed that comes down from the wall. We're home & we're in bed together — tho it is not Peter any more, but a slightly younger tougher kid — some grocer's delivery boy India — rather like Gopal the orphan saint of Deshbandu Leper's Park in Benares —

He has just finished some sort of puja, worship & prayers ceremony with others in the room who have left and we are together alone for the first time in bed. We're discussing "Wung" initiation Diksha and he's been initiated —

"Well, I've not been initiated" I say.

"That's alright" he says reaching for some dirt from a flower-pot, & he puts a tilak 3rd eye on my forehead with his thumb.

"But can you give that initiation too?" I say submitting myself to his hands.

"Well I have given this mark to you & I've given it to others too and I have the power to do that, tho I'm not certain you'd be satisfied it's a formal initiation. Still I've been initiated and that's good enough. Just accept whatever comes your way."

We're in bed and he's hovering over me, I have my head between his knees, lying there — My leg or my cheek on his thighs — I close my eyes and begin to feel a wavy soft friendliness from him — my own sensuality of wet dreams coming on my legs & breast — "Is *this* the excitement of initiation?"

"Well if that's what you're feeling that's your own so why not accept it?"

I think, well this is fine, but I am a little scared of spoiling the circumstance by making erotic scenes with him, reaching up & kissing his cheek & touching his thighs — I'm getting old — still he's here in bed — Who is he? —

"But am I supposed to act this out & feel this way"

"Why not? Do you see anything wrong?"

I have feeling I'm being trapped, meanwhile the blind wave of love is growing stronger & I don't want to resist —

"Well Teacher I'd be happy if this were the teaching. It's my old habit anyway — but I feel this may be a distracting test, & not the right manner of teaching?"

"Whatever you feel, as your heart tells you"

"But my heart tells me twice differently — on one hand the old lovely sensual temptation of Ordona Apartments — But flesh is crawling & unpermanent you know it says here"—

"Yes that's true too"—

"So that while pleasurable it may be a little childish"

And as I say that line & realised it seems it is childish to make this initiation a love scene —

I wake up. Not sure, but the love softness persists after the dream.

Joanna Macy, 1976 C.E.
18 February
    . . . I think about Shivaya's words yesterday:
how when you travel alone, you're both closer to the
people and nearer to God. He said that's because you're
simultaneously more open and more centered. Such
great freedom I feel. I reach my hand out into it, literally, tentatively, as if needing to ascertain that there really
is no solid barrier blocking me from the world. So deep
is the habit of constraint, of assuming limits. The freedom that is possible is far greater than what I can even
think into now. It just begins to begin to dawn on me
how radically and plausibly I could change my life. I
seem to take it for granted that there is an irresistible
force or immutable circumstances or unshirkable respon-
sibilities — that keep me harnessed to a particular role
and social identity. But the clear evidence of my dis-
pensability at home, on the one hand, and, on the other,
this appetite I discover in myself combine and nudge me
now to explore the illusoriness of that assumption.
    My Ceylonese seatmate speaks of his old bhikku-
ni friend whom I had seen with his party in Sanchi. That
little, orange-robed nun is still wandering across the land
as free as a bird, and as possessionless. My heart gives a
jolt, recognizing that her gay, devoted, footloose life
could be almost possible for me, too, theoretically. To
what am I in bondage? Was I, for example, beholden to
L.? Her ways and tastes are not mine, and tying myself
to them was like keeping a bird caged in my heart. Now
that we're apart and I am alone, I feel released into the
world, absorbed.
    My room at the Government Tourist Bungalow
here in Rajgir has doors front and back, their curtains
swing in the breeze blowing through from veranda and
garden. Even the john has an outside door, and *mirabile
dictu*, running water. I change after the 3-hour bus trip,

luxuriate in a breakfast of hot fried eggs and thick crispy toast and tea that is not goatmilk syrup.

At the Burmese temple in Rajgir there's a sign in Hindi and English and one which reads "Put off your shoes here." A wiry, springy, slightly zany monk ushers me in. Behind an assortment of wax flowers and gimcracks sits a dusty Buddha and behind him a "Visit India" poster blesses the hall. My host — I recognize him now as the monk smoking pot at the Tibetan prayer-drum in Bodh Gaya — insists, when I ask the way, on escorting me to the Nalanda bus and propels me there through a field of weeds. Cadging from a vendor a marigold the color of his robe, he presents it to me with a sweeping bow, asks me to extend his greetings to "the USA and the British High Commissioner," and tells me "Japanese no good." He also requests bus fare to Calcutta. I give him a somewhat maternal lecture before squeezing onto a seat for the ten miles to Nalanda. . . .

The Bamboo Grove

On King Bimbisara's invitation, the Buddha went back to Rajagriha after his enlightenment in Bodh Gaya. Bimbisara gave the Buddha and his new disciples a great feast, then presented them with a grant of land. Called the Bamboo Grove, it was the Buddhist order's first piece of property. The order built a monastery in the grove and established, with that first property, a tradition of rain retreats — yearly periods when, because of monsoon rains, the monks and nuns would leave their wanderings and gather together under the order's monastic roofs. Monasteries were generally located near important towns or cities and depended in large part on lay support. The monastic institution helped cement relations between the Buddhist order and the lay followers and sympathizers in the cities.

205

The Bamboo Grove

From *Tibetan Works in the* Bkah-Hgyur *and* Bstan-Hgyur.

[T]he Blessed One preached to the king and the people on form and its transitory nature . . . so that the king and a great multitude of Brahmans and householders were converted.

The king then invited the Blessed One to the city. . . . The king came to see him, and after having heard the Buddha preach, he invited him to a feast on the morrow. When the feast was over, the king poured water over the Blessed One's hands, and said, "I give the Kalantakanivasa Bamboo grove to the Blessed One to dispose of as may please him." The Buddha accepted it, and this was the first vihara or permanent residence that the Buddhist order possessed.

The origin of the name of Kalantakanivasa Veluvana is this. Before Bimbisara had ascended his throne, he took a great fancy to a park belonging to a householder of Rajagriha. He asked the owner for it, but he would not give it up, so the prince made up his mind that as soon as he should become king he would confiscate it. This he did, and the lawful owner became after death a venomous snake in his garden, and sought an occasion to bite the king. One day the king had gone into the park with his wives, and had fallen asleep while only one of the women was beside him. The snake was crawling near him, but some Kalantaka birds seized it and commenced crying, when the woman awaked and killed the snake.

To show his gratitude to the birds, the king had the place planted with bamboo groves, of which these birds were especially fond, so the park became known as the Bamboo grove, the place of the Kalantaka birds. In this grove the Buddha passed the rainy season of the first year of his ministry.

Thich Nhat Hanh, 1991 C.E.

[The Bamboo Forest] was an ideal location for the sangha, with nearly one hundred acres of healthy bamboo groves. Many kinds of bamboo grew there. At the center of the forest, Kalandaka Lake would be a perfect place for the bhikkhus to bathe, wash their robes, and do walking meditation along the shore. Because the bamboo was so plentiful, it would be easy to build small huts for the older monks to live in. The Buddha's senior students, including Kondanna, Kassapa, and Sariputta, were all delighted with the Bamboo Forest. They began planning at once how to best organize a monastery there.

The Buddha said, "The monsoon season is not a good time for travel. The bhikkhus need a place to study and practice together during the rains. Having a place like this will help the community avoid illness from exposure to the elements and also avoid stepping on the many worms and insects that are washed up on the ground during the rainy season. From now on, I would like the bhikkhus to return to a common place at the beginning of every rainy season. We can ask lay disciples of the area to bring food offerings during the three months of retreat. The lay disciples will also benefit from the teachings offered by the bhikkhus." Thus, the tradition of the rainy season retreat began.

Under Moggallana's supervision, the younger bhikkhus built huts from bamboo, thatch, and pounded earth for the Buddha and the older bhikkhus. The Buddha's hut, though small, was quite lovely. Behind it grew a thicket of golden bamboo and to one side grew a thicket of taller green bamboo which provided cool shade. Bhikkhu Nagasamala built a low, wooden platform for the Buddha to sleep upon. He also placed a large earthenware vessel for washing behind the Buddha's hut. Nagasamala was a young bhikkhu who had been Uruvela Kassapa's disciple. He was asked by Kassapa to serve as an attendant to the Buddha when the sangha moved to Bamboo Forest.

Sariputta arranged with a lay disciple from the capital to have a large bell donated to Bamboo Forest Monastery. He hung it from the branch of an ancient tree near Kalandaka Lake. The bell was used to announce times for study and meditation, and became a special part of the practice of mindfulness. The Buddha taught his bhikkhus to pause and observe their breath whenever they heard the bell ring.

Lay disciples assisted in many ways. Kassapa explained to them about the retreat season. "This retreat season will afford all the bhikkhus an opportunity to practice the way of liberation directly under the guidance of the Buddha. They will have time for more intensive study and practice. At the same time, they will avoid accidentally crushing worms and insects on the ground during the rainy season. You can assist the sangha during these three months of retreat by bringing food offerings. If possible, please try to coordinate your efforts to assure that there is the right amount of food each day, neither too much nor too little. Even the poorest of the poor, those who can only offer a chapati or two, will be invited to stay and listen to the Buddha or one of the senior students give a discourse on the Dharma each day. The retreat season will benefit bhikkhus and lay disciples alike."

2,500 Years Later

Maha Sthavira Sangharakshita (D. P. E. Lingwood), 1949 C.E.

Not a single bamboo was to be seen. In fact, there was hardly any vegetation, and what with the heaps of rubble that were lying all around, the appearance of the place was dreary and desolate.

Ascetics: True and False

Even before the Buddha's arrival in Rajagriha, the city was famous for its ascetics and holy wanderers. Some were truly wise; some ambitious, even treacherous. To this day, holy men and women can be found in Rajagriha's marketplace and on paths in the five hills. Here: glimpses, past and present, of Rajagriha's ascetics and of Rajagriha through its ascetics' eyes.

HINDU ASCETICS

By the thirteenth century, when Dharmasvamin described the city, there were very few Buddhist ascetics left in Rajagriha. Within a few hundred years of his visit, this community had probably disappeared. Only Hindu, Jain, and Muslim ascetics were to be found on the nine-teenth-century streets which Mr. Buchanan described.

The Dharmasvamin, 1234–36 C.E.

In general, one can say, that in India, the non-Buddhists were numerous, the Sravakas were fewer, and the followers of the Mahayana even fewer. The Indian followers of the Hinayana are distinguished by greater kindness than the Tibetan followers of the Mahayana. When on an alm's begging round, the non-Buddhists consider it their duty to give alms to [Buddhist monks]. Simple people, other than non-Buddhists, have a great faith, and whenever they meet a monk, they prostrate themselves with the words, "Rahula ke vandhanam . . ." i.e., "Salutation to the Master." They do not walk straight in front of holy images or the house of parents. A red cloth they call a saffron garment. Because it is the garb of a mendicant (*prabrajika*), when they find a piece of four inches on the road, even children pick it up.

Francis Buchanan, 1838 C.E.

At Rajagriha, a hermit of the kind called *Tapasya*, or penitent, has seated himself in an open gallery in front of a thatched hut. He sits all day in the posture, in which the Buddhas and Tirthangakars of the sect of Jain are represented, and is well besmeared with the ashes of cow dung. He neither moves nor speaks, and those, who choose, give him alms. If on any day he receives nothing, he fasts; for he never lays up for to-morrow, and whatever is superfluous he gives to the poor. He was one of the most humiliating objects that I have ever beheld. It was alleged by the people round, that some thieves had stolen his blanket; but I suspected, that this was a mere fetch to procure a rupee, as to their utter astonishment I had not given him anything. It seems scarcely credible, that any thief should have stolen from such an animal, who, besides his wretchedness, was supposed by all classes to enjoy a large proportion of divine favour.

John Blofeld, 1956 C.E.

[A]n old Hindu approached, crying:

"Alms in the name of God. I perish of hunger."

One of the young Thai monks, looking straight in his face, said slyly: "Which God?"

"This God," cried the old man, bursting into a peal of laughter and jabbing his finger into a toothless mouth. I was amused by such sincerity and gave him a few coins, whereupon the old fellow, perceiving the yellow garments my friends were just putting on, cried in a penetrating voice that echoed through the stone bath-house:

"Buddha Bhagawan ki-jai! Victory to the Blessed One, the Buddha!"

"It seems we've made a convert," I said laughing.

THE BUDDHA'S DISCIPLES

PINDOLA BHARADVAJA

In the legends, Asoka longed to get close to the real Buddha, to know how he looked, the sound of his voice, the feel of his presence. Encountering an ascetic so ancient he claimed to remember the Buddha, Asoka begged him to share what he had seen. Below, the ascetic recalls the Buddha as he appeared in Rajagriha:

From the Asokavadana, *second century C.E.*

"What?" cried the [Asoka], so thrilled that his hair stood on end and shivered like the blossoms of a kadamba tree, "is there a monk still alive who has seen the Buddha?"

"Indeed there is, great king," replied Yasas,

"Pindola Bharadvaja was with the Buddha, and he still lives."

"Would it be possible," Asoka enquired, "for me to see him?"

"Great king," the elder replied, "you will meet him presently, for the time of his arrival has come."

"Ah!" exclaimed the king, rejoicing in his heart,

> *Great would be my gain,*
> *and unprecedented my great bliss*
> *unsurpassed here on earth,*
> *were I to see with my own eyes*
> *that exalted being of the Bharadvaja clan.*

And folding his hands in reverence, Asoka stood with his eyes fixed on the vault of heaven.

Then the elder Pindola Bharadvaja, in the midst of several thousand arhats who formed a crescent moon around him, flew down from the heavens like a royal goose, and took his place on the seat of honor. Instantly those several hundred thousand monks rose to greet him, and Asoka too could see Pindola Bharadvaja — his body that of a pratyekabuddha, his hair very white, and his eyebrows so long that they hung down and covered his eyes. The king immediately fell full-length in front of the elder like a tree felled at the root. He kissed his feet, got up, and then knelt down again on the ground. Making an anjali, gazing up at the elder, he said, choked with emotion:

> *When I had cut down the enemy hosts*
> *and placed the earth and its mountains ringed by the*
> *sea*
> *under a single umbrella of sovereignty,*
> *my joy was not then what it is now*
> *that I have seen you, O elder.*

"By looking at you, I can, even today, see the Tathagata. You show yourself out of compassion, and that redoubles my faith. O elder! You saw him, the Lord of the Triple World, the Blessed Buddha, my Guru!"

Pindola then lifted up his eyebrows with his hands and looking straight at the king, he replied:

> *Indeed I saw him many times — that great*
> *incomparable Sage,*
> *whose brilliance matched that of the best polished*
> *gold,*
> *whose body bore the thirty-two marks,*
> *whose face was like the autumn moon,*
> *whose voice carried more authority than Brahma's*
> who dwelt ever free from passion.

"Elder," said the king, "where did you see the Blessed One and how?"

"Great king," replied the elder, "I saw him first after he had conquered Mara's hosts and was spending the rains retreat in Rajagriha together with five hundred arhats. I was there at the time and could not see him perfectly, he who is worthy of veneration."

And he added:

> *When the great Sage, the Tathagata,*
> *who is free from passion*
> *and surrounded by others equally free from passion,*
> *was spending the rains-retreat in Rajagriha,*
> *I was then right there*
> *in front of the enlightened Sage,*
> *and I saw him face to face*
> *just as you see me now with your own eyes.*

RAJADATTA
Pindola is a fictional creation and an eye without

much character. *The verses of the Buddhist elders are more revealing. They give us historic personalities and experiences which help us imagine what it would have been like to live in Rajagriha, an ascetic in the days of the Buddha. The elder Rajadatta recalls (all too vividly) that very burning ground mentioned in Hiuen Tsiang and Dharmasvamin's stories:*

From the Theragatha, **5th–1st c.** B.C.E.

When Rajadatta the trader was still young, a group of investors staked him to 500 carts of merchandise. He took them to the city of Rajagaha. There he met a beautiful prostitute whose body so intoxicated him he lavished 1,000 rupees a day on her. Before he could shake himself free, he'd squandered the whole caravan and ended up penniless. He took to wandering and one day joined a crowd of laymen who'd gone to hear the Buddha speak. Sitting at the edge of the assembly, he listened with deep concentration. The words rang so true and forcefully in his ears that he joined the assembly of monks that day. And recognizing his weakness for women, he took to a charnel ground to practice austerities.

Meanwhile, another caravan-leader was also spending thousands on the same prostitute. This man wore a lavishly wrought ring on his hand that the woman coveted fiercely. She hired some men to steal it for her. However, the police were tipped off, raided her house, found the wealthy merchant's ring, killed the prostitute on the spot, and flung her body into the charnel ground.

Rajadatta, tramping about in search of a suitably foul object to meditate on, stumbled across her corpse. "This will do," he thought, and began to brood on impermanence. But those parts of the prostitute no dog or jackal had mangled yet distracted him, and with horror he found himself terrribly aroused. Aghast at his fantasies he fled to a safe distance. There, sinking deeply into *dhyana*, with a supreme effort of will he achieved insight. This is his poem.

A recluse
went to the burning ground
found a woman's naked corpse
inside it a tangle of worms
Others blanched
& turned away at the sight
but that poor dead creature's golden
breasts and unshaved cunt
haunted me until I lost
control & shuddered with
violent urges

Quicker than boiling rice
overflows the pot
I fled the graveyard
fled that poor dead creature
fled until I reached
a safe secluded spot
to sit
& cross my legs &
calm my mind

I considered
the object
considered the hungry ignorant acts
that brought it where it lay
considered the tangle of worms
& corpses
I stared into countless
rounds of suffering
stared into greed & hunger

stared on vanity
stared until desire
blinked like a lamp
and went out
lust no longer assailed me
I made wisdom my own then
yes I accomplished
what had
to be done

DEVADATTA (The Story of Nalagiri)

Rajagriha's most notorious Buddhist disciple was Devadatta. A childhood aquaintance of the Buddha's, Devadatta was born in Kapilavastu. He remained close to the Buddha, drawn to him through feelings of jealousy and rivalry. It was a relationship that lasted for lifetimes. Devadatta seemed fated, by his own bad character, to be the perennial thorn in Buddha's side. At Rajagriha, Devadatta made two attempts on the Buddha's life. One, excerpted below, became a popular Buddhist story and is cited as the official reason for Rajagriha's fame.

From the Vinaya-Pitaka, Vol 5., 5th–1st c. B.C.E.

According to this often repeated story, Devadatta tried to incite a fierce elephant to kill the Buddha.

Now at that time there was a fierce elephant in Rajagaha, a man-slayer, named Nalagiri. Then Devadatta, having entered Rajagaha, having gone to the elephant stable, spoke thus to the mahouts: "We, my good fellows, are relations of the king. We are competent to put in a high position one occupying a lowly position and to bring about an increase in food and wages. Well now, good fellows, when the recluse Gotama is coming along this carriage road, then, having let loose this elephant, Nalagiri, bring him down this carriage road."

"Very well, honoured sir," these mahouts answered Devadatta in assent.

Then the Lord, having dressed in the morning, taking his bowl and robe, entered Rajagaha for alms-food together with several monks. Then the Lord went along that carriage-road. Then those mahout saw the Lord coming along that carriage-road; seeing him, having let loose the elephant Nalagiri, they brought him down that carriage-road. The elephant Nalagiri saw the Lord coming from afar; seeing him, having lifted up his trunk, he rushed toward the Lord, his ears and tail erect. Those monks saw the elephant Nalagiri coming in the distance; seeing him, they spoke thus to the Lord:

"Lord, this elephant Nalagiri, coming along this carriage-road, is a fierce man-slayer; Lord, let the Lord turn back, let the well-farer turn back."

"Wait, monks, do not be afraid; this is impossible, monks, it cannot come to pass that anyone should deprive a Truth-finder of life by aggression; monks, Truth-finders attain nibbana not because of an attack." And a second time. . . . And a third time these monks spoke thus to the Lord. . . .

"Wait, monks. . . . Truth-finders attain nibbana not because of an attack."

Now at that time people, having mounted up on to the long houses and the curved houses and the roofs, waited there. Those people who were of little faith, not believing, who were of poor intelligence, these spoke thus: "This great recluse is indeed lovely; he will be hurt by the bull elephant." But those people who had faith and were believing, who were wise and intelligent, these spoke thus: "Soon, good sirs, the bull-elephant will come into conflict with the elephant [among men]."

Then the Lord suffused the elephant Nalagiri

217

with loving-kindness of mind. Then the elephant Nalagiri, suffused by the Lord with loving-kindness of mind, having approached, he stood in front of the Lord. Then the Lord, stroking the elephant Nalagiri's forehead with his right hand, addressed the elephant Nalagiri with verses:

> "Do not elephant, strike the elephant [among men],
> for painful elephant, is the striking of the elephant
> [among men],
> For there is no good bourn, elephant, for a slayer of
> the elephant [among men] when he is hence beyond.
> Be not proud, be not wanton, for the wanton reach not
> a good bourn;
> Only that should you do by which you will go to a
> good bourn."

Then the elephant Nalagiri, having taken the dust of the Lord's feet with his trunk, having scattered it over his head, moved back bowing while he gazed upon the Lord. Then the elephant Nalagiri, having returned to the elephant stable, stood in his own place; and it was in this way that the elephant Nalagiri became tamed. Now at that time people sang this verse:

> "Some are tamed by stick, by goads and whips.
> The elephant was tamed by the great seer without a
> stick,
> without a weapon."

People looked down upon, criticised, spread it about, saying: "How evil is this Devadatta, how inauspicious, in that he tried to murder the recluse Gotama who is of such great psychic power, of such great might," and Devadatta's gains and honours declined; the Lord's gains and honours increased.

In the Hills

If you do not find a prudent companion, a wise associ-
ate leading a good life, then travel alone, like a king
abandoning a domain he has conquered, like an ele-
phant roaming the forest.

It is better to walk alone; there is no companionship
with a fool. Walk alone, like an elephant in the forest,
with few desires, doing no evil.

— The Dhammapada

Early Buddhism emphasized the individual's
struggle for enlightenment. Absorbed in that struggle,
Buddhist disciples in the hills around Rajagriha passed
their days in meditation and solitude.

From Sir Edwin Arnold, Light of Asia, *1879* C.E.

A winding track, paven with footworn slabs,
Leads thee, by safflower fields and bambu tufts,
Under dark mangoes and the jujube-trees,
Past milk-white veins of rock and jasper crags,
Low cliff and flats of jungle-flowers, to where
The shoulder of that mountain, sloping west,
O'erhangs a cave with wild figs canopied.
Lo! thou who comest thither, bare thy feet
And bow thy head! for all this spacious earth
Hath not a spot more dear and hallowed. Here
Lord Buddha sate the scorching summers through,
The driving rains, the chilly dawns and eves;
Wearing for all men's sake the yellow robe,
Eating in beggar's guise the scanty meal
Chance-gathered from the charitable; at night
Couched on the grass, homeless, alone; while yelped
The sleepless jackals round his cave, or cough

219

Of famished tiger from the thicket broke.
By day and night here dwelt the World-honoured,
Subduing that fair body born for bliss
With fast and frequent watch and search intense
Of silent meditation, so prolonged
That ofttimes while he mused — as motionless
As the fixed rock his seat — the squirrel leaped
Upon his knee, the timid quail led forth
Her brood between his feet, and blue doves pecked
The rice-grains from the bowl beside his hand.

Tapovan: The Hot Springs

The sacred resort: In Tapovan, the Buddha and his disciples, pilgrims, Hindus, Jains, Muslims, and tourists have bathed over the centuries in the hot springs.

Hiuen Tsiang, mid-seventh century C.E.

To the west of the north gate of the mountain city is the mountain called Pi-pu-lo (*Vipula-giri*). According to the common report of the county it is said, "On the northern side of the south-western crags of this mountain there were formerly five hundred warm springs; now there are only some ten or so; but some of these are warm and others cold, but none of them hot." These springs have their origin to the south of the Snowy Mountains from the Anavatapta . . . lake and flowing underground, burst forth here. The water is very sweet and pure, and the taste is like that of the water of the lake. The streams (*from the lake*) are five hundred in number (*branches*), and as they pass by the lesser underground fire-abodes (*hells*), the power of the flames ascending causes the water to be hot. At the mouths of the various hot springs there are placed carved stones, sometimes shaped like lions, and at other times as the

Hot Springs

heads of white elephants; sometimes stone conduits are constructed, through which the water flows on high (*aqueducts*), whilst below there are stone basins, in which the water collects like a pond. Here people of every region come, and from every city, to bathe; those who suffer from any disease are often cured. On the right and left of the warm springs are many *stupas* and the remains of viharas close together. In all these places the four past Buddhas have sat and walked, and the traces of their so doing are still left. These spots being surrounded by mountains and supplied with water, men of conspicuous virtue and wisdom take up their abode here, and there are many hermits who live here also in peace and solitude.

Francis Buchanan, 1838 C.E.
[A]t Tapoban . . . there are five pools considered holy. They are situated in a line parallel to the hill at its foot, and the ground on the plain near them is spouty and wet. . . . The heat being so moderate, the pilgrims bathe in them; and, as the annual assembly had been held the day before my arrival, the water was in a beastly state of filth; but at other seasons it is probably clear enough.

John Blofeld, 1956 C.E.
As darkness was falling, we came to an ancient bath-house fed by a hot spring once used for ablutions by the Buddha himself — or so it is said. The warm water came splashing out of stone pipes fashioned to resemble the heads of *Nagas*. The bath we enjoyed there was both refreshing and, to me, highly romantic. . . . We dried ourselves by the light of oil dips.

Vulture Peak (Gridhrakuta)

Vulture Peak is said to have been vital to the preservation, on the one hand, and the birth, on the other, of two branches of Buddhist thought: Hinayana and Mahayana Buddhism. After the Buddha's death, the sangha's elders met at Rajagriha's Vulture Peak to hammer out

The view from Vulture Peak

a Buddhist canon, the sum of the Buddha's teachings which they had learned by memory and hoped to preserve after his death. Their meeting is referred to as the First Council. Later written down in the Pali language, the Council's canon has come to be called the Pali Canon and forms the core of what was later named by Mahayana Buddhists, Hinayana Buddhism ("The Little Vehicle").

Mahayana Buddhism (the self-proclaimed "Greater Vehicle") developed between the first century B.C.E. and the eighth century C.E. According to the Greater Vehicle's texts, the Buddha delivered his popular Mahayana "Perfection of Wisdom" sutras at Gridhrakuta. His audience was a select group of enlightened beings, the only audience able at the time to comprehend the sutras' sophisticated teachings.

During the Buddha's lifetime, Gridhrakuta was a haven for Buddhist monks and nuns struggling on the path to nirvana. With its strange, beaklike formation (from which, it is often suggested, the hill got its name),

Gridhrakuta has probably changed little since the Buddha's day.

From the Teragatha, *fifth century* B.C.E.

> CITTA
> *Though I am thin, sick,*
> *and lean on a stick,*
> *I have climbed up Vulture Peak.*
>
> *Robe thrown down,*
> *bowl turned over,*
> *leaned on a rock,*
> *then great darkness opened.*

Fa-hsien, 400 C.E.

After entering the valley and travelling fifteen *li* to the mountains in the southeast, they reached Gridhrakuta Mountain. Three *li* from the summit of the mountain is a cave facing south, in which Buddha used to sit in meditation. About thirty paces to the north-west is another cave where Ananda was once sitting in meditation when Mara Pisuna took the form of a vulture and hovered in front of the cave to terrify him. But Buddha with his supernatural powers stretched his hand through the rock and patted Ananda's shoulder, so that his fears were allayed. The traces of the vulture and the hold made by the Buddha's hand can still be seen today. Thus the name of this mountain is called the Mountain of the Vulture Cave. . . . The Arhats each have a cave in which to meditate — several hundred in all. . . .

The hall in which Buddha preached the Law has been destroyed, and only the foundations of the brick walls remain. The peaks of this mountain are beautiful and imposing, and it is the highest of all the five hills. . . .

Fa-hsien bought incense, flowers and oil for

lamps in the new city, and requested two resident monks to guide him to Gridhrakuta Mountain. There he offered the incense and flowers and lit the lamps.

"This is where Buddha used to live," he said, shedding tears of emotion. "And here he expounded the *Surangama Sutra*. Fa-hsien, who was born too late to see Buddha himself, can only gaze at the traces left by him and the places where he lived."

He recited the *Surangama Sutra* in front of the cave and, after spending the night there, returned to the new city.

The Dharmasvamin, 1234–36 C.E.

The Gridhrakutaparvata of the Vulture Peak was not high. In general there are no mountains in India (ie. Magadha) and in Tibet the Vulture Peak would be considered a hill of middling height. The Vulture Peak was circular in shape and was surrounded on all sides by forest. Some [of the gullies] were rocky, the abode of numerous carnivorous animals, such as tiger, black bear and the brown bear, so that ordinary men did not dare to penetrate [into the forest], and only some Panditas, who had obtained *siddhis*, dwelt there unharmed by poisonous snakes and carnivorous animals. In the summer the peak was overgrown by shrubs and grass, and its colour appeared blue. In the winter, when the grass had withered away, the colour of the mountain appeared to be grey. There were many kinds of birds and trees on the mountain. There the Dharmasvamin Chag lo-tsa-ba distributed alms to a multitude of people among whom some were carrying bows and arrows. In order to frighten away the wild animals, some beat drums, many were carrying conches, cymbals and trumpets. Some carried bunches of fresh bamboos which emitted great sparks. Even nowadays, it is said that on the summit of the peak, in a pleasant and fragrant place, stands the seat from which the Buddha had formerly preached the Doctrine. There were also the ruins of a building; pieces of bricks of the size of the hand and some large ones were scattered about. The Peak's summit was treeless and was overgrown with soft grass. On the summit there was a Stupa built of bricks with terraced steps, each size of which had 2 1/2 fathoms. . . . [T]he Dharmasvamin said that in front of the Stupa was situated the blessed spot on which the Blessed One (Bhagavan) had preached the Doctrine. For three years a Siddha lived in a hole in the Stupa's foundation, unharmed by wild animals and snakes, and all venerated him.

John Blofeld, 1956 C.E.
Within sight of the little town is the Vulture's Peak. . . . My Thai friends took me to the foundations of a small cell upon that very peak which some believe to have been the Lord Buddha's dwelling. However doubtful this tradition, it is pleasant to sit there and indulge in one of those "perhaps-it-was-really-so" moods which most lovers of antiquity now and then permit themselves. Near the foot of that hill is the actual site of the prison where the unhappy King Bimbisara was imprisoned by his ambitious son. There, he was slowly tortured to death and from there, according to tradition, he used to lift up his eyes to the hill and take comfort whenever he observed a tiny moving spot of yellow, indicating that his beloved Teacher was present upon the Vulture's Peak.
One evening, as we strolled in the hills, I was startled to hear the familiar *dup-dup* of a Chinese handdrum. Presently a Japanese monk came running round a bend in the path, his feet seeming scarcely to touch the ground so lightly did he run. Energetically he tapped his drum, bellowing incessantly in a dramatic Kabuki-like voice: "Reverence to the Lotus Sutra." So inwardly con-

centrated was he that he almost collided with us, stopping himself only just in time. Whereupon he bowed
three-quarters of the way to the ground, smote his drum
with extra vigour, and roared out the same formula; but
this time it was intended as a greeting, rather as a medi-
aeval friar might have used "God is good" for "Good
morning." As it happened, I knew how to reply with the
same Japanese words in the same Kabuki-like voice, and
did so, bowing almost to the ground. Of course I expected his face to light up with surprise. Not at all. Without
the smallest flicker of astonishment, he bowed again and
continued running down the hill, as though a stray
Englishman reciting a Japanese sacred formula on an
India hillside was the commonest thing in the world. In
fact, his rhythmical tapping, his impressive roaring and
panther-like movements were a peculiar form of meditation. Probably he was barely aware of my existence and
had been much too absorbed to know or care whether I
was Japanese or not.

John Huntington, 1985 C.E.

The long walk up the hill must be taken slowly,
especially if the day is hot (one should be sure to carry
water). There is a tempting chairlift up the Chatha Hill
for those who might wish to take it, but it does not go to
the Grdhrakuta directly (there is still a long walk from
Chatha Hill to Grdhrakuta and the lift is often shut
down for repairs anyway). However, the history of the
place comes far more alive by walking the ancient road
and through the trails of the hills than by riding the
chairlift to the modern temple and *stupa* overlooking
Grdhrakuta and Chatha Hill.

As one passes the "Dismounting the Chariot"
stupa and turns off to the right fork in the trail to the
Grdhrakuta spur, there is a real sense of timelessness and
anticipation of things past. The road is the one used in

227

the time of the Buddha, the rocks were there when he lived, and even the direct descendants of the fauna from his time dart about on the hill. For much of the way, there is nothing to break the feeling that one could be approaching the potentially still active residing place of Sakyamuni Buddha. Even as one approaches the summit, passes the caves known as the "Two Houses," and circles to the right around the peak itself, passing yet another cave where it is possible the Buddha himself sat in meditation, there is no break in the mood of traveling in the past.

Only the garish pink stair railing installed by the Archaeological Survey of India . . . shatters the mood as one makes the final ascent to the platform at the top of Grdhrakuta. There, at the summit, are two small temple basements of Gupta period bricks — remnants of history's tribute to the great teacher who once sat there. At the westernmost of these, the visitor may offer his flower garlands at the tiny brick altar, just as Xuanzang once did before a life-size image of the preaching Buddha, and partake of his own meditations.

Allen Ginsberg, 1963 C.E.
>   *Vulture Peak — Rajgir April 18, 1963*

> GRIDHUAKUTA HILL
> *I've got to get out of the sun*
> *mouth dry and red towel wrapped*
> *round my head*
> *walking up crying singing* ah sunflower
> Where the traveller's journey
> *closed my eyes is done in the*
> *black hole there*
> *sweet rest far far away*
> *up the stone climb past where*
> *Bimbisara left his armies*

228

got down off his elephant
and walked up to meet
Napoleon Buddha pacing
back and forth on the platform
of red brick on the jut rock crag
Staring out Lidded-eyed beneath
the burning white sunlight
down on Rajgir kingdom below
ants wheels within wheels of empire
houses carts streets messengers
wells and water flowing
into past and future simultaneous
kingdoms here and gone on Jupiter
distant X-ray twinkle of the eye
myriad brick cities on earth and under
New York Chicago Palenque Jerusalem
Delphos Macchu Picchu Acco
Herculaneum Rajagriha
here below all windy with the tweetle
of birds and the blue rocks
leaning into the blue sky —
Vulture Peak desolate bricks
flies on the knee hot shadows
raven-screech and wind blast
over the hills from desert plains
south toward Bodh Gaya —
All the noise I made with my mouth
singing on the path up, Gary
Thinking all the pale youths
and virgins shrouded with snow
chanting Om Shantih all over the world
and who but Peter du Peru
walking the streets of San Francisco
arrived in my mind on Vulture Peak
Then turned round and around on my heels
singing and plucking out my eyes

229

ears tongue nose and balls as I whirled
longer and longer the mountains stretched
swiftly flying in circles
the hills undulating and roads speeding
around me in the valley
Till when I stopped the earth
moved in my eyeballs
green bulges slowly
and stopped . . .
My thirst in my cheeks and tongue
back throat drives me home.

Anne Cushman, 1993 C.E.

As we look out over the valley, I recall that it was on Vulture Peak that the Buddha is said to have delivered the Heart Sutra. Its cryptic words run through my mind: "Form is emptiness, emptiness is form. . . ." Nothing exists independently, the Heart Sutra tells us; everything is empty of a separate self, inextricably entwined with all things.

It was on Vulture Peak, too, that the Buddha gave his enigmatic "flower sermon": Gazing out over a crowd of monks eagerly awaiting his teachings, he wordlessly held up a single blossom. Most of the audience was bewildered; but one monk, Mahakasyapa, looked at the flower and smiled in perfect understanding.

The air is humming with crickets and the calls of unfamiliar birds; we can hear the distant clatter of the chair lift and the faint, tinny whine of recorded chanting from the Japanese temple. We sit in silence, watching the sun sink in tendrils of magenta clouds.

Joanna Macy, 1976 C.E.

I want to write about this morning on the hill. Gridhrakuta. Vulture Peak. How fortunate that Thursdays the lift to the top is closed, otherwise I would not have walked and found the way, off to the side, to the Vulture Peak itself. The fellows lounging by the empty parking lot tell me the foot path is unsafe for a woman alone, especially a foreigner, because of thieves. My rickshaw driver, who obviously hoped to hang out with them in the shade, is very reluctant to be hired to accompany me. When he finally agrees, he strides ahead at a fast clip, to get it all over with. He fairly fumes with impatience, when I pause to take in the view or to read the markers posted along the way. Soon I stop altogether and give him a talking to. "I come thousands and thousands of miles all the way from America to this very spot, where the Buddha gave many great teachings. This is a holy hill and I won't be hurried."

Path rising through rocks and scrub. Sounds from the road below growing fainter. Clear, empty bowl of sky ringing in my ears with buzz of insects where once the treasured words were spoken — words that have opened minds and hearts, over so many ages, in so many lands. I try to imagine how it was when the Buddha stayed here, coming year after year for the rainy season — conveniently close to his pals and patrons in the capital — organizing his growing Sangha, teaching, teaching. I try to picture the luxuriant forest, the half-tame deer, the bamboo garden given by King Bimbisara, the fountains described by Hsuan Tsang.

By the time H.T. (Hsuan Tsang . . .) got here — over a thousand years later — the viharas were already in ruins, but the fountains still bubbled and the *kanaka* trees still bore blossoms the color of gold. H.T.'s pilgrimage is so vivid to me, we could be climbing this hill together; wish I'd brought his staff. (The previous year I had loved reading the chronicles of Hsuan Tsang. Traveling alone on foot, he had crossed the Gobi desert to reach the land of the Lord Buddha and visited many sacred sites to acquire and translate Dharma scriptures for his people. At a recent "come-as-your-favorite-incarnation" party given by Huston and Kendra Smith, I had appeared as Hsuan Tsang, girded in a yellow sheet, with my face bronzed with turmeric, my short hair sprayed black, and a long stout stick for a pilgrim staff.)

Plaques show me where King Bimbisara would alight from his royal carriage; and where he sent back the crowd of courtiers, so he could have some privacy with the Buddha; and where the indefatigably nefarious Devadatta hurled the rock at his cousin; and where the monastery stood to which the injured Buddha was then brought.

I try to visualize the scene of the First Council, as H.T. relayed the legendary story that's always irritated me. How, right after the Buddha died, the disciples all gathered here en masse to repeat and formally agree on the teachings. And how Kassapa, presiding because Sariputra and Moggallana were already dead, excluded the beloved Ananda (the Buddha's aide), because he hadn't, in Kassapa's judgment, achieved total, spotless arhatship. And how Ananda — by dint of his own heart breaking, I imagine — struggled and achieved full enlightenment that very night, so he could join the rest and recite, as only he could, every word his blessed Lord ever uttered. All the discourses of the Pali Canon, I suppose.

Then I catch sight, up there on the right, of the craggy outcropping of Gridhrakuta, the Vulture Peak itself. Surprisingly, it's not the summit; but it's a very distinctive formation, as it juts out from the shoulder of the hill, stark and dramatic. Great jagged rocks thrust out on the diagonal, slicing the sky like a vulture's wing, as sharp and fierce as a vulture's beak. There are flat places in between, to sit, to gaze out over the misty plain below, a world away. It's a good spot for teaching. Insistent, rough, unadorned, it is a fitting podium for those early utterances that carved away the confusions and mystifi-

232

cations, that cut like a sword through illusion. An appropriate pulpit for so uncompromising a gospel.

When Ananda recited those discourses to the venerable assembly, he could not have imagined how many sutras would arise later — four, five, six centuries later — and would claim to have been spoken by the Buddha here, right here on the Vulture peak. They include my most beloved Prajnaparamita Astasahasrika (the Perfection of Wisdom in Eight Thousand Verses), though it's the Lotus Sutra with its extravagant descriptions that I associate more with this place. I have to scrunch my eyes and squint toward the sun to try to get the effect: the vast multitudes of scores of thousands of disciples and bodhisattvas and gods, all breathlessly hanging on the Buddha's each word, and the showers of flowers and incense and jewels that fall from the heavens as he speaks, and the beam of light from his third eye that illumines the universe from the highest reaches to the deepest hells, revealing numberless Buddhafields where identical Buddhas are teaching at this moment and at every moment, just like this. If you have faith, sings the sutra, you can always see that: the Buddha preaching the Dharma from the Vulture Peak surrounded by celestial hosts. Dear old Ananda would probably have understood, for I suspect he had a Mahayana heart.

The path curves down a ways and up again to the left, and farther up to the crown of the high hill, to the Viswa Shanti (World Peace) Pagoda, built by Japanese a few years back, along with the chair lift that serves it. I am glad the lift is motionless today, so that I come up to the summit like this, up a steep incline through scrub and rocks, a little fagged, a little fussed with my escort — in other words, up through the tangle and grit. And then — pow. Its lines are so clean, the shapes they carve so harmonious, yet assertive, that it seems to express and complete a dream. All I can think is: yes. Of the four golden Buddhas on the four sides, the one who greets me as I climb the final steps makes the mudra of namaskar [sign of greeting]. Yes, of course: homecoming. At the top, at the end of it all: this. Above the fuss and strife — in final vindication of all that had been hinted at and argued about and yearned for — this utter brilliance, this serene pure statement. This dazzling affirmation of the Dharmakaya feels as fitting to the Mahayana as the Vulture Peak to early Buddhism.

And you don't just see it before you, you enter it, surrounded. Walking into and around the curving passageways and parapets, beneath the belly of the main stupa in the blinding sun, you are a small, shadowy thing, being eclipsed into that incandescent purity.

My companion turns and gives me his name: Sitaram. He says if in the future I write Sitaram, cycle rickshaw, Tourist Bungalow, Rajgir, a postcard will reach him. He points to where he'll be waiting and says I can stay up here as long as I want, but not to start without him.

"THE HEART OF WISDOM SUTRA"

Said to have been delivered on Vulture Peak, "The Heart of Wisdom Sutra" is one of the most popular of the Mahayana "Perfection of Wisdom" or Prajnaparmita sutras.

The Heart of Wisdom Sutra, "Echoes of Voidness," fifth century B.C.E.

Thus I have heard. At one time the Lord was sitting on Vulture's Peak near the city of Rajgir. He was accompanied by a large community of monks as well as a large community of bodhisattvas. On that occasion the Lord was absorbed in a particular concentration called the profound appearance. Meanwhile the bodhisattva, the great being, the noble Avalokiteshvara was contemplating the profound discipline of the perfection of wisdom. He came to see that the five aggregates were void of any inherent nature of their own.

Through the power of the Buddha, the venerable Shariputra approached the noble Avalokiteshvara and asked him, "How should a son of the noble lineage proceed when he wants to train in the profound discipline of the perfection of wisdom?"

The noble Avalokiteshvara replied to the venerable Shariputra, "Whatever son or daughter of the noble lineage wants to train in the profound discipline of the perfection of wisdom should consider things in the following ways. First, he or she should clearly and thoroughly comprehend that the five aggregates are void of any inherent nature of their own. Form is void, but voidness is form. Voidness is not other than forms and forms are not other than voidness. Similarly, feelings, discernments, formative elements and consciousness are also void. Likewise, Shariputra, are all phenomena void. They have no defining characteristics; they are unproduced; they do not cease; they are undefiled, yet they are not separate from defilement; they do not decrease, yet they do not increase. This being the case, Shariputra, in terms of voidness there exist no forms, no feelings, no discernments, no formative elements, no consciousness; no eyes, no ears, no noses, no tongues, no bodies, no minds; no visual forms, no sounds, no smells, no tastes, no tactile sensations, no mental-objects. There exist no visual elements, no mental elements, and no elements of mental consciousness. There exist no ignorance and no exhaustion of ignorance, no ageing and death and no exhaustion of ageing and death. In the same way there exist no suffering, no origin of suffering, no cessation, no path, no wisdom, no attainment and no lack of attainment.

"Therefore, Shariputra, since bodhisattvas have no attainment, they depend upon and dwell in the perfection of wisdom; their minds are unobstructed and unafraid. They transcend all error and finally reach the end-point: nirvana.

"All the buddhas of the past, present and future have depended, do and will depend upon the perfection of wisdom. Thereby they became, are becoming and will be becoming unsurpassably, perfectly and completely awakened buddhas.

"Therefore, the mantra of the perfection of wisdom is a mantra of great knowledge; it is an unsurpassable mantra; it is a mantra that is comparable to the incomparable; it is a mantra that totally pacifies all suffering. It will not deceive you, therefore know it to be true! I proclaim the mantra of the perfection of wisdom: *tayatha gate gate paragate parasamgate bodhi svaha.* Shariputra, it is in this way that the great bodhisattvas train themselves in the profound perfection of wisdom."

At that moment the Lord arose from his concentration and said to the noble Avalokiteshvara, "Well said, well said. That is just how it is, my son, just how it is. The profound perfection of wisdom should be practised exactly as you have explained it. Then the tathagathas will be truly delighted."

When the Lord had spoken these words, the venerable Shariputra and the bodhisattva, the great being, the noble Avalokiteshvara, and the entire gathering of gods, humans, asuras and gandharvas were overjoyed, and they praised what the Lord had said.

Drum Beats

John Blofeld, 1956 C.E.

The memory of my last evening at Rajagriha, when my Thai friends had gone back to Nalanda, can hardly be described. Towards sunset, I paid a call on the Abbot of the Japanese Temple; and just as the rim of the sun dipped behind the hills I came out of the gate into the main road leading to the town. Just at that moment, the air about me throbbed with thunderous vibrations, as a splendid Japanese drum, probably of enormous size, poured forth its farewell to the sun from somewhere within the temple.

Bong bong bong bong-bong *bong*! On and on it went in just that familiar Chinese rhythm, loud as thunder in my ears, but thunder crashing on a magic note which seemed to dissolve *Sangsara*'s mirage, freeing men's Mind from their bodies, promising bliss inconceivable.

Often I have been moved by the sounds of percussion instruments used in the Far East for sacred purposes; they give forth an elemental music with stirring vibration of uncanny effect, whether they are of stone, bronze, wood or stretched skin. Instantly they induce a mood of profound meditation, so difficult to achieve otherwise without long-sustained effort. But the power of this drum exceeded anything in my experience. The whole world appeared to dissolve in a luminous mist as the spirit rose to a kind of ecstasy, so that the drum's sudden cessation wounded me like a knife-thrust, dragging me back to the world of forms. Of course the "luminous mist" and "knife-thrust" must not be taken too literally. It is just that they somewhat correspond to an inner experience not easily clothed in words. Perhaps silence is wiser than attempted descriptions of the subtler experiences of the spirit, for these seldom escape distortion when forced into the armour stiffness of words. Yet, were silence always to be maintained, we could not convey even the husks of our greatest experiences to others, and the literature of religion would become a collection of useless and misleading descriptions of externals.

Jetvana Park

Where the Buddha Performed the Great Miracles and Where He Descended from the Trayastrimsas Heaven

*Four places are always determined in advance:
where Buddhas shall attain Buddha-hood;
where they shall begin to preach;
where they shall expound the Law and refute
heretics; and where they shall descend from the
Trayastrimsas Heaven after having preached to
their mothers. Other places are chosen
according to circumstances.*

— From Fa-hsien

239

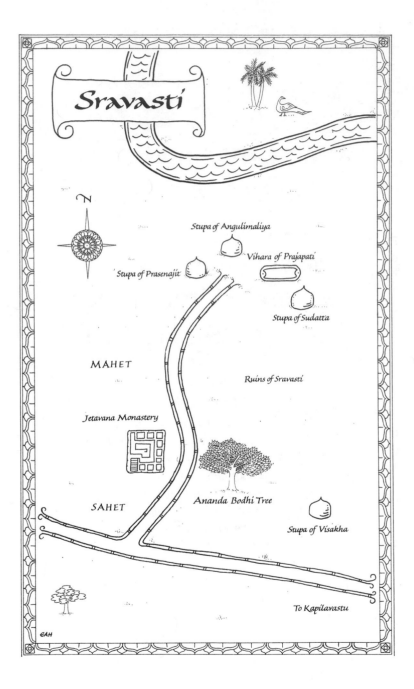

Sravasti

Stupa of Angulimaliya

Vihara of Prajapati

Stupa of Prasenajit

Stupa of Sudatta

MAHET

Ruins of Sravasti

Jetavana Monastery

SAHET

Ananda Bodhi Tree

Stupa of Visakha

To Kapilavastu

EAH

Sravasti and Sankasya lie closest on the pilgrim's map to Kapilavastu and Kusinagara, yet both places are a bit out of the way. Turning to the appropriate pages in the guidebook, the traveler reads about miracles, heretics and ladders in the sky. At Sravasti, the Buddha out-performed leaders of rival sects with his "Great Miracles." At Sankasya, he descended on a ladder from the Trayastrimsas Heaven, the Brahmanic gods paying him homage from either side.

Modern Buddhists are loath to recognize miracles, heavens and descents through the sky. Contemporary biographies of the Buddha, like Thich Nhat Hanh's *Old Path, White Clouds,* omit the miraculous episodes described in ancient texts. Yet stories of miracles have a metaphoric power: In the past, they have been used to suggest new ways of seeing. They have also served to spread the faith, working like the full-page ads in today's magazines. Stories about the Sankasya and Sravasti miracles were compelling advertisements for the Buddha's supremacy, aimed at, respectively, the border and the center of the religion's realm of influence.

Miracles or no, Sravasti memorializes the adult years of the Buddha's life, Sankasya the struggle to spread the Buddhist dharma. The significance of both cities continued to grow after the Buddha's death. Hiuen Tsiang, I-Tsing, and Fa-hsien were a few among millions of early Buddhist pilgrims to visit the two cities, transforming them into magnets of Buddhist faith and devotion.

In addition to the "Great Miracles," Sravasti is famous for its Jetavana Grove. In order to buy the Grove for the sangha, a rich merchant named Anathapindika had to cover every inch of its ground in gold. The Grove became the sangha's principal home during the rainy sea-

son. Thanks, in part, to a generous donation by the lay-woman Visakha, Sravasti also became home to a large community of Buddhist nuns. In the texts, the city abounds with Buddhist nuns and monks, a memorial to the sangha's and to the Buddha's accomplishments.

Ruled by King Prasenajit, Sravasti was, in the Buddha's time, the capital of the Kosala kingdom. Though its ancient ramparts still stand, the city has fallen into ruins. The area is now called Sahet-Mahet, with Sahet denoting the ruins of the Jetavana monastery, and Mahet the site of Sravasti proper. Sahet's extensive remains include the Ananda Bodhi tree, stupas, temples, and the stepped, gridded foundations of Jetavana's monasteries. Mahet, still surrounded by mud ramparts, contains a Jain temple and two stupas called the "Pakki"and "Kachchi Kuti." Judging from their ruins, Sravasti's monasteries underwent a revival soon after Hiuen Tsiang's time and harbored diminished activity well into the twelfth century, when the area was probably destroyed by Turkish raids.

After his enlightenment, the Buddha returned to Kapilavastu to preach the dharma to his family. His mother, Queen Maya, was not there to receive his teachings, having died shortly after his birth. To give her an opportunity to embrace his doctrine, the Buddha is said to have traveled from Sravasti to the Trayastrimsas Heaven, or Heaven of the Thirty-three, and to have spoken with her there before descending to earth at Sankasya. His voyage to the heavens was part of a series of activities prescribed for all Buddhas. Sankasya was said to be the site not only of Sakyamuni Buddha's descent but of all past Buddhas' descents to earth.

The old ramparts of Sankasya stand today, as do several stupas, an Asokan pillar, and the pillar's elephant capital, housed separately. The Temple of the Stairs exists as well, but has been subsumed into a Hindu shrine.

Temple in Jetvana Park

I. SRAVASTI
(SAVATTHI, SAHET-MAHET)

This world is blind; few can see here.
Few go to heaven, like birds escaped from a net.

Arise, do not be negligent; practice the principle
of good conduct. One who acts on truth is happy
in this world and beyond.

— The Dhammapada

243

On the Road to Sravasti

Before his birth, the Buddha carefully examined the many places from which he could choose a birthplace. He rejected Sravasti. Though Sravasti's "people [were] numerous, and the king [was] powerful," it had an unattractive history: "The kings of Kosala have descended from Matangas, both on the mother's and father's side, of impure birth; and in former days they were of small repute, without any personal courage or nobleness of heart; the country [was] comparatively poor, although there are the seven precious substances there; yet they are in no abundance. Therefore, I cannot be born there!" Despite its unsuitabilities, the city became a vital center of Buddhism during the Buddha's life. The Buddha passed a great deal of his post-enlightenment years in Sravasti and delivered a majority of his sermons in its Jetavana Grove. Among the pilgrims who have recorded their visits to Sravasti, opinions vary strikingly from impressions of dullness to inspiration. The road that takes travelers to Sravasti, modern Sahet-Mahet, is straight and tree-lined.

Fa-hsien, 400 C.E.

Travelling northward for eight *yojanas*, they reached the city of Sravasti in the country of Kosala. This city is sparsely populated, having only about two hundred families in it.

S. R. Wijayatilake, 1963 C.E.

At Balrampur there were no taxis available and for our ten mile trip to Saheth-Maheth the choice was between the omnibus and the cycle-rickshaw. Despite the twenty mile trip up and down, we opted for the latter. . . . Riding early in the morning against the cold breeze was invigorating but we made the mistake of shedding our monkey-caps, shawls and over-coats so that at the end of the day some of us had developed bad colds. . . .

The road to Sravasti is a bee-line, as straight. It is really an avenue of mango trees. These mango trees are all numbered and leased out to the villagers in the area. . . . Except for a stray motor-bus the only other vehicles we met were huge bullock carts laden with bags of paddy and of course the pony carts without any hoods — the passengers hanging on to them like bats. . . . While riding along our thoughts went back to the time of the Buddha when his presence was a familiar sight in this area for nearly twenty-four years. We could picture to ourselves the mango groves in which he sought shelter from the sweltering sun. Within two hours we reached Sravasti.

Major Rowland Raven-Hart, 1956 C.E.

The road to Sahet-Mahet is dull to unsufferableness, nearly always straight, and with trees set so far back that their shade is usable only when it is useless, with the long shadows of morning or evening. At one place a group of itinerant entertainers were sitting in their shade, all in brown-yellow stuffs and with stringed instruments on their laps or slung to their shoulders. . . . I think they were gypsies, but whence and whither bound? There were no women with them, but at least one of the boys was a dancer, a slim, limber child of about fourteen: he sketched a couple of dance-poses at me with an inviting, impudent grin that made me wish I could see their whole performance.

And at another place there were monkeys, the common brown ones. . . . Only once was there a patch of thick jungle-scrub, full of Babblers scuttling about on the ground more like beasts than birds, and Grey Tits on the twigs above them more often upside-down than right way up. And I just caught a glimpse of a Tree-Pie, or rather of its black-tipped tail, though its "Bobolink"

245

call was annoyingly clear and persistent.

That was all that the road had to offer, except for the dust; but it was good dust, blinding and suffocating when a rare car passed. The only reasonable thing to do was to dismount and wait, with muffled eyes and nose: one could no more ride through that turbid swirl than through pitch darkness. The surface was fair, under repair in stretches which compelled detours over deep ruts: it was a boy from one of the road-gangs who took time out to show me where the site lay.

The Miracles of Sravasti: A Contest of Faiths

At Sravasti, six non-Buddhist philosophers challenged the Buddha to a contest of words and miracles. Having heard that he refused to perform miracles, they hoped to make a fool of their rival. The Buddha accepted their challenge, explaining that his interdiction against miracles applied to his disciples, not to himself. He proceeded to outdo the six, causing fire and water to leap from his body and multiplying himself in the air around them.

THE BUDDHA'S INTERDICTION AGAINST MIRACLES

From the Digha Nikaya, *Sutta 11: The Kevaddha Sutta, 5th–1st c. B.C.E.*
. . .[T]he householder Kevaddha came to the Lord, prostrated himself before him, and sat down to one side. He then said: "Lord, this Nalanda is rich, prosperous, populous, and full of people who have faith in the Lord. It would be well if the Lord were to cause some monk to perform superhuman feats and miracles. In this way Nalanda would come to have even more faith in the Lord."

246

The Lord replied: "Kevaddha, this is not the way I teach Dhamma to the monks, by saying: 'Go, monks, and perform superhuman feats and miracles for the white-clothed laypeople!'"

[Kevaddha repeats his request two more times.]

When Kevaddha repeated his request for a third time, the Lord said: "Kevaddha, there are three kinds of miracles that I have declared, having realised them by my own insight. Which three? The miracle of psychic power, the miracle of telepathy, the miracle of instruction.

"What is the miracle of psychic power? Here, Kevaddha, a monk displays various psychic powers in different ways. Being one he becomes many, being many he becomes one . . . and he travels in the body as far as the Brahma world. Then someone who has faith and trust sees him doing these things.

"He tells this to someone else who is sceptical and unbelieving, saying: 'It is wonderful, sir, it is marvellous, the great power and skill of that ascetic. . . .' And that man might say: 'Sir, there is something called the Gandharan charm. It is by means of this that that monk becomes many. . . .' What do you think, Kevaddha, would not a sceptic say that to a believer?" "He would, Lord." "And that is why, Kevaddha, seeing the danger of such miracles, I dislike, reject and despise them.

"And what is the miracle of telepathy? Here a monk reads the minds of other beings, of other people, reads their mental states, their thoughts and ponderings, and says: 'That is how your mind is, that is how it inclines, that is in your heart.' Then someone who has faith and trust sees him doing these things.

"He tells this to someone else who is sceptical and unbelieving. . . . And that man might say: 'Sir, there is something called the Manika charms. It is by means of this that that monk can read the minds of others. . . .'

And that is why, seeing the danger of such miracles, I . . . despise them.

"And what is the miracle of instruction? Here, Kevaddha, a monk gives instruction as follows: 'Consider in this way, don't consider in that, gain this and persevere in it.' That, Kevaddha, is called the miracle of instruction."

THE STORY OF THE GREAT MIRACLES

According to one version of the story, the contest was called when one of the Buddha's disciples put non-Buddhist disciples (schismatics) to shame with a show of magic powers. Wanting to recover face, the schismatics challenged the Buddha to match his skills with theirs. In response, he performed the "Twin Miracles" or "Great Miracles" of Sravasti.

From the "Srabha-Miga Jataka," 5th–1st c. B.C.E.
[Responding to a challenge, a Buddhist monk flew through the air to retrieve a wooden bowl perched high on a pole. The Buddha chided him for his miracle.]

The schismatics thought, "The ascetic Gotama has forbidden the use of miraculous power: now he will do no miracle himself." [The schismatics'] disciples were disturbed, and said to the schismatics, "Why didn't you take the bowl by your supernatural power?" They replied: "This is no hard thing for us, friend. But we think, 'Who will display before the laity his own fine and subtle powers for the sake of a paltry wooden bowl?' And so we did not take it. The ascetics of the Sakya class took it, and showed their supernatural power for sheer foolish greed. Do not imagine it is any trouble to us to work miracles. Suppose we leave out of consideration the disciples of Gotama the ascetic; if we like, we too will show our supernatural powers with the ascetic

Gotama himself: if the ascetic Gotama works one miracle, we will work one twice as good."

The Brethren who heard this told the Blessed One of it: "Sir, the schismatics say they will work a miracle." Said the Master, "Let them do it, Brethren; I will do the like." Bimbisara, hearing this, went and asked the Blessed One: "Will you work a miracle, Sir?" "The command, O king, was given to my disciples; there is no command which can rule the Buddhas. When the flowers and fruit in your park are forbidden to others, the same rule does not apply to you." "Then where will you work this miracle, Sir?" "At Savatthi, under a knot-mango tree." "What have I to do, then?" "Nothing, Sire."

Next day, after breaking his fast, the Master went to seek alms. "Whither goes the Master?" asked the people. The Brethren answered to them, "At the gate of the city of Savatthi, beneath a knot-mango tree, he is to work a twofold miracle to the confounding of the schismatics." The crowd said, "This miracle will be what they call a masterpiece; we will go see it." Leaving the doors of their houses, they went along with the Master. Some of the schismatics also followed the Master, with their disciples: "We too," they said, "will work a miracle, in the place where the ascetic Gotama shall work his."

By and by the Master arrived at Savatthi. The king asked him, "Is it true, Sir, you are about to work a miracle, as they say?" "Yes, it is true. . . . Proclaim it, O king." The king sent forth the Crier of the Truth on an elephant richly caparisoned, to proclaim thus: "News! the Master is about to perform a miracle, for the confounding of the schismatics, at the Gate of Savatthi, under a knot-mango tree, seven days from now!" Each day was this proclamation made. When the schismatics heard this news, that the miracle will be done under a knot-mango tree, they had all the mango trees near to Savatthi cut down, paying the owners for them.

On the night of the full moon the Crier of the Truth made the proclamation, "This day in the morning the miracle will take place." By the power of the gods it was as though all India was at the door and heard the proclamation; whosoever had it in his heart to go, they all beheld themselves at Savatthi: for twelve leagues the crowd extended.

Early in the morning the Master went on his rounds seeking alms. The king's gardener, Ganda or Knot by name, was just taking to the king a fine ripe mango fruit; thoroughly ripe, big as a bushel, when he espied the Master at the city gate. "This fruit is worthy of the Master," said he, and gave it to him. The Master took it, and sitting down then and there on one side, ate the fruit. When it was eaten, he said, "Ananda, give the gardener this stone to plant here on the spot; this shall be the mango knot-tree." The Elder did so. The gardener dug a hole in the earth, and planted it. On the instant the stone burst, roots sprouted forth, up sprang a red shoot tall as a plough-pole; even as the crowd stared it grew into a mango tree of a hundred cubits, with a trunk fifty cubits and branches of fifty cubits in height; at the same time flowers bloomed, fruit ripened; the tree stood filling the sky, covered with bees, laden with golden fruit; when the wind blew on it, sweet fruits fell; then the Brethren came up and ate of the fruit and retired. . . . The Master, having for the confounding of the schismatics performed a twofold miracle passing marvellous among his disciples, caused faith to spring up in multitudes, then arose and, sitting in the Buddha's seat, declared the Law.

THE CONTEST OF FAITHS

After this first contest of miracles, the site became associated with heretics and the struggle between

Buddhism and other faiths. Centuries later, Fa-hsien described another "contest" of faiths taking place at the site between Buddhists and Brahmans.

Fa-hsien, 400 C.E.

Stupas were later built in this city on the sites of the ruined monastery of Mahaprajapati and the home of the elder Sudatta, and over the spots where Angulimalya attained sainthood and was cremated after he entered Nirvana. Out of jealousy, heretical Brahmans planned to destroy these stupas; but the heavens thundered and lightning flashed so that they were foiled. . . .

On the east of the road is a temple named "Overshadowed." This is also about sixty feet in height and was built by Brahman heretics just opposite the shrine erected over the debating place [where the Great Miracles were performed]. This temple is so named because, when the sun is in the west, the shadow of the Buddhist shrine covers the heretics' temple; but when the sun is in the east, the shadow of the heretics' temple falls towards the north and can never overshadow the Buddhist shrine.

The heretics sent men regularly to look after their temple, sweep it, water it, burn incense, light the lamps and present offerings. But by the morning their lamps always disappeared, and they would discover them in the Buddhist shrine. The Brahmans grew angry, and said, "The monks are taking our lamps to offer to Buddha. We must stop them." So they kept a watch by night. Then they saw the gods they worshipped take the lamps, circle the Buddhist shrine three times, offer the lamps before the image of the Buddha, then suddenly disappear. At that the Brahmans realized that Buddha was greater than their gods, and they forsook their homes to become his followers. It was said that this had occurred only recently. . . .

Exploring Sravasti

Sravasti is divided into two parts, now called respectively Sahet and Mahet. At the height of its glory, Sravasti was a heavily fortified city, its ponderous walls packed with houses, shops, and life.

John Huntington, 1985 C.E.

Contrary to ancient pilgrims who may have seen structures similar to those shown in the Barhut and Sanci reliefs, the modern visitor [to Sravasti] is treated only to the foundations of buildings that date from the sixth century and later. This is not to say that the early remains are missing but that the excavation levels have not been taken down that far. To excavate to further depths would necessitate destroying, at least in part, what is presently at the site. Perhaps, someday, partial excavation (for example, the north half of each building site) will reveal the foundations of the buildings of greater antiquity. Even with this limitation of not being able to see the foundations of the ancient buildings themselves, the continuity of purpose at the site still gives one a profound sense of the presence of Sakyamuni. Indeed, for anyone aware of the history of Buddhism, a visit to the excavated Jetavana and, by contrast, totally unexcavated Sravasti is to bask in the full vitality of the period of the Buddha's ministry. Indeed, the poignancy of this experience was experienced by Faxian [Fa-hsien], the fifth-century Chinese pilgrim. . . .

Even today, walking among the ruined structures of the Jetavana one is reminded at every turn of the presence of Sakyamuni Buddha. Here he walked; at this well he drew water; he stayed in the Kosambakuti, where he taught. . . .

Regrettably, the entire city remains an unexcavated archaeological field. Yet within the low walls,

rolling mounds and few *stupas* and tanks which are all
that are perceptible to the modern visitor, Sakyamuni
and his contemporaries created much of the history of
Buddhism, and it was here that many of the great teachings of Buddhism were offered for the first time. One
can only hope that interest in the site by visitors and pilgrims will encourage future excavation. More than at
any other site, at Sravasti there is the possibility of laying
bare the very streets on which the Buddha walked during his alms rounds and the places where his conversions and ministrations occurred. In spite of the fact
that actual remains of Sakyamuni survive at other sites
and some sites are more intimately associated with his
attainments, it is at Sravasti that his ministry — his special relationship with his disciples and lay devotees —
still may be felt and understood.

Major Rowland Raven-Hart, 1956 C.E.

[I]t was cool and shady there . . . and I lingered,
trying to picture what the city must have been like when
the Buddha knew it. A fortified nucleus, of course,
defended with walls and moat and the river. Outside that
nucleus a huddle of thatched mud huts, separated by
narrow lanes: inside it, more huts and lanes, but with a
few wider streets on which stood lines of windowless
shops, shuttered by night, and the houses of the richer
citizens. On the streets, not in gardens or compounds,
though within those houses there were at least flower-
beds and perhaps fountains, in patio style. Two-storeyed,
probably, wood or brick over brick or stone; and very
probably a third storey in the form of a wall-less pavilion
which was the real living-room. A gateway to the street,
a pompous one with huge doors; and in this gate-house
the store-rooms and treasure, since it was the safest and
best-built part. Within this a courtyard with rooms opening off it, especially for servants and dependents.

Indoors but little furniture, no tables or chairs. No pictures, but plenty of gay decorations, frescoes on plaster over skin linings to the brick or wood walls: decorative foliage patterns, geometrical designs, but also paintings of people, scenes from everyday life and legend. No ceiling, but ceiling-cloths, still useful in many Dak Bungalows to keep snakes and scorpions out of your soup. No sewers, I fear: drains for bath- and rain-water but otherwise lots of "sweepers" as in India to-day. . . .

[T]hat evening I found dust caked on areas of me where I had thought no dust could reach, and it took two buckets of water and one amused room-boy to evict it.

The Jetavana Grove

Village or forest, hill or dale, anywhere that saints
dwell is pleasant.

People compelled by fear go to many a refuge —
mountains, forests, resorts, trees, and shrines.
That is not a safe refuge, that is not the ultimate
refuge; one is not freed of all miseries by going
to that refuge.

But one who takes refuge in the enlightened,
the teaching, and the community, sees the four noble
truths with accurate insight: misery, the origin
of misery, and the overcoming of misery; and the
noble eightfold path that leads to cessation of misery.

This indeed is a safe refuge; this is the ultimate refuge.
Having come to this refuge,
one is freed from all misery.

— The Dhammapada, 5th–1st c. B.C.E.,
translated from the Pali by Thomas Cleary

The old Bodhi tree

During the Buddha's lifetime, the Jetavana Grove sheltered the sangha's most active monastery. The story of the Grove's donation is the subject of popular legend, illustrated in early Buddhist reliefs and related in numerous sermons and stories. To buy the land for the sangha, a mer-

255

chant named Sudatta covered the entire ground of the Grove with gold pieces, the price demanded by its owner, Prince Jetavana. Sudatta, also known as Anathapindika, exhausted his funds with just a corner of land left to cover. Impressed by the merchant's devotion, the Grove's owner, Prince Jetavana, decided to donate the rest.

The Grove figures in hundreds of Buddhist texts. Here, the Buddha delivered the majority of his sermons. And here travelers stop longest to meditate on the Buddha's life in Sravasti.

THE DONATION

From Tibetan Works in the Bkah-Hgyur *and* Bstan-Hgyur, *8th–14th c.* C.E.

While stopping at the Citavana of Rajagriha, the Blessed One was invited to a feast by a householder of the city, at whose house was then stopping a rich merchant of Cravasti called Sudatta, better known on account of his generosity and charitableness as "the incomparable almsgiver," or Anathapindada. The night before the feast Sudatta heard the master of the house giving his orders; and having inquired the reason of these preparations, he heard of the Buddha and his disciples, and conceived great admiration for the Master. Early on the morrow he went to Citavana, and finding the Buddha walking in front of the house, he was led by him into the room, and there the Blessed One talked to him of charity, morality, &c., so that he saw the truth, and became a lay follower.

Then the Blessed One questioned him as to his name, his country, &c., and Sudatta besought him to come to Cravasti in Kosala, and assured him that he would provide him and his disciples with all which they might require.

"Householder," the Buddha inquired, "is there any vihara at Cravasti?"

"There is none, Blessed One."

"If there were such a place, householder, bhik-shus could go, come, and stay there."

"Only come, Blessed One, and I will provide a vihara also."

The Buddha promised him, and with that assurance Sudatta departed.

After a little while he came back and asked the Buddha to send a bhikshu with him who could superintend the building of the vihara. The Buddha chose Cariputra, for well he knew that he would also work at the conversion of the people of Cravasti.

Sudatta sought to procure a suitable piece of ground for the vihara, and his choice fell upon a park belonging to Jeta, son of King Prasenadjit. He asked the prince for it; [the prince] at first refused, but finally agreed to sell it if Sudatta covered all the ground with gold pieces. To this the householder consented. When he had nearly finished having the ground covered with gold, Jeta thought that it would be good for him to offer something to this Buddha for whose sake Sudatta was sacrificing so much, so he asked him to let him retain that part of the park not yet covered with gold. Sudatta let him have it; and on this ground the prince afterwards built a vestibule, which he gave to the order. . . .

PILGRIM ACCOUNTS
OF THE JETAVANA GROVE

Fa-hsien, 400 C.E.

The Jetavana Grove evoked from Fa-hsien one of his most personal and emotional responses. Describing his reaction to the site, Fa-hsien refers to himself in the third-person.

About 1,200 paces out of the South Gate of [the] city and on the west side of the road is a temple built by the elder Sudatta. Its door faces east and it has two chambers before which stand two stone pillars. On the top of the left pillar is the image of a wheel, and on top of the right one the image of an ox. The water in the pool is clear, the trees and plants luxuriant, and flowers of many colours make a lovely sight. This place is called the Jetavana Retreat. . . .

The Jetavana Retreat originally had seven storeys. And the rulers and citizens of many countries vied with one another in making offerings here, hanging silk pennants and canopies, scattering flowers and lighting lamps which burnt day and night without ever being extinguished. . . .

On arriving at the Jetavana Retreat, when Fa-hsien and Tao-chen reflected that the Blessed One had lived here for twenty-five years, they regretted having been born in a far-off country. Of the companions who had travelled with them through many lands, some had returned to their homes and some had died. As they gazed at the places where the Buddha could no longer be seen, they were deeply moved and their hearts were filled with sorrow.

The monks there came forward to question them.

"Where do you come from?" they asked

"We come from China," replied Fa-hsien and Tao-chen.

"How wonderful," exclaimed the monks, "that men from a far-off country should come all this way to seek for the Law!" And they commented to each other, "Not from the earliest times has any of our teachers ever seen a Chinese monk here!"

. . . The spacious grounds of the Jetavana Retreat have two gates, one facing east and the other north. It was in this garden that the elder Sudatta covered the ground with gold coins to buy the site for Buddha. The retreat is at the centre of the garden, and Buddha spent longer here than in any other place. Stupas, each with a distinctive name, have been built where he preached for the salvation of men, and where he walked and sat. . . . Around the Jetavana Retreat are ninety-eight monasteries, of which all but one are occupied by monks.

Anne Cushman, 1993 C.E.

The Jeta Grove itself is an exquisite, wooded park that feels dreamily serene despite the incessant commentary of the hoopoes and parakeets and the quarrelling of the giant langur monkeys who romp through the bel trees. Tradition holds that this piece of land was bought for the Buddha by the wealthy merchant Anathapindika from a prince, who demanded that Anathapindika cover the entire grove with pieces of gold as a purchase price; as we stroll down the path used by the Buddha for walking meditation, I imagine the grass around us buried in sparkling coins.

S. R. Wijayalitake, 1963 C.E.

Going through the excavated area of Jethavanarama one could see only the foundations and remnants of crumbling massive walls of bricks. . . .

The fact that this monastery afforded shelter to the Master for twenty-four rainy seasons should endear this place to all his followers. It's a pity that pilgrims to India sometimes do not include this sacred site in their itinerary. Probably there's not a square-foot on this site the revered feet of the Buddha have not trod on and it was in a spirit of humility we surveyed the place. There is the rostrum from which the Buddha addressed his disciples in a fair state of preservation. It is possible that parts of what is to be seen today have been rebuilt but at least they give an indication as to what this place must have looked like in the time of the Buddha. There are two huge well-built wells about 20 to 30 feet in depth. There can be no doubt that the Buddha must have used them for his ablutions. . . .

It is fascinating to see even now deer roaming about Jetavana undisturbed by the many pilgrims. . . .

Our minds went back 2,500 years. . . . We could see the Buddha in deep meditation in the grove beside the pool. The hour was late and suddenly the place became lit up with the glowing beauty of the devas. The Jeta Grove became transformed into a land of fairies. The chief of them approached the Buddha and posed the question: "Oh tell us, Sir, what is the greatest blessing?" The Master anticipated this question and he had no hesitation in replying. There was a hushed silence. The dazzling light became more subdued and the music in the air ceased for the moment. Thus spake the Buddha:

> Not to follow after fools, the worship of the
> worshipful, To dwell in a pleasant spot,
> To have set oneself in the Right Path. . . .

We bowed our heads in reverence and we rode back to Balrampur and we took the night mail to Lucknow.

Sravasti's Bhikkhus (Monks)

> Few among men reach the other shore (Nibbana);
> all the others only run up and down on this shore.
> But those who practise according to the well-
> expounded Dhamma will reach the other shore
> (Nibbana), having passed the realm of Death (i.e.
> Samsara), very difficult as it is to cross.

> — The Dhammapada, 5th–1st c. B.C.E.,
> translated from the Pali by Daw Mya Tin

Those who have no accumulation, who eat with
perfect knowledge, whose sphere is emptiness,
signlessness, and liberation, are hard to track,
like birds in the sky.

— The Dhammapada, 5th–1st c. B.C.E.,
translated from the Pali by Thomas Cleary

The Buddhist texts abound with stories of the
monks and nuns of Sravasti, many of whom had known
the city in their lay youth. One of the largest cities in North
India, Sravasti was a considerable source of converts to the
faith. Below are stories about the monks of Sravasti,
including verses by two monks who hailed, as laypeople,
from Sravasti.

NANDAKA

From the Theragatha, *circa fifth century* B.C.E.
One day [Nandaka] was wandering in search of
alms through the town of Savatthi, when he met his former wife face to face. She gave a little laugh, an amorous
little laugh, remembering the nights Nandaka had
shared her bed. Divining her thoughts, Nandaka lec-
tured her on Dharma, emphasizing repugnance for the
body and cautioning how Mara the temptor sets his
snares.

> *That wretched malodorous thing,*
> *that woman's body,*
> *its nine streams always leaking —*
> *piss, shit, blood and tears*
> *cum, saliva, snot*
> *thin milk and sweat —*
>
> *Yet you smirk*
> *over past conquests and imagine*
> *it might lure a son of Buddha?*

Sex in heaven couldn't sway this beggar,
how much less what's
done on earth?

Instruments of Mara these
legs and arms
hips, breasts and sex —
Mara sets out charms
to snare dark hearts and
muddy minds.

But there are men untouched by lust
or ignorance who've got
no appetite for leaky
sweating bodies.
These ones have cut the cords, woman,
these have gotten free.

MAHANAMA

From the Theragatha, circa fifth century B.C.E.
Reborn in this Buddha age to a Brahmin clan at
Savatthi, [Mahanama] joined a company of monks after
hearing the Enlightened One speak. Hungry for insight
he scaled Hunter's Point to meditate, but a host of ugly
thoughts and painful desires swarmed over him. "What
good is life with a mind so wretched?" he cried, and
climbed a steep crag in disgust. "I'll kill him!" he shouted, as though it were somebody else, and preparing to
throw himself down muttered this verse —

Agh! what a ghastly
end you've brought yourself to,
Mahanama,
your grave a desolate
cliff at Hunter's Point

smothered with sal trees
and tangled with brush —

As he stood cursing over the cliff's edge, working up courage to cast himself off, an abrupt and unshakable insight tore through him. Thus Mahanama became an Arhat.

MONKS IN TODAY'S SRAVASTI

Anne Cushman, 1993 C.E.

As we walk, Nancy tells us that back in New York City, a monk at a Sri Lankan temple gave her a package to deliver to one of his teachers, whom he assured her she'd find meditating under a pipal tree at the Jeta Grove. To our amazement, she actually does find the monk she is looking for; and after she presents him with her gift, he invites us all to return for an unspecified ceremony late that afternoon.

So at four o'clock on the last day of our pilgrimage, we find ourselves assembling under the giant pipal known as the Anathapindika tree. . . .

As we take our seats in a semicircle under the branches, eight Sri Lankan monks in brilliant saffron robes file in and sit opposite us. The head monk, an elderly man with the ageless, compassionate face of a Buddha statue, unreels a white silk cord, which is passed from monk to monk, then from pilgrim to pilgrim, until all of us are linked. We raise our hands into prayer position as the monks begin to chant in the lilting, melodic Sri Lankan style: *Buddham saranam gacchami, Dhamman saranam gacchami.* . . . It's the oldest Buddhist chant of all: "I take refuge in the Buddha, I take refuge in the dharma, I take refuge in the sangha."

This, I think, is where the Buddha can be found: not in the ruins of ancient stupas, but in the lives of the

A monk reading in Jetvana Park

people all around the world who practice the teachings they were built to commemorate. The buildings are far less durable than the insights; the temples disintegrate with time, but the realizations are born again and again with each generation of practitioners.

When the chanting is finished, Larry asks the head monk the question that I started the trip with: "What is the spiritual value of pilgrimage?"

"When you come to places where the Buddha lived, you become happier. You increase the well-being within you," he answers in Hindi as Shantum translates. "In America, it might be more difficult to remember the Buddha with every step you take."

He pauses, then smiles at us, and concludes, "Besides, there is a special kind of *sukkha*, or joy, that comes from sharing the dharma with friends."

John Blofeld, 1956 C.E.

My only experience there worthy of record was a touching little incident connected with my Burmese or Thai style sunshade of orange-coloured oiled paper. It happened that the Burmese monk who guided me round the ruins had an identical sunshade which he was carrying that day. The simple Hindu villagers, seeing the local holy man approach, followed by another man with the same kind of sunshade, supposed that I was a "holy man" also. Accordingly, when they had "taken the monk's *Darshan*" by humbly touching his foot or knee, they hastened forward to obtain mine. My attempt to make them understand that I am far from holy fell on deaf ears as we had no language in common. (The "making of *Darshan*" is a Hindu rite with several variations. The theory is that some virtue can be transferred from a sacred image or holy man to the person who "takes *Darshan*," usually by gazing at or touching the object of veneration.) The most moving and instructive aspect of this little incident is that it illustrates the noble catholicity of the Hindus who accept a holy man for the real or supposed sanctity of his life and do not stop to argue as to whether he is a co-religionist or not.

265

Visakha's Convent:
Sravasti's Bhikkhunis (Nuns)

VISAKHA'S DONATION

From **The Dhammapada, 5th–1st c. B.C.E.**

Visakha was the daughter of a rich man of Bhaddiya, named Danancaya, and his wife Summanadevi, and the granddaughter of Menadaka, one of the five extremely wealthy men of King Bimbasara's dominions. When Visakha was seven years old, the Buddha came on a tour to Bhaddiya. On that occasion, the rich man Mendaka took Visakha and her five hundred companions with him to pay homage to the Buddha. After hearing the discourse given by the Buddha, Visakha, her grandfather and all her five hundred companions attained *Sotapatti* Fruition.

When Visakha came of age, she married Punnavaddhana, son of Migara, a fairly rich man from Savatthi. One day, while Migara was having his meal, a bhikkhu stopped for alms at his house; but Migara completely ignored the bhikkhu. Visakha, seeing this, said to the bhikkhu, "I am sorry, your reverence, my father-in-law only eats leftovers." On hearing this, Migara flew into a rage and told her to leave his house. But Visakha said she was not going away, and she would send for the eight elderly rich men who were sent by her father to accompany her and to advise her. It was for them to decide whether she was guilty or not. When the elders came, Migara said to them, "While I was having my rice-with-milk in a golden bowl, Visakha said that I was taking only dirt and filth. For this offence, I'm sending her away." Thereupon, Visakha explained as follows: "When I saw my father-in-law completely ignoring the bhikkhu standing for alms-food, I thought to myself that my father-in-law was not doing any meritorious deed in this existence, he was only eating the fruits of his past good deeds; so I said, 'My father-in-law only eats left-overs.' Now Sirs, what do you think, am I guilty?" The elders decided that Visakha was not guilty. Visakha then said that she was one who had absolute and unshakable faith in the Teaching of the Buddha and so could not stay where the bhikkhus were not welcome; and also, that if she was not given permission to invite the bhikkhus to the house to offer alms-food and make other offerings, she would leave the house. So permission was granted her to invite the Buddha and his bhikkhus to the house.

The next day, the Buddha and his disciples were invited to the house of Visakha. When alms-food was about to be offered, she sent word to her father-in-law to join her in offering food; but he did not come. When the meal was over, again she sent a message, this time requesting her father-in-law to join her in hearing the discourse that would soon be given by the Buddha. Her father-in-law felt that he should not refuse for a second time. But his ascetic teachers, the Niganthas, would not let him go; however, they conceded that he could listen from behind a curtain. After hearing the Buddha's discourse Migara attained *Sotapatti* Fruition. He felt very thankful to the Buddha and also to his daughter-in-law. Being so thankful, he declared that henceforth Visakha would be like a mother to him, and Visakha came to be known as Migaramata [the mother of Migara].

Visakha gave birth to ten sons and ten daughters, and ten sons and ten daughters each were born to everyone of her children and grandchildren. Visakha possessed an immensely valuable gem-encrusted cloak given by her father as a wedding present. One day, Visakha went to the Jetavana monastery with her entourage. On arrival at the monastery, she found that her bejewelled cloak was too heavy. So, she took it off, wrapped it up in her shawl, and gave it to the maid to hold it and take care of it. The maid absentmindedly left it at the monastery. It was the custom for the Venerable Ananda to look after the things left by any one of the lay disciples. Visakha sent the maid back to the monastery saying, "Go and look for the bejewelled cloak, but if the Venerable Ananda had already found it and kept it in a place do not bring it back; I donate the bejewelled cloak to the Venerable Ananda." But the Venerable Ananda did not accept her donation. So Visakha decided to sell the bejewelled cloak and donate the sale proceeds. But there was not one who could afford to buy that bejewelled cloak. So Visakha bought it back for nine crores and one lakh. With this money, she built a monastery on the eastern side of the city; this monastery came to be known as Pubbarama.

After the libation ceremony she called all her family to her and on that night she told them that all her wishes had been fulfilled and that she had nothing more to desire. Then reciting five verses of exultation she went round and round the monastery. Some bhikkhus hearing her, thought she was singing and reported to the Buddha that Visakha was not like before, and that she was going round and round the monastery, singing. "Could it be that she had gone off her head?" they asked the Buddha. To this question, the Buddha replied, "Today, and on account of that sense of achievement, she was feeling elated and contented; Visakha was just reciting some verses of exultation; she certainly had not gone off her head. Visakha, throughout her previous existences, had always been a generous donor and an ardent promoter of the Doctrine of successive Buddhas. She was most strongly inclined to do good deeds and had done much good in her previous existences, just as an expert florist makes many garlands from a collection of flowers."

Then the Buddha spoke in verse as follows:

*As from a collection of flowers many a garland
can be made by an expert florist, so also, much good
can be done (with wealth, out of faith and
generosity) by one subject to birth and death.*

THE BHIKKHUNIS

*Visakha and her grant of land came to be associ-
ated with the community of Buddhist nuns which possessed a thriving convent in Sravasti. Because of the convent, nuns had a strong presence in the city.
Consequently, stories about nuns often take Sravasti as
their setting.*

FAT NANDA
From the "Suvannahamsa Jataka," 5th–1st c. B.C.E.

A lay-brother at Savatthi had offered the
Sisterhood a supply of garlic, and sending for his bailiff,
had given orders that, if they should come, each Sister
was to receive two or three handfuls. After that they
made a practice of coming to his house or field for their
garlic. Now one holiday the supply of garlic in the house
ran out, and the Sister Fat Nanda, coming with others to
the house, was told, when she said she wanted some garlic, that there was none left in the house, it had all been
used up out of hand, and that she must go to the field
for it. So away she went and carried off an excessive
amount of garlic. The bailiff grew angry and remarked
what a greedy lot these Sisters were! This piqued the
more moderate Sisters; and the Brethren too were piqued
at the taunt when the Sisters repeated it to them, and
they told the Blessed One. Rebuking the greed of Fat
Nanda, the Master said, "Brethren, a greedy person is
harsh and unkind even to the mother who bore him; a
greedy person cannot convert the unconverted, or make
the converted grow in grace, or cause alms to come in, or

save them when they come in; whereas a moderate person can do all these things."

KISAGOTAMI

From the Samyutta Nikaya, 5th–1st c. B.C.E.

Thus have I heard. Once when at Savatthi, the Lord stayed at Anathapindika's Jeta Grove. The nun, Kisagotami, having dressed, went one morning into town with her robe and bowl to beg for food. After her almsround and after she had returned with her almsfood, she ate, then went into the dark forest to spend the day there. Arriving in the dark forest, she sat down at the foot of a tree.

Then Mara, the Evil One, wanting to inspire fear and terror and to ruin her meditation, went to that same place. Having gone there, he spoke this verse to her:

> [Mara:] What's going on?
> You look as if your child has died.
> You sit alone;
> tears streak your face.
> You've come to the woods alone —
> are you looking for a man?

But Kisagotami thought, "Is this a human being or not? It must be Mara. He has spoken this verse because he wants to terrify me and ruin my meditation." When she knew this for certain, that this was none other than the Evil One, Mara, she addressed him as follows:

> [Kisagotami:] I have finished with the death of my child,
> and men belong to that past.
> I don't grieve.
> I don't cry.
> I'm not afraid of you, friend.

Everywhere the love of pleasure is destroyed,
the great dark is torn apart,
and Death,
you too are destroyed.

A TWENTIETH-CENTURY BHIKKHUNI
Marie Beuzeville Byles, 1953 C.E.

The Ceylonese nun Gotami was Byles's hostess in Sravasti.

[S]he did so much work at the temple that she could not spare a great deal of time to take me sightseeing. Each day at sunset she would spend about two hours burning incense and camphor, and reciting sutras under the bodhi tree which overhung the ruins of the kuti or cottage of Ananda, the most intimate of the Buddha's disciples. An occasional peasant would pass by or a monkey or two swing from tree to tree. For the rest, we were alone, with only the jungle around us. I would sit on the walls of the kuti and meditate beside her. She liked puja or worship-ritual — she had little time for her countrymen who did not. . . . She looked very picturesque in her yellow robes standing on the long grey walls of the ruins where her spiritual forebears may have walked in meditation.

THE ANANDA BODHI TREE

The Ananda Bodhi tree is a dual memorial. While intended to remind disciples of the Buddha, the monument equally memorializes the monk Ananda who planted it. The story of the Ananda tree lays out the Buddha's strictures on objects and means of worship.

From the "Kalinga-Bodhi Jataka," 5th–1st c. B.C.E.

When the Tathagata had set forth on pilgrimage, for the purpose of gathering in those who were ripe for conversion, the citizens of Savatthi proceeded to Jetavana, their hands full of garlands and fragrant wreaths, and finding no other place to show their reverence, laid them by the gateway of the perfumed chamber and went off. This caused great rejoicings. But Anathapindika got to hear of it; and on the return of the Tathagata visited Elder Ananda and said to him, — "This monastery, Sir, is left unprovided while the Tathagata goes on pilgrimage, and there is no place for the people to do reverence by offering fragrant wreaths and garlands. Will you be so kind, Sir, as to tell the Tathagata of this matter, and learn from him whether or no it is possible to find a place for this purpose." The other, nothing loth, did so, asking, "How many shrines are there?" — "Three, Ananda." — "Which are they?" — "Shrines for a relic of the body, a relic of use or wear, a relic of memorial." — "Can a shrine be made, Sir, during your life?" — "No, Ananda, not a body-shrine; that kind is made when a Buddha enters Nirvana. A shrine of memorial is improper because the connection depends on the imagination only. But the great bo-tree used by the Buddhas is fit for a shrine, be they alive or be they dead." — "Sir, while you are away on pilgrimage the great monastery of Jetavana is unprotected, and the people have no place where they can show their reverence. Shall I plant a seed of the great bo-tree before the gateway of Jetavana?" — "By all means do so, Ananda, and that shall be as it were an abiding place for me."

S. R. Wijayatilake, 1963 C.E.
The Ananda Bodhi stands as a lone sentinel guarding the ruins. . . . The tree as it stands today looks very ancient, and with reverence we picked up a few leaves which lay fallen to take home to our friends as souvenirs of our pilgrimage. . . .

Noeyal Peiris, 1976 C.E.

Before leaving Sri Lanka for India, Noeyal Peiris declared his intention to leave in veneration a consecrated robe at the Ananda Bodhi tree in Sravasti.

[We] left Lucknow on the 30th January, 1976, to Sravasti by bus, to meet Ven. M. Sangharatana, Maha Thera at Sravasti, as I had to offer one of the Robes I had taken to be offered as Poojas [worship] at Sravasti, to the place where Lord Buddha preached the whole Tripitaka and spent 27 rainy seasons. . . .

The [robe] at Sravasti was offered on the 30th night, after the lighting of coconut oil lamps, joss sticks, camphor, and flowers were offered and Suttas were recited and chanted at the Ananda Bodhi Tree at Jethavanaramaya. We did meditation and kept the Robe where Lord Buddha sat and preached the Tripitaka. Early next morning we went again and offered flowers, lighted lamps and chanted Pirith and covered the Ananda Bodhi Tree with the Robe.

II. SANKASYA
(KAPITHA, SANKISSA)

Fa-hsien, 400 C.E.

This country is rich and fertile, with a people prosperous and happy beyond compare. The men of other lands, coming here, are entertained and provided with all they need.

Hiuen Tsiang, mid-seventh century C.E.

This country is about 2,000 li in circuit, and the capital 20 li or so. The climate and produce resemble those of P-lo-shan-na. The manners of the people are soft and agreeable. The men are much given to learning.

John Huntington, 1985 C.E.

Unfortunately, except for the identification of an "Asokan" elephant capital by Cunningham, virtually nothing has been accomplished in the way of excavation at either the city of Sankasya or the Stupa of the Triple Stairs. Today, the site is difficult to reach by a very long drive from either Delhi or Lucknow and has no rest house facilities. The ancient city of Sankasya is one of the largest archaeological areas in northern India, for it covers several square kilometres. Some archaeologists at the University of Kanpur have initiated a site survey, but their work has only begun in the last few years and nothing has been published so far. Although the vast expanse of the ruined city (about equal in size to imperial Rome) beckons those concerned with archaeology in a more general way, from the viewpoint of the Buddhist pilgrim, only the closely fenced "Asokan" capital . . . and the ruined Stupa of the Triple Stairs are there to visit. . . .

Difficult to reach and offering little to see once one arrives there, the Sankasya site at once both defines the westernmost activity of Sakyamuni and is the place of the demonstration of the pre-eminence of the Buddhist religion in the Indic sphere. For the true pilgrim, it is one of the key sites of the route.

The Descent from the Heavens

From Tibetan Works in the Bkah-Hgyur *and* Bstan-Hgyur
After performing miracles in Sravasti,

. . . the Buddha vanished from amidst his disciples and went to the Trayastrimcat heaven, where, seated on a slab of white stone in a beautiful grove of parijataka and kobidaraka (*sic*) trees, he instructed his mother and a host of devas. He was prompted to leave Varanasi lest the people should suppose that the great wonders he had shown were intended as a means of acquiring gifts and honours.

The disciples were greatly worried at the Buddha's disappearance, and questioned Maudgalyayana, who told them where the Blessed One was. When three months had passed away the disciples sought Maudgalyayana again, and told him that they wanted to see the Buddha, that they thirsted after him. Maudgalyayana, by the power of samadhi, went to the Trayastrimcat devas' heaven, and told the Buddha how all the people of Jambudvipa [India] longed to see him. The Blessed One bid him return and tell the disciples that after seven days he would return to them, and would be at the foot of the udumbara tree of the Avadjaravana (*sic*) of the town of Samkacya in Jambudvipa. Then the Buddha visited many other abodes of the devas, teaching them all the truth; after which he descended to the earth by a vaidurya (lapis lazuli) staircase, while Brahma, bearing a jewelled yak tail, descended a golden one on his right together with all the gods . . . and Cataketu (Indra), bearing a hundred-ribbed parasol over him, descended by a crystal staircase on his left accompanied by all the devas of the Kamaloka.

The Monuments

SANKASYA'S MONASTERY

The story of the Buddha's descent from the heavens turned Sankasya into an important early pilgrimage and monastic center. Even in Hiuen Tsiang's day, the city harbored a substantial monastic community.

Hiuen Tsiang, mid-seventh century C.E.

There are four *sangharamas* [monasteries] with about 1,000 priests, who study the Ching-liang

(Sammatiya) school of the Little Vehicle. There are ten
Deva temples, where sectaries of all persuasions dwell.
They all honour and sacrifice to Mahesvara. . . .

To the east of the city 20 li or so is a great *sang-harama* of beautiful construction, throughout which the
artist has exhibited his greatest skill. The sacred image of
the holy form (*of Buddha*) is most wonderfully magnificent.
There are about 100 priests here, who study the doctrines of
the Sammatiya . . . school. Several myriads of "pure men"
(*religious laymen*) live by the side of this convent.

Fa-hsien, 400 C.E.

Here are about a thousand monks and nuns,
who take their meals together and study both Mahayana
and Hinayana Buddhism. At their dwelling place is a
white-eared dragon that acts as their patron. It brings
this region rich harvests and rain in season and preserves
it from all misfortunes, so that the monks may live in
security. The monks, grateful for its favours, have built a
house for the dragon and provided it with a seat.
Moreover, sacrificial food is prepared and offered to it,
and every day three monks are selected to take their
meal in the dragon's house. At the end of each summer
retirement, the dragon often assumes the form of a little
serpent whose ears are edged with white. The monks,
recognizing it, place it in a copper vessel filled with
curds, and carry it around from the highest seat to the
lowest as if to pay greetings to all. After making the
rounds it disappears. It comes out once every year.

THE LADDERS THAT
DESCENDED FROM HEAVEN

Hiuen Tsiang, mid-seventh century C.E.

Within the great enclosure of the *sangharama*
there are precious ladders, which are arranged side by

side from north to south, with their faces for descent to the east. This is where Tathagata came down on his return from the Trayastrimsa heaven. . . .

Some centuries ago the ladders still existed in their original position, but now they have sunk into the earth and have disappeared. The neighbouring princes, grieved at not having seen them, built up of bricks and chased stones ornamented with jewels, on the ancient foundations (*three ladders*) resembling the old ones. They are about 70 feet high. Above them they have built a *vihara* in which is a stone image of Buddha, and on either side of this is a ladder with the figures of Brahma and Sakra, just as they appeared when first rising to accompany Buddha in his descent.

John Huntington, 1985 C.E.

The *stupa* is presently topped by a Saivite shrine, and because the shrine is in active daily worship, it is not eligible for excavation under present Indian guidelines for religious monuments. Circumambulation demonstrates conclusively that the mound is a *stupa*, indeed, a very large one of the exact type that would have been raised at so important a location as the place where the Buddha demonstrated his dominion over the traditional gods.

Fa-hsien, 400 C.E.

King Asoka, wishing to know how deep into the ground the ladders had penetrated, sent men to dig down and find out. They went on digging till they reached the Yellow Spring at the base of the earth, yet still did not reach the bottom. This increased the king's faith and reverence, and he built a temple over the steps. On the central step he placed a full-length statue of Buddha sixteen feet high. Behind the temple he erected a stone pillar thirty cubits high, on the top of which he placed the figure of a lion. On the four sides of the pillar, which was clear and transparent as glass, images of Buddha were carved.

Once a heretical teacher came to the monks and contested their right to live there.

Defeated in argument, the monks prayed together: "If this is where we should live, let there be some miracle to prove it!"

As they uttered this prayer, the lion on top of the pillar gave a loud roar as a sign. Then the heretic was frightened and, humbled, went away.

The Story of Utpala

When the Buddha descended to earth at Sankasya, a bhikkhuni named Utpala, fearing that she, a mere woman, would not be able to greet him properly, is said either to have transformed herself or been transformed by the Buddha into a powerful king.

Fa-hsien, 400 C.E.

Fa-hsien tells a fairly conventional version of the Utpala story. When the Buddha returned to earth, he writes,
. . . a nun by the name of Utpala thought: "Now the kings, ministers and people have all come here to meet Buddha. I am only a woman — how can I see him first?"

Thereupon, by means of supernatural power, she transformed herself into a holy, universal monarch, and as such she was the very first to render homage to Buddha.

From Tibetan Works in the Bkah-Hgyur and Bstan-Hgyur
The Tibetan tale is slightly different:
Now the bhikshuni Utpalavarna saw the Blessed One descending the earth, so she took the appearance of

an emperor (*Chakravartin*), and came to honour him. Udayin, who was also there, recognised her by the sweet odour her body emitted; but the Blessed One rebuked her, saying, "It is not seeming in a bhikshuni to perform magical feats in the presence of the Master." Then he sent her away

From the "Kanha Jataka," fifth century B.C.E. to first century C.E.

Though the Buddha scolds Utpala in the Tibetan tale, several versions of the story imagine him transforming her into a king. Ultimately, their relationship seems to have been a good one. According to the Jatakas, the two enjoyed a fruitful relationship in past lives.

Once upon a time when Brahmadatta was reigning in Benares, the Bodhisatta came to life as a bull. And while he was still a young calf, his owners, who had been lodging with an old woman, made him over to her in settlement of their reckoning. She reared him like her own child, feeding him on rice-gruel and rice and on other good cheer. The name he became known by was "Granny's Blackie." Growing up, he used to range about with the other cattle of the village, and was as black as jet. The village urchins used to catch hold of his horns and ears and dewlaps, and have a ride; or they would hold on to his tail in play, and mount on his back.

One day he thought to himself, "My mother is very poor; she has painfully reared me, as if I were her own child. What if I were to earn some money to ease her hard lot?" Thenceforth he was always looking out for a job. Now, one day a young merchant at the head of a caravan came with five hundred waggons to a ford the bottom of which was so rough that his oxen could not pull the waggons through. And even when he took out the five hundred pairs of oxen and yoked the lot together to form one team, they could not get a single cart by itself across the river. Close by that ford the Bodhisatta was about with the other cattle of the village. And the young merchant, being a judge of cattle, ran his eye over the herd to see whether among them was a thoroughbred bull who could pull the waggons across. When his eye fell on the Bodhisatta, he felt sure *he* would do; and to find the Bodhisatta's owner, he said to the herdsmen, "Who owns this animal? If I could yoke him on and get my waggons across, I would pay for his services." Said they, "Take him and harness him, then; he has got no master hereabouts."

But when the young merchant slipped a cord through the Bodhisatta's nose and tried to lead him off, the bull would not budge. For, we are told, the Bodhisatta would not go till his pay was fixed. Understanding his meaning, the merchant said, "Master, if you will pull these five hundred waggons across, I will pay you two coins per cart, or a thousand coins in all."

It now required no force to get the Bodhisatta to come. Away he went, and the men harnessed him to the carts. The first he dragged over with a single pull, and landed it high and dry; and in like manner he dealt with the whole string of waggons.

The young merchant tied round the Bodhisatta's neck a bundle containing five hundred coins, or at the rate of only *one* for each cart. Thought the Bodhisatta to himself, "This fellow is not paying me according to contract! I won't let him move on!" So he stood across the path of the foremost waggon and blocked the way. And try as they would, they could not get him out of the way. "I suppose he knows I've paid him short," thought the merchant; and he wrapped up a thousand coins in a bundle, which he tied round the Bodhisatta's neck, saying, "Here's your pay for pulling the waggons across." And away went the Bodhisatta with the thousand pieces of money to his "mother."

"What's that round the neck of Granny's Blackie?" cried the children of the village, running up to him. But the Bodhisatta made at them from afar and made them scamper off, so that he reached his "mother's" all right. Not but what he appeared fagged out, with his eyes bloodshot, from dragging all those five hundred waggons over the river. The pious woman, finding a thousand pieces of money round his neck, cried out, "Where did you get this, my child?" Learning from the herdsmen what had happened, she exclaimed, "Have I any wish to live on your earning, my child? Why did you go through all this fatigue?" So saying, she washed the Bodhisatta with warm water and rubbed him all over with oil; she gave him drink and regaled him with due victuals. And when her life closed, she passed away. . . .

After his lesson to shew that only "Blackie" could draw the load, [the Buddha] shewed the connexion, and identified the Birth by saying, "Uppala-Vanna was the old woman of those days, and I myself 'Granny's Blackie.'"

A Last Word

Hiuen Tsiang, mid-seventh century C.E.

To the south-east of the great *stupa* is a Naga [semi-divine snake] tank. He defends the sacred traces with care, and being thus spiritually protected, one cannot regard them lightly. Years may effect their destruction, but no human power can do so.

281

A Tibetan nun

Where the Buddha Accepted Women into the Sangha

"Ananda, Vaisali is delightful. . . ."

— *The Buddha*

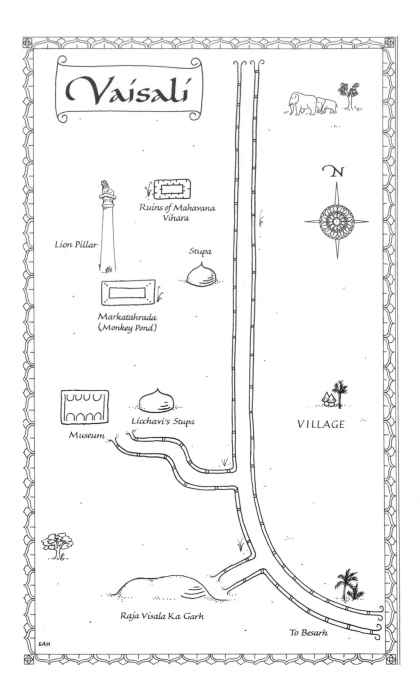

Vaisali

Ruins of Mahavana Vihara

Lion Pillar

Stupa

Markatahrada
(Monkey Pond)

Museum

Licchavi's Stupa

VILLAGE

N

Raja Visala Ka Garh

To Besarh

EAH

*P*iecing together the past from its traces, travelers like to conjure themselves into the historical picture. They picture themselves, perhaps, as members of the sangha listening to the Buddha's sermons or as laypeople giving alms to the Buddha's disciples. Women may have a harder time making this imaginative projection. In the Buddha's time, a woman's value to society depended on her worth to men, to her father, her husband, and her sons: barren women were reviled, widows were outcast, most women were slaves to their husbands' households, and wealthy women typically shared their husbands with several wives and concubines. It is one of the peculiar twists of the Buddha's story that when he departed Kapilavastu, he is said to have left behind, along with the life of a prince, a harem full of women useless, adrift, and confused.

What could such women do? They had one narrow path of escape: the homeless life. They could abdicate family ties to join a loosely defined community of wanderers, living outside of society and propagating non-Brahmanic practices and beliefs. However, it was hard for a woman to brave unfrequented roads and woods alone. Few women ventured to follow this path. With Buddhism, that situation changed.

Attracted to the Buddha's teachings, a number of exceptional women sought to enter on the path to enlightenment. Forming a group, they asked the Buddha to accept them into the sangha. Headed by the Buddha's stepmother, Mahaprajapati, the group included some of the concubines whom the Buddha had left behind in the harem at Kapilavastu. The Buddha initially refused their request. He feared, some suggest, that society would turn against his teachings if people saw that Buddhists were luring away their wives and daughters. But Mahaprajapati and her followers would not except a refusal. They made a pilgrimage by foot from Kapilavastu to Vaisali, hoping to demonstrate to the Buddha the depth of their sincerity. Seeing them dusty, ragged, and determined, the Buddha relented. If women agreed to submit to more stringent rules than monks, he would ordain them into the sangha and assist them on their quest for enlightenment.

As they began to join Buddhist lay and ordained communities, women entered Buddhist history. Consequently, the female traveler who visits Lumbini, Sravasti, Rajgir, Vaisali need not look in on the past from an imagined distance. Women were not only present in these places, they were active — wandering, begging, meditating, learning, and teaching. More than any other place on the pilgrimage route, Vaisali invites the female traveler to muse on the independently minded women of the early Buddhist community. Here, in Vaisali, Mahaprajapati won for women the right to become Buddhist nuns. And here, too, the courtesan Amrapali earned the Buddhist community's centuries-long respect with her donation to the sangha. At Vaisali, women found an outlet for their energies in a restricted society. Among Vaisali's ruins, their voices resound:

> *I'm free. Ecstatically free*
> *I'm free from three crooked things:*
> *the mortar*
> *the pestle*
> *& my hunchbacked husband*
> *All that drags me back is cut — cut!*
>
> — *the bhikkhuni Mutta*

Each pilgrimage site is associated with an event in the Buddha's life. At Vaisali, that event is an act of lay devotion. Eager to demonstrate his love for the Buddha, a

monkey offered him a morsel of honey on a leaf. The Buddha accepted his humble offering and the monkey, wild with delight, broke into insane acrobatics, springing from tree to tree. His elation threw him clear out of his monkey senses. Falling mid-jump, he was impaled on the stub of a dead tree. Dying a noble death, on the heels of a humble and well-meant service, he went straight to heaven, where he was installed in a palace and surrounded with sensuous, slavishly attentive maid-servants.

A touching story, yet it does not begin to express Vaisali's historic importance to the Buddhist community. The Buddha and his disciples spent, off and on, many years of their lives at Vaisali. Those years are associated with a number of stories: with the courtesan Amrapali's donation of land to the sangha; with the sangha's admission of women; with the last days of the Buddha's life, and with the announcement of his approaching death. After the Buddha's cremation, Vaisali's leaders took one-eighth of his relics and enshrined them in a stupa at Vaisali which still stands.

The city was capital of the Vrijian confederacy. A union of eight local clans, Vaisali is said to be the earliest republic, earlier even than the Greek. It was the birthplace of the Jain founder, Mahavira, and home to the great Mahayana Buddhist sage Vimalakirti. One hundred and ten years after the Buddha's death, the Buddhist "Second Council" was held in Vaisali, fracturing the sangha's unity.

Vaisali:
From Splendor to Ruin

"All things rush on." Vaisali is a lesson in the transitory nature of "all compounded matter." The city is not what it once was — the glorious capital of history's *earliest republic, the Vrijian confederacy. Yet it is a worth-while trip off the tourist track: here, no ritzy hotels, no pushy merchants, no "spares" hanging about to prey on the traveler's pocket, innocence, and patience. Vaisali's historic remnants, a few only guessed at beneath unexca-vated mounds in the earth, give themselves up most oblig-ingly to the traveler's imagination.*

Richard Terrell, 1980 C.E.

We had a long way to go next morning, for I wanted to visit Vaishali, where an ancient city had once stood, and to see the pillar erected there by Ashoka, the great ruler of the Mauryan empire, to mark the conversion of his people to Buddhism. To reach Vaishali we turned off the main road at about midday and travelled for several miles along a winding country road through a fresh green landscape of rice fields and small villages, a scene proba-bly unchanged for centuries. Nothing is left of Vaishali except the Ashoka pillar itself and a partially excavated mound quite close to it. The interior of the mound con-sists of brickwork whose purpose is not evident. The pillar, perhaps sixty feet high, is surmounted by a squatting stone lion which, gazing in tranquillity over the plain, has had a remarkable view of the landscape over the past 2,000 years. The pillar stands upon a brickwork base and is itself made of bricks covered over with very strong cement to form a smooth, slightly tapering cylinder. All round are scrawled the names of visitors going back at least to the time of the Napoleonic Wars and all through the nineteenth century. Most of the names are written in various Indian scripts but there are many British names among them, usually with dates. The British names could have belonged to soldiers or clerks employed by the East India Company, and I wondered how some had managed to chip or scratch their names with such elegance a long way above the present ground level.

An undulating area of grassland nearby must conceal the unexcavated remains of Vaishali. I walked over this area, a few hundred yards in diameter, and found in the grass many fragments of terracotta which, for all I could tell, could have been of great antiquity. The experience reminded me of a walk in the Alban hills near Frascati, a few miles from Rome, where, at every other step, one disturbs with one's feet small fragments of Roman mosaic or little coins, bits of broken marble.

Allan Hunt Badiner, 1990 C.E.

> *Ah, this path*
> *With no person travelling it.*
> *An autumn twilight.*
> — *Basho*

The first thing I noticed about Vaisali was the trees. Rare, isolated, tall, with immense foliage in the shape of a parasol, their silhouettes against the sky give the surrounding countryside a look of great peace and majesty. Since the time of Christ a depiction of Vaisali has been enshrined on the great stupa of Sanchi. It features beautiful mango trees under which a monkey is moved to offer the Buddha some honey.

North of the Ganges river, and one day's journey from Patna, Vaisali was the urbane capital of the Licchavi republic, and one of the most beautiful cities in India. It played an important role in Buddhist history and in the evolution of its canonical literature. Vaisali's charms included hundreds of lotus ponds and ten square miles of broad lanes lined with banana and mango trees.

"Pleasant is Vaisali," said the Buddha to his aide Ananda, "pleasant are its shrines and gardens." Surrounded by walls on three sides, replete with ornate gates and watchtowers, Vaisali was a popular stopping place and *tirtha* (a place of pilgrimage) along major trade routes.

Vaisali is still beautiful, perhaps even more so. The city is completely gone, and only the grand coronation pool known as Abhisekha Pushkarna, now a large tank surrounded by exceptionally lovely old trees, and some important ruins remain. The sounds of children playing in the water, and the penetrating drumbeat of a single Nipponzan Myohoji monk slowly circumambulating the tank greeted me on arrival.

For less than one dollar, I was able to stay in the circuit-riders room of the government guest house facing the tank, clearly the finest accommodations available. I wondered how Vaisali managed to stay so serene, and later learned its proximity to Patna, just across the seven mile bridge, has spared it the fate of becoming a resort. Sleek air conditioned double decker tourist coaches slide in here regularly. Out will pour two dozen Western, or Japanese, or Korean, or Thai pilgrims toting flash cameras. After a quick look around, they will line up at the now deserted ramshackle souvenir stand for little clay buddhas. Moments later they'll be gone.

To the pilgrim, Vaisali has special significance as it was here that Buddha first traveled after leaving the comforts of home. He became a student of the elder teacher Alara Kalama, who was immediately taken with Gotami's beauty. Kalama was famous for his powers of concentration, able to maintain meditative states even on noisy streets. As Vaisali was already well known as a Jain religious center, it is conceivable to some that Siddhartha Gotami became a Jain, or *Nigantha* as they were known then, in the first stage of his spiritual odyssey.

While in the tutelage of Kalama, Buddha learned about the practice of austerities, and how to reach the higher stages of meditation, known as *jnanas*. Within a year he had excelled to such an extent that Kalama invited him to co-lead his community of 300 followers. Not having reached his goal of total liberation from suffering, he declined Kalama's offer and continued his search. For the balance of his life, both in his sermons and by example, Buddha emphasized the importance of the teaching over the teacher.

Five years later, Buddha would return to this fair city as a great teacher of the Way accompanied by 500 monks. Vaisali became a flourishing center in which to practice freedom from obsession, or the *asavas*. The general of the Vijjian army, Siha, led a wave of conversions from Jainism to the ranks of those "gone forth." Eight major sutras were delivered here while Buddha and his minions spent at least two rainy seasons in the *Mahavana*, or great forest outside of Vaisali. Places known to be graced with the steady presence of the Buddha were the Ambapali-vana, a meeting hall and mango grove donated by the famous courtesan Ambapali, and the Kutagarasala monastery, erected by the Licchavi people as a gift to the Sangha.

The city of 42,000 homes with its noisy streets has been replaced by soft dirt roads and the sound of water slapping against the stone banks of the coronation tank. Vaisali's peacefulness reflects its great history of wrestling with the challenges of power politics and resolving conflicts in a sustainable manner. "Very old trees," my guide kept saying. The soil supporting these trees nourished the roots of democracy, as well as Jainism and Buddhism.

As I stood at the site of the Second Buddhist Council, I could almost hear the sweet soundwave of the *sangiti*, 700 monks chanting the teachings in unison. It was also the scene of the great discordance in Buddhism, into what ultimately became the two basic schools of Mahayana and Theravada. Spurred by rebellious Vajji monks — known as the *Mahasanghika* — who wanted a relaxing of the rules, and inflexible elders who would

291

tolerate no revisions, the Council convened one hundred years after the Buddha's death, but failed to completely resolve the schism. By the 7th century, the pilgrim I-tsing observed four principal schools and eighteen subdivisions of Buddhism, although they seemed to coexist harmoniously.

Twenty-five hundred years later, Buddhism is found in a vast array of ethnic, philosophical, and religious envelopes, enabling, at the very least, some semblance of Dharma to be heard in everyone's language. Diversity is latent in the founder's teachings which repudiate authority, and fixed views, or *ditthi*, in every form. The tension between the schools may have served to keep them honest, preserving elements of the Dharma that survived among the spectrum of teachings.

The Buddha was known to have admired the ancient stupas of Vaisali. Stepping among the excavation trenches, and markers for archaeological digs, I had the sense of being in an odd kind of twilight realm; not the present, with a character all its own, so much as a dialogue between the future, from where we can look back clearly, and the past, which continues to unfold around us. The amount of careful archaeological investigation done since British archaeologist Alexander Cunningham discovered the site in 1861, pales next to the awesome riches in numbers of places left to study. I saw numerous large overgrown circular mounds in the area, indicating unexcavated stupas. In continuation of an ancient practice, a new stupa is going up. Currently under construction in Vaisali is a 160 foot stupa by the Nipponzan Myohoji order, similar but larger than their impressive new stupa in Rajgir above Vulture Peak.

In nearby Kolhua, the crumbling Ashokan stupa sits over ruins dating back to the 5th century B.C. A beautiful soapstone casket containing earth and ashes was removed from the core in 1958. Amidst the ashes was a

Three nuns passing before prayer flags

thin gold leaf, a conch, a glass bead, and a copper coin. Archaeological and historical evidence indicates the discovery was none other than Vaisali's one-eighth portion of the Buddha's charred remains brought here from the cremation in Kushinagar. Both the old texts and the archaeological record suggest it was opened under Ashoka who redistributed relics into thousands more stupas across the subcontinent.

I spent hours studying the Ashokan stupa and imagining the great Mauryan empire that these ruins are a vestige of. Disturbing the soil under my feet with the toe of my shoe, I was able to uncover an old shard of black

293

pottery. As in all places that have been continually inhab-
ited for many centuries, there are innumerable shards of
various ages and types commingled in the ground.
Examining the shard closely, I could almost see the royal
palaces, the pillared halls, and the busy shops selling
goods from Greece and the Orient. A small museum next
to the tank established in 1971 houses antiquities of
recent excavations, including stone sculptures, terra-cotta
pieces, and objects of art from bone, ivory, and shell.

The morning sun reflected sharply off the straw
huts. I toured the nearby village of Bhagavanpur
(Buddha was always addressed as Bhagavan), while my
driver held a meeting with forty locals to discover directions to Buddhatola, the village I was seeking. Most of
the discussion centered around how to break the news to
me that cars can't go there. Two years earlier, Thich
Nhat Hanh had found his way to this small Buddhist village and left a bond of friendship between them and
Plum Village, his meditation center in southern France.

Carefully I walked through the fields on a raised
path of hardened mud. Only our heads could be seen
through the towering wheat as we traversed the winding
paths between villages. I remembered the story of the
wicked young Licchavi prince whose parents brought
him to the Buddha from a neighboring village, perhaps
the one to which I was headed. In his characteristic style,
the Buddha charmed him into humility, even as he
helped him see the law of karma, leaving him "gentle as
a snake devoid of fangs, or as a crab with broken claws,
or as a bull with broken horns."

Alerted to my arrival from a relay of voice calls
over the fields, it seemed as though the entire village, of
all ages — over forty people — gathered to welcome me.
All of the residents are converted or born Buddhists. Their
healthy glow and warm smiles made them seem strange-
ly modern and familiar, yet there was no visible trace of

industrial culture. After touring the village fragrant from mogra blossoms, the elder showed me a series of ancient wells, evenly spaced along a part of the village fields. He confided that they were not wells at all, but city toilets. He remembered villagers discovering marble casts of footprints adjacent to the wells. The entire area, he explained, was once a part of the ancient city of Vaisali.

Extensive excavations are underway in and around Vaisali. I visited the archaeologists' tent city, located on what is believed to be the grounds of the ancient Kutagarasala monastery. The chief of the project, a formal man, whose silvery-white hair contrasted sharply with his dark skin, seemed skeptical about my discovery of the ancient latrines, but promised to investigate. Hinting that "significant" findings were being made, he quickly added that his mouth was sealed about any specifics. The size of the operation, and the wealth of excavated objects in full view, including complete human skeletons, suggested major findings here.

Back in New Delhi, I paid a visit to M.C. Joshi, chief of the Archaeological Survey of India. He couldn't have been more dismissive about the findings in Vaisali. "Oh, some bones here, and some monastic seals there." He did mention that in Orissa, near Ratnagiri, there was a discovery of another reliquary quite possibly containing relics of the Buddha. I had the strong impression that he was riding a fast wave of discoveries from this period, but lacked the enthusiasm, funding, or both, that one would expect would be appropriate for such exciting prospects.

Architecture, sculpture, terra-cotta work, and other arts reached great heights here during Ashoka's time. In many respects, the ancient empire two centuries after Buddha's death was more advanced and developed than the India of today. Stretching from the northern mountains of Nepal to the southern tip of the subcontinent, Ashokan India was peaceful and prosperous. Pilgrims and traders travelled the length of it unhindered along tree-lined highways, with state operated rest houses every few miles. But the moral development of the time was even more impressive. It was a period of religious and intellectual freedom unparalleled in human history. Although Ashoka was Buddhist, he generalized the Dharma in his numerous stone carved edicts, laying the template for tolerance and respect for diversity that has been culturally embedded ever since.

When word of the courtesan Ambapali's death reached the Buddha, he made his way with his disciples to her cremation. He held up the lighting of her corpse with a lengthy sermon, forcing both his sangha and the gentlemen of Vaisali to watch her beautiful physiognomy decompose. In this way, Buddha enabled Ambapali to use her body one last time for an important teaching on the nature of beauty. It was a teaching that he felt one of his monks, known to be hopelessly in love with her, particularly needed.

Sojourning in Beluva, a village to the south of Vaisali, Buddha suffered what has been attributed from ancient times to be a gastric upset, probably dysentery. Feeling the weight of his 80 years, he called himself a "worn out cart," announced his intention to go to Kusinagar, and predicted his death three months later. As he left, he turned around and looked at the city longingly, with "the eyes of an elephant king" embracing fully the beauty of Vaisali.

Devotion:
The Gift of the Monkey

Early pilgrims revered Vaisali above all for the story of the monkey who, in the excitement of his devo-

tional feelings for the Buddha, plunged to his death from a tree in Vaisali. The monkey became a symbol of the depth to which devotion could be felt and expressed.

> *Weeds are the bane of the fields, passion is the*
> *bane of humankind; so a gift to those free of desire*
> *bears great fruit.*
> — *The Dhammapada, 5th–1st c. B.C.E.,*
> *translated from the Pali by Thomas Cleary*

"The Monkey's Gift," fifth century B.C.E. to first century C.E.

[After observing an elephant attend the Buddha by bringing water and fruits, a monkey said to himself,] "I'll do something too." One day as he was running about, he happened to see some stick-honey free from flies. He broke the stick off, took the honey-comb, stick and all, broke off a plantain-leaf, placed the honey on the leaf, and offered it to the Teacher [the Buddha]. The Teacher took it. The monkey watched to see whether or not he would eat it. He observed that the Teacher, after taking the honey, sat down without eating. "What can be the matter?" thought he. He took hold of the stick by the tip, turned it over, carefully examining it as he did so, whereupon he discovered some insect's eggs. Having removed these gently, he again gave the honey to the Teacher. The Teacher ate it.

The monkey was so delighted [because the Buddha had accepted his offering] that he leaped from one branch to another and danced about in great glee. But the branches he grasped and the branches he stepped on broke off. Down he fell on the stump of a tree and was impaled. So he died. And solely because of his faith in the Teacher he was reborn in the World of the Thirty-three [Trayastrimsa] in a golden mansion thirty leagues in measure, with a retinue of a thousand celestial nymphs.

Hiuen Tsiang, mid-seventh century C.E.

[A tank] was dug by a band of monkeys (Markatahrada) for Buddha's use. . . . Not far to the south of this tank is a *stupa*; it was here the monkeys, taking the alms-bowl of Tathagata, climbed a tree and gathered him some honey.

Not far to the south is a *stupa*; this is the place where the monkeys offered the honey to Buddha. At the north-west angle of the lake there is still a figure of a monkey.

Sermon in Amrapali's Grove: On Mindfulness

The Buddha offered a sermon on mindfulness at Vaisali. The practice of mindfulness is an important form of Buddhist meditation and a valuable practice for travelers, whose minds, while journeying, are likely to be more open, more distracted, and more vulnerable to change.

From The Digha Nikaya, *Sutta 16*:
The Mahaparinibbana Sutta, 5th–1st c. B.C.E.

Buddha went with a large company of monks to Vesali, where he stayed at Ambapali's grove.

And there the Lord addressed the monks: "Monks, a monk should be mindful and clearly aware, this is our charge to you!

"And how is a monk mindful? Here, a monk abides contemplating the body as body, earnestly, clearly aware, mindful and having put away all hankering and fretting for the world, and likewise with regard to feelings, mind and mind-objects. That is how a monk is mindful.

"And how is a monk clearly aware? Here, a monk, when going forward or backward, is aware of what he is doing; in looking forward or back he is aware of what he is doing; in carrying his inner and outer robe and bowl he is aware of what he is doing; in eating, drinking, chewing and savouring he is aware of what he is doing; in walking, standing, sitting or lying down, in keeping awake, in speaking or in staying silent, he is aware of what he is doing. That is how a monk is clearly aware. A monk should be mindful and clearly aware, this is our charge to you!"

Amrapali: Courtesan of Vaisali

It is not inappropriate that the Buddha should have delivered a lesson on mindfulness in Amrapali's grove at Vaisali. Amrapali was the most beautiful, most popular, and most rich courtesan in Vaisali. On one level, she represented everything from which the Buddha would have his followers turn away: slavery to the senses and to luxury. However, courtesans in India were often great artists, singers, dancers, and poets. Their talents were coupled with a unique wisdom, gained through their professional experiences, of the weaknesses that assault the mind and body. In order to gain power over her clients and seduce from them her living, the courtesan had to be able to understand and manipulate her clients' sexual and emotional vulnerabilities. The client is no helpless victim: He knows he is entering a dangerous game, and while he does not want to win that game, he does not want to lose it wholly either. Thus the courtesan must find and play on vulnerabilities stronger than her client knows to lie within him. Because of her keen knowledge of the human temper, the courtesan has often been understood to keep herself at a cynical distance from the webs of lust and love. She must be mindful, if cynically so, in order to win the love game many times over. She must win early and often, for she knows, more trenchantly than many lay disciples, that the body's beauty is fleeting. If the courtesan is cynically mindful of physical frailty, she may be, at the same time, poignantly and wisely so. At the height of her powers, Amrapali invited the Buddha to dine at her house and then donated her mango grove to his order. Her verse in the Therigatha, composed when she had joined the order in her later years, is a moving expression of the body's fickle changes.

From the Therigatha, 5th–1st c. B.C.E.

Once my hair was black like the color of bees
Alive — curly
Now it is dry like bark fibers of hemp
I'm getting old
This is true, I tell you the truth

Covered with flowers, my head was fragrant
As a perfumed box
Now, because of old age, it smells like dog's fur

Thick like a grove it used to be beautiful —
Ends parted by comb & pin
Now it's thin, I'm telling the truth

This was a head with fine pins once,
Decorated with gold, plaited, so beautiful
Now bald

My eyebrows were like crescents
Exquisitely painted by artists
Now because of old age they droop down with wrinkles
Ah, I'm telling the truth

My eyes used to be shiny, brilliant as jewels
Now they don't look so good

My nose was like a delicate peak
Now it's a long pepper
This scarecrow is telling the truth

My earlobes once — can you believe it?
Were like well-fashioned bracelets
Now they're heavy with creases

Formerly my teeth were pearly white
like the bud of a plaintain
Now they're broken & yellow
Indeed, this is the truth

Sweet was my singing like the cuckoo in the grove
Now my voice cracks & falters
Hear it? These words are true

My neck used to be soft like a well-rubbed
conch shell
Now it bends, broken

My arms were round like crossbars
Now they're weak as the petali tree

My hands were gorgeous — they used to be
gorgeous —
Covered with signet rings, decorated with gold
Now they are like onions & radishes
This is true, I tell you

Formerly my breasts looked great —
round, swelling, close together, lofty
Now they hang down like waterless waterbags

My body used to be as shiny as a sheet of gold
Now it is covered with very fine wrinkles

Both thighs — & this was once considered
a compliment —
looked like elephants trunks —
very interesting
I swear I'm telling the truth
Now they're like stalks of bamboo

My calves too, like stalks of sesame

My feet used to be elegant
like shoes of soft cotton wool
Now they are cracked & wrinkled
This hag speaks true

Once I had the body of a queen
Now it's lowly, decrepit, an old house
plaster falling off
Sad, but true.

Mahaprajapati: Women Are Admitted to the Sangha

In the Buddhist sangha, many people discovered a chance not only to break free from the web of mortal suffering, but to escape the inequalities of caste, position, and wealth. At first, the fruits of the Buddhist homeless life and the supportive community of the sangha were open only to men. This changed when Mahaprajapati, the Buddha's aunt and the woman who had raised him after his mother's death, succeeded in persuading her reluctant nephew to admit women into the monastic fold.

Thich Nhat Hanh, 1991 C.E.

Mahaprajapati:
"If you will allow women to be ordained, many

will benefit. Among our clan, many princes have left home to become your disciples. Many of them had wives. Now their wives desire to study the Dharma as nuns. I want to be ordained myself. It would bring me great joy. This has been my sole desire since the king died."

The Buddha was silent for a long moment before he said, "It is not possible."

Lady Prajapati pleaded, "I know this is a difficult issue for you. If you accept women into the sangha you will be met with protest and resistance from society. But I do not believe you are afraid of such reactions."

Again the Buddha was silent. He said, "In Rajagaha, there are also a number of women who want to be ordained, but I don't believe it is the right time yet. Conditions are not yet ripe to accept women in the sangha."

Gotami pleaded three times with him, but his answer remained the same. Deeply disappointed, she departed. When she returned to the palace she told Yasodhara of the Buddha's response.

A few days later, the Buddha returned to Vesali. After his departure, Gotami gathered all the women who wished to be ordained. They included a number of young women who had never been married. All the women belonged to the Sakya clan [the Buddha's clan]. She told them, "I know beyond a doubt that in the Way of Awakening, all people are equal. Everyone has the capacity to be enlightened and liberated. The Buddha has said so himself. He has accepted untouchables into the sangha. There is no reason he should not accept women. We are full persons too. We can attain enlightenment and liberation. There is no reason to regard women as inferior.

"I suggest we shave our heads, get rid of our fine clothes and jewels, put on the yellow robes of bhikkhus, and walk barefoot to Vesali where we will ask to be ordained. In this way we will prove to the Buddha and everyone else that we are capable of living simply and practicing the Way. We will walk hundreds of miles and beg for our food. This is the only hope we have to be accepted into the sangha."

All the women agreed with Gotami. They saw in her a true leader. Yasodhara [the Buddha's wife] smiled. She had long appreciated Gotami's strong will. Gotami was not one to be stopped by any obstacle, as proved by her years of working on behalf of the poor with Yasodhara. The women agreed on a day to put their plan into action.

Gotami said to Yasodhara, "Gopa, it would be best if you didn't come with us this time. Things may go more smoothly. When we have succeeded, there will be plenty of time for you to follow."

Yasodhara smiled in understanding.

Early one morning on his way to the lake to get some water, Ananda met Gotami and fifty other women standing not far from the Buddha's hut. Every woman had shaved her head and was wearing a yellow robe. Their feet were swollen and bloody. At first glance, Ananda thought it was a delegation of monks, but suddenly he recognized Lady Gotami. Hardly able to believe his eyes, he blurted, "Good heavens, Lady Gotami! Where have you come from? Why are your feet so bloody? Why have you and all the ladies come here like this?"

Gotami answered, "Venerable Ananda, we have shaved our heads and given away all our fine clothes and jewels. We no longer have any possessions in this world. We left Kapilavatthu and have walked for fifteen days, sleeping by the roadsides and begging for our food in small villages along the way. We wish to show that we are capable of living like bhikkhus. I beseech you, Ananda. Please speak to the Buddha on our behalf. We wish to be ordained as nuns."

Ananda said, "Wait here. I will speak to the Buddha at once. I promise to do all I can."

Ananda entered the Buddha's hut just as the Buddha was putting on his robe. Nagita, the Buddha's assistant at that time, was also present. Ananda told the Buddha all he had just seen and heard. The Buddha did not say anything.

Ananda then asked, "Lord, is it possible for a woman to attain the Fruits of Stream Enterer, Once-Returner, Never-Returner, and Arhatship?"

The Buddha answered, "Beyond a doubt."

"Then why don't you accept women into the sangha? Lady Gotami nurtured and cared for you from the time you were an infant. She has loved you like a son. Now she has shaved her head and renounced all her possessions. She has walked all the way from Kapilavatthu to prove that women can endure anything that men can. Please have compassion and allow her to be ordained."

The Buddha was silent for a long moment. He then asked Nagita to summon Venerable Sariputta, Moggallana, Anuruddha, Bhaddiya, Kimbila, and Mahakassapa. When they arrived, he discussed the situation with them at length. He explained that it was not discrimination against women which made him hesitant to ordain them. He was unsure how to open the sangha to women without creating harmful conflict both within and outside of the sangha.

After a lengthy exchange of ideas, Sariputta said, "It would be wise to create statutes which define the roles of nuns within the sangha. Such statute would diminish public opposition which is certain to erupt, since there has been discrimination against women for thousands of years. Please consider the following eight rules:

"First, a nun, or bhikkhuni, will always defer to a bhikkhu, even if she is older or has practiced longer than he has.

"Second, all bhikkhunis must spend the retreat season at a center within reach of a center of bhikkhus in order to receive spiritual support and further study.

"Third, twice a month, the bhikkhunis should delegate someone to invite the bhikkhus to decide on a date for *uposatha*, the special day of observance. A bhikkhu should visit the nuns, teach them, and encourage them in their practice.

"Fourth, after the rainy season retreat, nuns must attend the Pavarana ceremony and present an account of their practice, not only before other nuns, but before the monks.

"Fifth, whenever a bhikkhuni breaks a precept, she must confess before both the bhikkhunis and the bhikkhus.

"Sixth, after a period of practice as a novice, a bhikkhuni will take full vows before the communities of both monks and nuns.

"Seventh, a bhikkhuni should not criticize or censure a bhikkhu.

"Eighth, a bhikkhuni will not give Dharma instruction to a community of bhikkhus."

Moggallana laughed. "These eight rules are clearly discriminatory. How can you pretend otherwise?"

Sariputta replied, "The purpose of these rules is to open the door for women to join the sangha. They are not intended to discriminate but to help end discrimination. Don't you see?" . . .

The Buddha turned to Ananda, "Ananda, please go and tell Lady Mahaprajapati that if she is willing to accept these Eight Special Rules, she and the other women may be ordained."

The sun had already climbed high into the sky, but Ananda found Lady Gotami and the other women patiently waiting. After hearing the Eight Rules, Gotami was overjoyed. She replied, "Venerable Ananda, please tell the Buddha that just as a young girl gladly accepts a garland of lotus flowers or roses to adorn her hair after washing it with perfumed water, I happily accept the Eight Rules. I will follow them all my life if I am granted permission to be ordained."

Ananda returned to the Buddha's hut and informed him of Lady Gotami's response.

The other women looked at Gotami with concern in their eyes, but she smiled and reassured them, "Don't worry my sisters. The important thing is that we have earned the right to be ordained. These Eight Rules will not be barriers to our practice. They are the door by which we may enter the sangha."

All fifty-one women were ordained that same day.

VERSES OF THE BHIKKHUNIS (NUNS)

When the Buddha opened his order to women, he created a haven for women who were trapped in painful situations they had not chosen or could not escape: bad marriages, the degradations of widowhood, the humiliations of a ruined reputation, or the pain of neglect brought on them in old age. The Terigatha, *a compilation of verses composed by the first Buddhist nuns, includes the voices of lowly prostitutes, courtesans like Amrapali, abused housewives, widows, women who have lost their sons, daughters who hate the thought of marriage . . .*

From the Therigatha, *5th–1st c.* B.C.E.

ADDHAKASI
I was a prostitute with fees as large
as the whole country of Kasi
The sheriff fixed it: I was priceless
Then I got disgusted with my figure

307

No one was interested in it anymore
Used up, tired, weary — this old body,
good for sex, this sex-money body
Where does it go?
How far does it go?
Never gain, chasing rebirth after
rebirth after rebirth

SUMANGALA'S MOTHER SPEAKS
I'm free
Free from kitchen drudgery
no longer a slave dirty among my cooking pots
(My pot smelled like an old water snake)
& I'm through with my brutal husband
& his boring sunshades
I purge lust & hate with a sizzling sound — POP
I sit at the foot of a tree & think
"O happiness," meditate upon
This as happiness

VASITTHI
Out of my mind
deranged with love of my lost son
Out of my senses
Naked — hair disheveled
I wandered here, there
I lived on rubbish heaps
in a cemetery, on a highway
I wandered three years in hunger & thirst
Then I saw the Buddha
gone to Mithila
I paid homage
He pitied me
& taught me the Dharma
I went forth into the homeless state

MAHAPRAJAPATI
*Her verses are offered in thanks to the Buddha for
accepting women into the* sangha.

*Homage to you Buddha,
best of all creatures,
who set me and many others
free from pain.*

*All pain is understood,
the cause, the craving is dried up,
the Noble Eightfold Way unfolds,
I have reached the state where everything stops.*

*I have been mother,
son,
father,
brother,
grandmother;
knowing nothing of the truth
I journeyed on.*

*But I have seen the Blessed One;
this is my last body,
and I will not go
from birth to birth again.*

*Look at the disciples all together,
their energy,
their sincere effort.
This is homage to the buddhas.*

*Maya gave birth to Gautama
for the sake of us all.
She has driven back the pain
of the sick and the dying.*

The Buddha Announces
His Approaching Death

*The Buddha spent his last days at Vaisali. There
he announced his approaching death before journeying on
to Kusinagara to die.*

From **The Digha Nikaya, Sutta 16:**
The Mahaparinibba Sutta, 5th–1st c. B.C.E.
"Ananda, whoever has developed the four roads
to power, practiced them frequently, made them his
vehicle, made them his base, established them, become
familiar with them and properly undertaken them,
could undoubtedly live for a century, or the remainder of
one. The Tathagata has developed these powers . . .
properly undertaken them. And he could, Ananda,
undoubtedly live for a century, or the remainder of one."

But the Venerable Ananda, failing to grasp this
broad hint, did not beg the Lord: "Lord, may the Blessed
Lord stay for a century, may the Well-Farer stay for a century for the benefit and happiness of the multitude, out
of compassion for the world, for the benefit and happiness of devas and humans," so much was his mind possessed by Mara.

Then the Lord said: "Ananda, go now and do
what seems fitting to you." "Very good, Lord," said
Ananda and, rising from his seat, he saluted the Lord,
passed by on the right, and sat down under a tree some
distance away.

Soon after Ananda had left, Mara the Evil One
came to the Lord, stood to one side, and said: "Lord, may
the Blessed Lord now attain final Nibbana, may the Well-
Farer now attain final Nibbana. Now is the time for the
Blessed Lord's final Nibbana. Because the Blessed Lord
has said this: 'Evil One, I will not take final Nibbana till
I have monks and disciples who are accomplished,

trained, skilled, learned, knowers of the Dhamma, trained in conformity with the Dhamma, correctly trained and walking in the path of the Dhamma, who will pass on what they have gained from their Teacher, teach it, declare it, establish it, expound it, analyze it, make it clear; till they shall be able by means of the Dhamma to refute false teaching that has arisen, and teach the Dhamma of wondrous effect.'

"And now, Lord, the Blessed Lord has such monks and disciples. May the Blessed Lord now attain final Nibbana, may the Well-Farer now attain Nibbana. Now is the time for the Blessed Lord's final Nibbana. And the Blessed Lord has said: 'I will not take final Nibbana till I have nuns and female disciples who are accomplished, . . . till I have laymen-followers . . . till I have laywomen-followers.'. . . May the Blessed Lord now take final Nibbana. . . . And the Blessed Lord has said: 'Evil One, I will not take final Nibbana till this holy life has been successfully established and flourishes, is widespread, well-known far and wide, well-proclaimed among mankind everywhere.' And all this has come about. May the Blessed Lord now attain finally Nibbana. Now is the time for the Blessed Lord's final Nibbana."

At this the Lord said to Mara: "You need not worry, Evil One. The Tathagata's final passing will not be long delayed. Three months from now, the Tathagata will take final Nibbana."

Ananda went to the Lord and the Lord said:

"The Tathagata has mindfully and in full awareness renounced the life-principle."

At this the Venerable Ananda said: "Lord, may the Blessed Lord stay for a century, may the Well-Farer stay for a century for the benefit and happiness of the multitude, out of compassion for the world, for the ben-

efit and happiness of devas and humans!" "Enough,
Ananda! Do not beg the Tathagata, it is not the right
time for that . . . yours is the fault, yours is the failure
that, having been given such a broad hint, such a clear
sign by the Tathagata, you did not understand and did
not beg the Tathagata to stay for a century. . . . If,
Ananda, you had begged him, the Tathagata would twice
have refused you, but the third time he would have consented. Therefore, Ananda, yours is the fault, yours is
the failure.

"Ananda, have I not told you before: All those
things that are dear and pleasant to us must suffer
change, separation and alteration? So how could this be
possible? Whatever is born, become, compounded, is
liable to decay — that it should not decay is impossible.
And that has been renounced, given up, rejected, abandoned, forsaken: the Tathagata has renounced the life-
principle."

The Second Council

*Vaisali hosted the Buddhist "Second Council." It
is a dubious distinction: The council initiated critical
breaks in Buddhist unity. However, these breaks allowed
Buddhist philosophy to take new paths, some of which led
to Mahayana Buddhism, a form of Buddhism followed
today by Buddhists in many parts of Asia and in the
West.*

From Tibetan Works in the Bkah-Hgyur **and** Bstan-
Hgyur, *8th–14th c.* C.E.
One hundred and ten years after the death of
the Blessed Buddha the sun of the Conqueror was
obscured, and the bhikshus of Vaisali imagined ten false
propositions which transgressed the law and the rules,

which were not of the Master's teaching, which were not comprised in the Sutranta, nor to be found in the Vinaya, which transgressed the Dharma; and the bhikshus of Vaisali taught that these things were right. . . .

The bhikshus of Vaisali [said], "Venerable sirs, enjoy yourselves"; and indulging in enjoyment in the congregation of bhikshus, they made enjoyment lawful. . . .

Moreover, the bhikshus of Vaisali held as lawful that [a bhikshu] might dig the earth with his own hand. . . .

Moreover, the bhikshus of Vaisali held as lawful the practice of keeping salt as long as one lived, if he added to [his supply] at the right time some consecrated salt. . . .

Moreover, the bhikshus of Vaisali practiced as being lawful during journeys, going a yojana and a half yojana [away from their viharas], then meeting and eating.

Moreover, the bhikshus of Vaisali having deemed it lawful to take food, hard or soft, that was not left-over food, with two fingers, did practice as lawful eating with two fingers. . . .

Moreover, the bhikshus of Vaisali held it lawful to suck fermented drinks as would a leech, though one was made ill by drinking [thus]. . . .

Moreover, the bhikshus of Vaisali held it lawful to eat between ties a mixture of half-milk and half-curds. . . .

Moreover, the bhikshus of Vaisali held it lawful to use a new mat without patching it around the edge [the width of] a Sugata span. . . .

Moreover, the bhikshus of Vaisali held it lawful to take a round alms-bowl and to besmear it with perfumes, to make it redolent with sweet burnt incense and adorn it with different kinds of sweet-smelling flowers. Then they put a mat on a cramana's head and on it [the bowl], and he went through the highroads, the lanes, the crossroads, saying, "Hear me, all ye people who live in Vaisali, ye town's people and ye strangers; this alms-bowl is a most excellent one; he who gives here, who gives very much, he who makes many offerings here, will receive a great reward; it will profit him much, it will avail him much." And in this way they got riches, gold, and other treasures, which they [the bhikshus of Vaisali] made use of, thus holding it lawful to have gold and silver.

From the Dipavansa, *fourth to fifth centuries* C.E.

> *The monks of the Great Council turned the religion*
> *upside down;*
> *They broke up the original Scriptures, and made a*
> *new recension;*
> *A discourse put in one place they put in another;*
> *They distorted the sense and the teaching of the Five*
> *Nikayas.*
> *Those monks — knowing not what had been*
> *spoken at length, and what concisely,*
> *What was the obvious, and what was the higher*
> *meaning —*
> *Attached new meaning to new words, as if spoken by*
> *the Buddha,*
> *And destroyed much of the spirit by holding to the*
> *shadow of the letter.*
> *In part they cast aside the Sutta and the Vinaya*
> *so deep,*
> *And made an imitation Sutta and Vinaya,*
> *changing this to that.*
> *The Pariwara abstract, and the Six books of*
> *Abhi-dhamma;*
> *The Patisambhida, the Niddesa,* and a portion of
> the Jataka —
> *So much they put aside, and made others in their*
> *place!*

The Buddha Leaves Vaisali

From The Digha Nikaya, *Sutta 16:*
Mahaparinibbana Sutta, 5th–10th c. B.C.E.
The teacher said this:

> *"Ripe I am in years. My life-span's determined.*
> *Now I go from you, having made myself my refuge.*
> *Monks, be untiring, mindful, disciplined,*
> *Guarding your minds with well-collected thought.*
> *He who, tireless, keeps to law and discipline,*
> *Leaving birth behind will put an end to woe."*

Then the Lord, having risen early and dressed, took his robe and bowl and went into Vesali for alms. Having returned from the alms-round and eaten, he looked back at Vesali with his "elephant-look" and said: "Ananda, this is the last time the Tathagata will look upon Vesali. Now we will go. . . ."

A Monk standing before the Nirvana temple and main stupa

KUSINAGARA
(Kusinara; Kasia)

Where
the Buddha
Passed Away

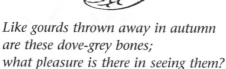

*Like gourds thrown away in autumn
are these dove-grey bones;
what pleasure is there in seeing them?*

*Knowing the body is like froth,
realizing it is insubstantial,
breaking the flowery arrow of the Killer,
one goes to a realm invisible to the King of Death.*

*Whoever looks upon this world as a bubble,
as a mirage, is not seen by the King of Death.*

— *The Dhammapada*

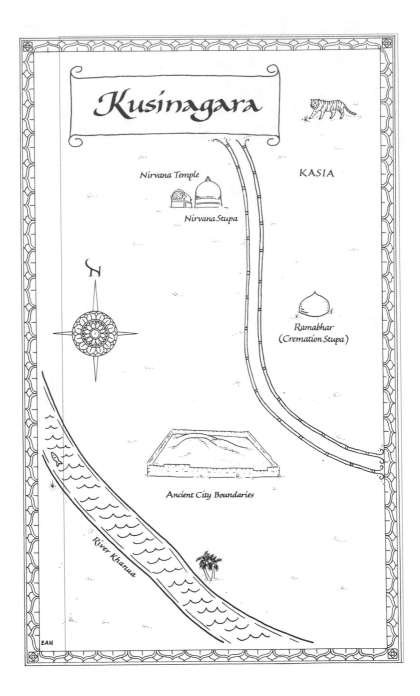

Kusinagara

Nirvana Temple

Nirvana Stupa

KASIA

Ramabhar
(Cremation Stupa)

Ancient City Boundaries

River Kharua

EAH

*T*he body is like "froth," a "bubble." Rarely are we more aware of the body's fragility than on a journey. Many of us have fallen sick during the course of our travels. We have lain in strange rooms, been served by unfamiliar faces, received assistance from unknown doctors. Then, after a time, we recover, thank the people who have assisted us, and continue our journeys. Our bodies, though fragile, surprise us again and again with their resilience and strength.

The Buddha, it is said, died of food poisoning, saying, as he died, "All conditioned things are of a nature to decay." Even he was subject to death. Yet, his body must have been strong to have served him so long — eighty years, by most accounts, despite a life on the road and an ascetic's diet of berries and rice. Like all "conditioned" things, the Buddha may be forgotten one day. But memory of him does not show signs of fading yet — twenty-five hundred years after his death.

Travelers confront the problem of decay and memory even as they explore the geography of Buddhist India. For centuries, the places where the Buddha lived and taught lay virtually forgotten. Today, what were ruins have been unearthed, brushed up, and kept, for the moment, from further destruction. Still, they are ruins, reminders of impermanence. Rajagriha, Vaisali, Sravasti were prosperous, hectic cities once, the Delhi, Bombay, and Madras of ancient North India. Today, they earn a meager paragraph or two in most Indian guidebooks. By contrast, Kusinagara has remained surprisingly unchanged. When the Buddha went there to die, Kusinagara was — his disciples noted — a run-down, provincial nowhere, and it has remained that way to this day. If the once prosperous city of Kapilavastu can disappear from memory, how has a small village like Kusinagara resisted time's obliterations? No more than chance, perhaps. Kusinagara takes the traveler far off the tourist track and into small-town India. Its inconvenient smallness has not deterred adventurous travelers in the past and should serve as an encouragement to modern pilgrims who want to experience an India free of tourists. Here, at last, travelers see something of what the Buddha saw — the "wattle-and-daub" village where the founder of Buddhism lay down under two sal trees to die.

Kusinagara belonged to the Malla republic. A small republic in the Buddha's day, it was taken over by the Magadha empire (whose capital had been Rajagriha) soon after the Buddha's death. Asoka erected a number of monuments on his pilgrimage to Kusinagara. However, none of these have been identified from Kusinagara's ruins, which include two large stupas, a vihara enshrining an image of the reclining Buddha, the remains of a monastery, and several small pilgrims' stupas. Though the town appears to have been a thriving pilgrimage center during the fifth century, it was in lamentable condition when Hiuen Tsiang visited it in the eighth century and has today returned to little more than a village.

The Buddha is said to have fallen ill after eating bad meat or a poisonous mushroom inadvertently served him by the householder Cunda. Though the Buddha fell ill just outside of Kusinagara, he had anticipated his death even before visiting Cunda and had planned to pass away in Kusinagara. After his death, the Mallas oversaw the Buddha's cremation. They were not powerful enough to take control of his relics, and following a dispute among the eight major powers of North India (called the "War of the Relics"), a decision was made to split the relics into eight parts. The eight recipients took their share of the relics to their respective homelands and enshrined them, according to the Buddha's prescription, in memorial stupas. Though the Mallas got one share, no sign of that share can be found at Kusinagara.

Asoka Visits Kusinagara

From the Asokavadana, *second century* C.E.

[T]the elder took King Asoka to Kusinagari. Stretching out the palm of his right hand, he said, "In this place, great king, the Blessed One, having finished doing the work of a Buddha, entered the state of complete nirvana without any remaining attributes."

And he added:

"The great, wise, most compassionate Sage converted
everyone to the eternal Dharma and Vinaya —
gods, men, asuras, yaksas, and nagas.
Then he went to rest, his mind at ease,
because there was no one left for him to convert."

Hearing these words, Asoka collapsed on the ground in a faint. His attendants splashed some water in his face, and as soon as he had somewhat regained consciousness, he made an offering of a hundred thousand pieces of gold to the site of the parinirvana, and built a caitya there.

The Twin Sal Trees: The Buddha Arrives in Kusinagara

The scent of flowers cannot go against the wind;
not sandalwood, not aloes wood, nor jasmine.
But the scent of the virtuous does go against the
winds; the fragrance of righteousness perfumes all
directions.
　　　　　　　　　　　　　　　　　— The Dhammapada

321

From The Digha Nikaya, *Sutta 16:*
The Mahaparinibbana Sutta, 5th–1st c. B.C.E.

The Lord said: "Ananda, let us cross the Hirannavati River and go to the Mallas' sal-grove in the vicinity of Kusinara." "Very good, Lord," said Ananda, and the Lord, with a large company of monks, crossed the river and went to the *sal*-grove. There the Lord said: "Ananda, prepare me a bed between these twin *sal*-trees with my head to the north. I am tired and want to lie down." "Very good, Lord," said Ananda, and did so. Then the Lord lay down on his right side in the lion-posture, placing one foot on the other, mindful and clearly aware.

And those twin *sal*-trees burst forth into an abundance of untimely blossoms, which fell upon the Tathagata's body, sprinkling it and covering it in homage. Divine coral-tree flowers fell from the sky, divine sandal-wood powder fell from the sky, sprinkling and covering the Tathagata's body in homage. Divine music and song sounded from the sky in homage to the Tathagata.

And the Lord said: "Ananda, these *sal*-trees have burst forth into an abundance of untimely blossoms. . . ."

Thich Nhat Hanh, 1991 C.E.

". . . It is not yet spring, but the sal trees are covered with red blossoms. Do you see the petals falling on the Tathagata's robes and the robes of all the bhikkhus? This forest is truly beautiful. Do you see the western horizon all aglow from the setting sun? Do you hear the gentle breeze rustling in the sal branches? The Tathagata finds all these things lovely and touching. Bhikkhus, if you want to please me, if you want to express your respect and gratitude to the Tathagata, there is only one way, and that is by living the teaching."

On the Road to Kusinagara

Fa-hsien, *400* C.E.

[T]hey reached the city of Kusinagara. . . . Here are stupas and monasteries. . . . This city is almost deserted, with only a handful of monks and a few laymen as its inhabitants.

Hye-Ch'o, *early eighth century* C.E.

After a month's journey, I arrived at the country of Kusinagara. . . . The city is desolate and no people live there. The *stupa* was built at the site where the Buddha entered *nirvana*. There is a *dhyana* master who keeps the place clean. Every year on the eighth day of the eighth month, monks, nuns, clergy and laymen hold a great assembly of worship there. [On this occasion], numerous banners which were seen by all people would appear in the sky. On the same day, many people would resolve their minds [for the religion].

Marie Beuzeville Byles, *1953* C.E.

I had been warned that Kusinara, now the village of Kusinagara, was no place in which to meditate on the truths revealed by that solemn scene. The grove of the sal trees and the end of the river exist no more, nor the small town with its little cottages of bamboo and mud in which the Mallians dwelt, and which Ananda felt unworthy to be the site of the death of the All-Compassionate.

Tripathi and I had spent the night at Gorakhpur railway station where there was a good restaurant and spacious waiting-rooms with excellent washing facilities as well as settees on which to sleep. But what with the temple gongs and bells the night before, and the mosquitoes and trains at Gorakhpur this night, I was nearly crazy with weariness by the time the bus dropped us at Kusinagara. And here the noise continued. There was a

school run by the Maha Bodhi Society next to the dharmasalas, the sacred shrines and the temples, and hosts of
school children — and other children — played and
shouted, and poked inquisitive faces through the bars of
one's window after one had shut the door. I wandered
around searching for a quiet place in which to lay my
weary head, and eventually found a semi-secluded ditch
under the shadow of the stupa, where the Buddha's giant
image lay reclining with two poor little twin sal trees
struggling to grow at the foot of the steps beneath it.

Allan Hunt Badiner, 1990 C.E.

"Long have you wandered, and filled the grave-
yards full." Buddha's words ricocheted through my head
as dust sprayed the bus windows opaque and we lurched
to a metal-grinding stop. I thought I'd die getting to
Kusinagar. Not because the state of Bihar through which
we passed is a bizarrely primitive place, although it is.
And not because the public bus within which I navigat-
ed the thirty miles of potholes from Gorakhpur to
Kusinagar was so comically dilapidated and painfully
uncomfortable as to defy description. What gave me
pause to question my immediate survival was the hundreds of angry jeering people who surrounded the bus.

My odyssey to the places of the Buddha's life was
a search for some accommodation between ancient wisdom and the harsh realities of modern life, a bridge
between the past and the present. I wanted to make a
bond with the Buddha; to "see" him through the ruins,
the stories and the symbols that pilgrims throughout
time have touched at the great places of pilgrimage. Was
it auspicious to die here? I wondered. When I heard the
unhappy reception given to our bus driver, such an out-
come did not seem unlikely. Passengers watched in
mindful horror as he pleaded his case to a sea of shaking
fists. They turned out to be local communist guerrillas

324

blockading the main highway in a fervent protest of election fraud.

The seven-hour standstill included an intense interrogation of every passenger by a semi-toothless cadre waving sharpened wood spears, chewing betel nut and spitting what looked like blood. Their attention was diverted by a more determined bus carrying Japanese pilgrims also bound for Kusinagar at which they threw stones. As if things weren't exciting enough, I overheard a BBC report from a Korean monk's shortwave radio announcing the bombing of Baghdad. The sound of the buses' ignition rescued me from some grim imaginings. Shaken, but with even greater resolve, we were back on the bumpy path of pilgrimage to the place of Buddha's death.

Maha Sthavira Sangharakshita (D. P. E. Lingwood), 1949 C.E.

Sangharakshita and his companion Buddharakshita were both refused ordination in Sarnath and traveled on foot to Kusinagara in search of a monk who would ordain them into the sangha.

The concluding stages of our journey were the worst, and had it not been for the hope that every step was bringing us nearer to the goal of our desires it might have been difficult for us to carry on. It was still early May, and the heat, having risen in fiery crescendo to its terrific climax, now seemed likely to remain there indefinitely. Not a drop of rain fell. Day by day the hot dry wind from the desert, laden with dust, blew more strongly and more scorchingly than ever upon the hard, sunbaked earth, which by this time had become crisscrossed with a network of innumerable cracks and fissures, some of them several inches wide. Travelling during the less hot hours of the day, and taking advantage of every scrap of shade, grimly and wearily Satyapriya and I plodded on from temple to temple and from

325

Reclining Buddha in the Nirvana temple

ashram to ashram, mile after mile across the heat-stricken land. In some of the temples and ashrams at which we halted we were given a cordial welcome, in others our reception was more reserved. Towards the end of our journey our stops became more and more frequent. At one place we took our bath in a pond full of lotuses. At another, where we came across an unusually clean ashram standing within a secluded mango grove, a friendly Nanak Panthi, or follower of Guru Nanak, not only put us up for the night but treated us with exceptional kindness.

On our last morning we were less fortunate. Indeed, this was the least fortunate part of the whole journey. We had intended to halt for an hour or two at the Buddhist Rest House which had been built, so the Nanak Panthi had informed us, not half a dozen miles from our destination. On our arrival there we found that the Rest House had been converted into a school, and the headmaster received us in a very unfriendly fashion. We had no alternative but to set off again at once. Before long we were heartened by the sight of the dome of the

326

Maha Paranirvana Stupa rising majestically from behind a cluster of trees in the far distance, and leaving the road we cut straight across the fields towards it. I could not help thinking with what exultation, only ten or twelve days earlier, we had seen the pinnacle of the Mulagandhakuti Vihara rising above the tree-tops of Sarnath. Did Kusinara hold a similar disappointment in store for us? Or were we destined to receive here the ordination on which we had set our hearts?

Rick Fields, 1994 C.E.

ON THE WAY TO KUSINAGARA

I.
Passing by
Silver and gold sari
Covered corpse
in Sarnath
Dawa
Hip 20 year old
Dharmsala-born
Tibetan girl
says:
"Tibetans say
When you see dead
It's good luck."
"Why?"
"Makes people pray."

AT KUSINAGARA

II.
At the foot of Buddha
Kusinagar shrine
A card —

327

Sang Gu Lee
Buddhist Chaplain of Korea
Air Force.

"May the Lord Not Pass Away in This Miserable Little Town . . ."

From the "Mahasudassana Jataka," 5th–1st c. B.C.E.

"Nay, Ananda," said the Master; "call not this a sorry little town, a little town in the jungle, a little suburban town. In bygone days, in the days of Sudassana's universal monarchy, it was in this town that I had my dwelling. It was then a mighty city encompassed by jewelled walls twelve leagues round." Therewithal, at the Elder's request, he told this story of the past. . . .

"Then it was that Sudassana's queen Subhadda marked how, after coming down from the Palace of Truth, her lord was lying hard by on his right side on the couch prepared for him in the Palm-grove which was all of gold and jewels, — that couch from which he was not to rise again. And she said, 'Eighty-four thousand cities, chief of which is the royal-city of Kusavati, own your sovereignty, sire. Set your heart on them.'"

"Say not so, my queen," said Sudassana; "rather exhort me, saying, 'Keep your heart set on this town, and yearn not after those others.'"

"Why so, my lord?"

"Because I shall die to-day," answered the king.

In tears, wiping her streaming eyes, the queen managed to sob out the words the king bade her say. Then she broke into weeping and lamentation; and the other women of the harem, to the number of eighty-four thousand, also wept and wailed; nor could any of the courtiers forbear, but all alike joined in one universal lament.

"Peace!" said the Bodhisatta [Sudassana]; and at his word their lamentation was stilled. Then, turning to the queen, he said, — "Weep not, my queen, nor wail. For, even down to a tiny seed of sesamum, there is no such thing as a compound thing which is permanent; all are transient, all must break up." Then, for the queen's behoof, he uttered this stanza: —

> *How transient are all component things!*
> *Growth is their nature and decay:*
> *They are produced, they are dissolved again:*
> *And then is best, — when they have sunk to rest.*

Thus did the great Sudassana lead his discourse up to ambrosial Nirvana as its goal. Moreover, to the rest of the multitude he gave the exhortation to be charitable, to obey the Commandments, and to keep hallowed the fast days. The destiny he won was to be re-born thereafter in the Realm of Devas.

His lesson ended, the Master identified the Birth by saying, "The mother of Rahula was the Queen Subhadda of those days; Rahula was the King's eldest son; the disciples of the Buddha were his courtiers; and I myself the great Sudassana."

Exploring Kusinagara

Hiuen Tsiang, mid-seventh century C.E.
The capital of this country is in ruins, and its towns and villages waste and desolate. The brick foundation walls of the old capital are about 10 li in circuit. There are few inhabitants, and the avenues of the town are deserted and wasted.

John Blofeld, 1956 C.E.
The last stage of my pilgrimage before its culmi-

nation in Delhi took me to Kusinagara, where the Lord Buddha at last abandoned his worn-out body which, since his Enlightenment nearly fifty years before, had stood between him and utter absorption into the state of *Nirvana*. From pure compassion he, who had already won freedom from bondage to the Wheel, had clung to and tended that body that the whole of his Wisdom could be transferred to others and handed down for the enormous benefit of posterity.

By the time the bus from the nearest railway station had set me down at Kusinagara just opposite the Burmese rest-house, it was close on midday and the heat so frightful that I feared collapse. A very aged Burmese monk advised me to lie down in one of the bedrooms for pilgrims until the heat had somewhat abated. On that day, the thermometer crossed the 120 mark! I found myself gasping for breath, sucking in the air through my mouth. But at about five o'clock in the afternoon I felt able to walk across to the well which served for bathing. In good Thai style, I girded my loins with my *pakaoma*, allowing the trouser to slip from under it, and was thus able to bathe in full view of anyone who happened to be passing. Winding up a bucket of water, too cold for me on account of the well's great depth, and using my silver *kan* (Thai-style bowl), I sluiced water over myself. It was almost like bathing in iced water. Again I found myself gasping for air. India had taught me never to travel even for half a day without a change of underwear; and for this I was thankful, as my vest and pants were as wet with perspiration as if they had been retrieved from the well. Much refreshed, but still languid from the scarcely abated heat, I set out to explore.

Anne Cushman, 1993 C.E.

We arrive [at Kusinagar] late at night; but although it's almost midnight by the time we finish our dinner, my roommate and I head out for a moonlight stroll through the temple park across the street from our government lodgings.

The park entrance is barred with a locked iron gate; but as seems to be standard procedure in India, an informal, unbarricaded path leads in to the left of the official entry. The night watchman is asleep on the steps of the squat modern temple marking the Buddha's place of death. The light of the almost-full moon pours down over teak and ashoka trees and the by-now-familiar jumble of ruined brick walls. For a few moments, I mistake the distant grumble of a truck engine for the sound of chanting.

What ubiquitous human impulse insists that we throw up these structures of stone and brick? It's as if we desperately want to reassure ourselves that the Buddha's life really took place. But what moves me most is not the disintegrating remnants of ancient houses of worship — the discarded skins of Buddhism — but the almost unspeakable beauty of the land itself; the silver light on the sal leaves, the owl drifting under the full moon.

The next morning, Kushinagar is revealed as a sleepy little town, too far off the beaten track to attract any but the most dedicated of pilgrims. (In fact, the Buddha's disciples berated him for choosing to die in such an insignificant "mud-and-daub" village.) Even the inevitable children soliciting money seem less professional than their counterparts in Bodh Gaya or Sarnath.

Allan Hunt Badiner, 1990 C.E.

The stillness in the area near the Buddhist monuments contrasts with the rest of the town. The air is thick with a mixture of spices, dust, mango, and the smoke of small fires. Other than the occasional bus of pilgrims unloading at the conveniently located and pleasant government tourist motel across from the main stupas, few cars or trucks impose their sonic reminders of modern life. It is even more peaceful at the site of Buddha's cremation, now marked by the crumbling but massive remains of the Ramabhar stupa.

The Buddha's Death and Paranirvana

Hiuen Tsiang, mid-seventh century C.E.
To the north-west of the city 3 or 4 li, crossing the Ajitavati (O-shi-to-fa-ti) river, on the western bank, not far, we come to a grove of *sala* trees. The *sala* tree is like the *Huh* tree, with a greenish white bark and leaves very glistening and smooth. In this wood are four trees of an unusual height, which indicate the place where Tathagata died.

From The Digha Nikaya, *Sutra 16:*
The Mahaparanibbana Sutra, 5th–1st c. B.C.E.
Ananda was probably the Buddha's closest friend as well as one of his most devoted disciples. Learning of the Buddha's approaching death, he began to weep.
And the Lord said: "Enough, Ananda, do not weep and wail! Have I not already told you that all things that are pleasant and delightful are changeable, subject to separation and becoming other? So how could it be, Ananda — since whatever is born, become, compounded is subject to decay — how could it be that it should not pass away? For a long time, Ananda, you have been in the Tathagata's presence, showing loving-kindness in act of body, speech and mind, beneficially, blessedly, whole-heartedly and unstintingly. You have achieved much merit, Ananda. Make the effort, and in a short time you will be free of the corruptions." . . .
And the Lord said to Ananda: "Ananda, it may be

that you will think: 'The Teacher's instruction has ceased, now we have no teacher!' It should not be seen like this, Ananda, for what I have taught and explained to you as Dhamma and discipline will, at my passing, be your teacher.

"And whereas the monks are in the habit of addressing one another as 'friend,' this custom is to be abrogated after my passing. Senior monks shall address more junior monks by their name, their clan or as 'friend,' whereas more junior monks are to address their seniors either as 'Lord' or as 'Venerable Sir.'

"If they wish, the order may abolish the minor rules after my passing." . . .

Then the Lord addressed the monks, saying: "It may be, monks, that some monk has doubts or uncertainty about the Buddha, the Dhamma, the Sangha, or about the path or the practice. Ask, monks! Do not afterwards feel remorse, thinking: 'The Teacher was there before us, and we failed to ask the Lord face to face!'" At these words the monks were silent. The Lord repeated his words a second and a third time, and still the monks were silent. Then the Lord said, "Perhaps, monks, you do not ask out of respect for the Teacher. Then, monks, let one friend tell it to another." But still they were silent.

And the Venerable Ananda said: "It is wonderful, Lord, it is marvellous! I clearly perceive that in this assembly there is not one monk who had doubts or uncertainty. . . ."

"You, Ananda, speak from faith. But the Tathagata knows that in this assembly there is not one monk who has doubts or uncertainty about the Buddha, the Dhamma or the Sangha or about the path or the practice. Ananda, the least one of these five hundred monks is a Stream-Winner, incapable of falling into states of woe, certain of Nibbana."

Then the Lord said to the monks: "Now, monks, I declare to you: all conditioned things are of a nature to decay — strive on untiringly." These were the Tathagata's last words.

Then the Lord entered the first jhana. And leaving that he entered the second, the third, the fourth jhana. Then leaving the fourth jhana he entered the Sphere of Infinite Space, then the Sphere of Infinite Consciousness, then the Sphere of No-Thingness, then the Sphere of Neither-Perception-Nor-Non-Perception.

Then the Venerable Ananda said to the Venerable Anuruddha: "Venerable Anuruddha, the Lord has passed away." "No, friend Ananda, the Lord has not passed away, he has attained the Cessation of Feeling and Perception."

Then the Lord, leaving the attainment of the Cessation of Feeling and Perception, entered the Sphere of Neither-Perception-Nor-Non-Perception, from that he entered the Sphere of No-Thingness, the Sphere of Infinite Consciousness, the Sphere of Infinite Space. From the Sphere of Infinite Space he entered the fourth jhana, from there the third, the second and the first jhana. Leaving the first jhana, he entered the second, the third, the fourth jhana. And, leaving the fourth jhana, the Lord finally passed away.

And at the Blessed Lord's final passing there was a great earthquake, terrible and hair-raising, accompanied by thunder. And Brahma Sahampati uttered this verse:

> *"All beings in the world, all bodies must break up:*
> *Even the Teacher, peerless in the human world,*
> *The mighty Lord and perfect Buddha's passed away."*

And Sakka, ruler of the devas, uttered this verse:

> *"Impermanent are compounded things, prone to rise*
> *and fall,*

*Having risen, they're destroyed, their passing truest
bliss."*

And the Venerable Anuruddha uttered this verse:

*"No breathing in and out — just with steadfast heart
The Sage who's free from lust has passed away to peace.
With mind unshaken he endured all pains:
By Nibbana the Illumined's mind is freed."*

And the Venerable Ananda uttered this verse:

*"Terrible was the quaking, men's hair stood on end,
When the all-accomplished Buddha passed away."*

And those monks who had not yet overcome
their passions wept and tore their hair, raising their
arms, throwing themselves down and twisting and turning, crying: "All too soon the Blessed Lord has passed
away, all too soon the Well-Farer has passed away, all too
soon the Eye of the World has disappeared!" But those
monks who were free from craving endured mindfully
and clearly aware, saying: "All compounded things are
impermanent — what is the use of this?"

The Cremation

Major Rowland Raven-Hart, 1956 C.E.

Once, when I was a boy, I lay naked on a sand-
dune after a warm swim, my body slowly sinking into
the fine sand that moved to receive it; and for a
moment I *was* that sand, and the coarse grass on which
my head rested, and the hot sun, and the cool wind that
chased shivers over my skin, and the hawk floating high
above me, and the clumsy green beetle that bumbled

335

angrily through the sparse forest of my new-grown belly hair. . . .

If Nirvana is such union, and far more, union not only with all material things but with all intellect and all spirit — if it is this, you can keep your harps and houris.

From the Tibetan Works in the Bkah-Hgyur *and* Bstan-Hgyur, *8th–14th c. C.E.*

On the seventh day, having prepared a golden bier, and got together all the perfumes, garlands, and musical instruments within twelve yojanas, from Kusinara to the Hiranyavati river, from the twin sala grove to the crested tchaitya of the Mallas . . . they went out of the town to the twin sala tree grove to honour the Buddha's remains. When they came there, the principal Mallas of Kusinara said, "O Vasishtas, let the Mallas women and maidens make a canopy of their garments over the Blessed One; then when we have honoured his remains with perfumes and garlands, they will carry his body to the western gate of the city, which we will traverse and leave by the eastern gate. . . ."

Now at that moment there fell in the town of Kusinara such a quantity of mandarava flowers . . . that they were knee-deep. . . .

When the Mallas tried to light the funeral pile, they were unable to do so, and Aniruddha told Ananda that it was because Mahakacyapa [Kasyapa, an elder Buddhist monk] had not arrived. . . .

When the people saw Mahakacyapa coming from afar off, they took perfumes and wreaths, &c., and went out to meet him; then they bowed down at his feet and followed after him to the place where the Blessed One's body was. He uncovered and worshipped it. . . . He had a store of robes, alms, bedding, medicines, and other necessaries . . . so he changed the garments which enshrouded the Blessed One for others from his store; and having replaced the cover of the coffin, the fire burst forth from the pile and consumed the body. . . .

When the body was consumed, the Mallas put out the fire with milk, and putting the remains . . . in a golden vase, they placed it on a golden bier, and having honoured it with perfumes and the sound of music, &c., they took it to Kusinara, to the center of the town, where they again paid it honors.

Pilgrims circle the Cremation stupa

The Cremation Stupa

Hiuen Tsiang, mid-seventh century C.E.

To the north of the city, after crossing the river, and going 300 paces or so, there is a *stupa*. This is the place where they burnt the body of Tathagata. The earth is now of a blackish yellow, from a mixture of earth and charcoal. Whoever with true faith seeks here, and prays, is sure to find some relics of Tathagata.

V. S. Naravane, 1965 C.E.

Although Kusinara offers us very few monuments, there are spots concerning which strong local traditions persist. We are shown the place where the people of Kusinara decked out the body of the Blessed One in costly raiment and honoured it with perfumes and garlands. They did not have the heart to burn it. "Not today, friends, not today," they said. "Let us cremate the body tomorrow." But on the morrow they again said the same thing, and so also on the day after that. At last on the seventh day they carried the body outside the city gates and in the premises of an ancient prayer cremated it. And when the body was consumed they put out the pyre with scented water.

Allan Hunt Badiner, 1990 C.E.

Bright orange robes of a Burmese monk swept into my field of vision interrupting my meditation on impermanence. Looking studious, with round spectacles, and long chocolate brown arms extending into wise weathered looking hands, the monk half-smiled as if to apologize for the interruption. After some polite conversation, I asked him if he was afraid to die. The monk displayed no sign of surprise or discomfort. He claimed to be neither fearful nor hopeful, yet he seemed genuinely tuned to the imminent reality of death.

The monk spoke of the need to balance one's will to live with the acceptance of death. Surely death was more fundamental to his culture than my own, where it has been all but dislodged completely from consciousness. Westerners live like immortals, I explained. Death is considered a fiasco, and if it befalls one of your own, its unpleasant procedures must be completed as quickly as possible so that people can get back to business.

We walked to the Ramabhar stupa and exchanged stories about what the Buddha ate during his final meal at the nearby home of the blacksmith Chunda. The monk was intrigued to hear of ethnobotanist Gordon Wasson's theory that Chunda may have confused fungi and served his distinguished guest some psychedelic Putika, a fungi related to the legendary soma. The wise Buddha instructed Chunda to bury the rest in the ground after serving him. Clear to both of us was the great extent of Buddha's compassion, such that even on his deathbed, he worried about how Chunda would feel after hearing of his death. The monk told me Chunda's home was marked by a stupa for many centuries, and described in the writings of the Chinese pilgrim, Hiuen Tsiang.

A wobbly wagon carrying a load twice its own size slowly overtook us and dropped fresh cut sugar cane stalks at our feet. Reaching the banks of the Hiranyavati River we sat in full view of the cremation stupa listening to the loud cries of crows circling above. I was still processing the news that Baghdad was in flames from American bombs, and civilian casualties were high. Why, I wondered, is humanity so forgetful? With his last breath, the Buddha warned us to make haste. We're told to pursue our liberation "as though there were a fire in our hair," and yet most of us fall swiftly back into doubt, complacency and the everyday business of fulfilling short-term needs.

The monk and I fell silent. The calls of the crows grew louder. My eyes fixed on the stupa and my thoughts turned to the accounts of Buddha's final moments. Having uttered his last words, the Buddha began to meditate. It was unclear after some time whether he had ceased to breathe or was still in a deep state of meditative absorption. His faithful assistant

Ananda prevented anyone from disturbing him for many hours. Only after it was totally clear to him that his master had passed on did he allow the body of the Buddha to be washed, wrapped in shrouds, placed in a casket adorned with jewels, and prepared for cremation.

The cremations I had recently seen in Banaras came to mind, and I imagined the body of the Buddha frying in the pyre. "The body is an island of suffering," said the Buddha, "a framework of bones, bound by sinews, clothed with soft flesh, and enclosed in the cuticle and covered with the epidermis, pierced and perforated with pores, swarming with vermin, pernicious for living creatures, and the dwelling of evil deeds." Further, the Buddha urged us to be continually mindful of the fact that the body "has pains, suffers decay, breaks down, becomes lame, wrinkled and decrepit."

My eyes remained fixed on the stupa. It was decaying and dying itself, like just another kind of body for the Buddha. Is building a shrine or monument to a person in conflict with the dharma itself? I wondered. Thich Nhat Hanh, when asked what he thought of someone building a stupa for him, said, "I would laugh." His close confident and friend, Sister Chan Khong, actually chuckled. "I devote my life to lessening my attachment to the body," said Thich Nhat Hanh, "and you would enshrine it forever?"

. . . I asked the monk what he thought would be an enlightened view of death. Buddhism, he suggests, makes death the mirror for one's life. Death is a very important teaching. When death is present in your mind, life is less a struggle to make moments more meaningful or enjoyable as it is a wondrous journey with each moment being inherently thrilling. "Contemplating our mortality is unexpectedly liberating," he said, "and it inspires compassion." I reflected on how the precarious beginnings of my Kushinagar experience helped me into a deeper relationship with fear and negativity.

Being here, walking in the Buddha's footsteps, and seeing the land as he saw it, has restored my spirit. The Himalayan peaks were barely discernible, appearing like orange dots in the horizon. Thrilled was I to have such a deep sense of the continuity of history, to be present with a timeless Buddha presence, and to witness the inspiring and unbroken stream of human devotion to his teachings. The monk and I rose and exchanged good wishes and safe passage for the rest of our respective pilgrimages.

It was late in the afternoon when I returned to the large park that contains most of the ancient shrines. The dome of the two-hundred feet high Nirvana stupa was emblazoned against a fluorescent field of crimson clouds. Years earlier, in the very place I was standing, I remember Thich Nhat Hanh describing a poignant moment between Ananda and Buddha at the end of his life. "Don't you think nature is lovely and wonderful?" Buddha asked. Born under a tree, enlightened under a tree, the Buddha was enjoying mindful breathing for the last time under two stately sala trees. Their falling red blossoms framed a special and most beautiful sunset. Buddha wondered if Ananda could really see it.

Remembering the Buddha: Kusinagara's Monuments

From The Digha Nikaya, *Sutra 16:*
The Mahaparanibbana Sutta

"Lord, formerly monks who had spent the Rains in various places used to come to see the Tathagata, and we used to welcome them so that such well-trained monks might see you and pay their respects. But with the Lord's passing, we shall no longer have a chance to do this."

"Ananda, there are four places the sight of which should arouse emotion in the faithful. Which are they? 'Here the Tathagata was born' is the first. 'Here the Tathagata attained supreme enlightenment' is the second. 'Here the Tathagata set in motion the Wheel of Dhamma' is the third. 'Here the Tathagata attained the Nibbana-element without remainder' is the fourth. And, Ananda, the faithful monks and nuns, male and female lay-followers will visit those places. And any who die while making the pilgrimage to these shrines with a devout heart will, at the breaking-up of the body after death, be reborn in a heavenly world."

". . . Lord, what are we to do with the Tathagata's remains?" "Ananda, they should be dealt with like the remains of a wheel-turning monarch." "And how is that, Lord?" "Ananda, the remains of a wheel-turning monarch are wrapped in a new linen-cloth. This they wrap in teased cotton wool, and this in a new cloth. Having done this five hundred times each, they enclose the king's body in an oil-vat of iron, which is covered with another iron pot. Then having made a funeral-pyre of all manner of perfumes they cremate the king's body, and they raise a stupa at a crossroads. That, Ananda, is what they do with the remains of a wheel-turning monarch, and they should deal with the Tathagata's body in the same way. A stupa should be erected at the crossroads for the Tathagata. And whoever lays wreaths or puts sweet perfumes and colours there with a devout heart, will reap benefit and happiness for a long time.

"Ananda, there are four persons worthy of a stupa. Who are they? A Tathagata, Arahant, fully-enlightened Buddha is one, a Pacceka Buddha is one, a disciple of the Tathagata is one, and a wheel-turning monarch is one. And why is each of these worthy of a stupa? Because, Ananda, at the thought: 'This is the stupa of a Tathagata, of a Pacceka Buddha, of a disciple of the Tathagata, of a wheel-turning monarch,' people's hearts are made peaceful, and then, at the breaking-up of the body after death they go to a good destiny and rearise in a heavenly world. That is the reason, and those are the four who are worthy of a stupa."

THE NIRVANA TEMPLE AND STUPA

An inscription, dating from the fifth century C.E., attributes the donation of a large, reclining statue of the Buddha to "Haribala." Inside the Nirvana Temple, the statue, carved from reddish sandstone, is flanked by three mourning figures, one of whom may be the donor Haribala. The temple and statue were found and restored in 1876 by A. C. L. Carlleyle. Carlleyle's restoration of the building is now thought to be based on a late reconstruction of the temple described by Hiuen Tsiang below. Next to the temple is the large brick stupa which Hiuen Tsiang attributed to King Asoka. Also excavated by Carlleyle, the stupa was found to contain several fifth-century silver coins and a copper plate inscription with the name "Haribala." First restored in 1927, the Nirvana stupa has undergone a second restoration since Blofeld, Raven-Hart, and Wijayatilake's visit.

Hiuen Tsiang, mid-seventh century C.E.

There is *(here)* a great brick *vihara*, in which is a figure of the *Nirvana* of Tathagata. He is lying with his head to the north as if asleep. By the side of this *vihara* is a *stupa* built by Asoka-raja; although in a ruinous state, yet it is some 200 feet in height. Before it is a stone pillar to record the *Nirvana* of Tathagata; although there is an inscription on it, yet there is no date as to year or month.

John Blofeld, 1956 C.E.

The ancient temple enclosing a famous reclining image of the Buddha was closed, so I had little to do but to sit gazing at the *stupa* (bottle-shaped reliquary tower) which marks the actual site of the Lord Buddha's *Parinirvana* or final passing. As had become my custom in sacred places, I first prostrated myself towards the *stupa* and then sat down to meditate and to read the scriptures appropriate to that place. As the Maha Bodhi Society's guide-book declares so truly, Kusinagara is the only one of the Buddhist shrines which arouses melancholy. I found it easy to visualize the Lord reclining in his favourite position, lying on his right side with his head resting upon a cupped hand supported by his elbow. Above him were twin sala trees similar to the one beneath whose shade he had been born. Their falling flowers sprinkled him as he and his mother had been sprinkled at the time of his birth exactly eighty years before. And all about him were weeping disciples and the hastily assembled villagers from round about. But he exhorted them not to weep, reminding them that "everything born, brought into being or created by having its various parts assembled contains within itself the inherent necessity of dissolution." So saying, he commended his cousin and most devoted disciple, Ananda, for his years of selfless devotion to his Master and for his excellent effect upon the others. To the villagers who wept, dishevelled their hair and rolled on the ground in anguish, he explained that, though their Teacher would soon be no more, they must not grieve, for the Truths he had taught and the Rules he had provided for the Order would forever be Teacher to them all. Then, speaking to the whole assembly of monks and laymen, he exclaimed, "Behold now, brothers, I exhort you saying: Decay is inherent in all compounded things! Work out your own salvation with diligence."

Those were his last words. Entering into the successive stages of meditation, he withdrew further and further from the consciousness of outward things and peacefully passed away.

It is hard for a Buddhist to contemplate this scene, while meditating in Kusinagara itself, without weeping. I had to remind myself that the Lord Buddha had chidden his disciples for their tears, requiring of them a firm resolution to work out, each one for himself, salvation from the Wheel. I put away my book and meditated for a while, sharply aware of the voices of birds and insects all around.

Anne Cushman, 1993 C.E.

We walk to the ruins and meditate inside the temple next to an enormous fifth-century reclining Buddha, draped in a gold blanket emblazoned with the slogan "Thailand 1993."

After a period of silent sitting, Shantum guides us through the Buddha's meditation on death: "The practitioner compares his own body with a corpse that he imagines he sees thrown onto a charnel ground and lying there for one, two, or three days — bloated, blue in color, and festering — and he observes, 'This body of mine is of the same nature. It will end up in the same way. There is no way it can avoid that state.' As we finish, we hear chanting beginning outside: a middle-aged Korean man in casual slacks is circling the temple, praying to Amitabha Buddha.

"I came here partly to deal with my own death — but I feel much more alive than I ever have," says Jan that evening, as we sit in a circle on the floor of a tiny Chinese temple in downtown Kushinigar. The temple is run by a nun who befriended Shantum on a previous visit; we've gathered there to sip chai, nibble on the nun's homemade candied ginger, and check in about

345

how our pilgrimage is unfolding.

"Being at the place the Buddha died — and realizing that for all his accomplishments, he had to die too — somehow makes me feel more at ease with my own mortality," adds Larry. "And it somehow helps me see the possibility of dying peacefully, without attachment, as I'm fairly sure the Buddha did."

What's hitting home for all of us, we discover as we talk, is the essential humanity of the Buddha. We've seen the places he walked, sat, struggled, triumphed, and taught, and now we sit in the place where his body returned to the earth. Somehow, this realization makes the task of achieving the liberation he spoke of seem more accessible to all of us.

Maha Sthavira Sangharakshita (D. P. E. Lingwood), 1949 C.E.

Not far from the Stupa was the Temple of the Recumbent Buddha. This was a place of no architectural pretensions whatever. Indeed, it was nothing more than a white-washed brick shed, long and narrow, with a barrel roof that had been put up to protect the celebrated image which, next to the Stupa itself, in the heyday of Kusinara had been the principal object of worship at the sacred site. This image, which belonged to the Gupta period, was about thirty feet in length, and represented the Buddha at the time of the Great Decease. One foot on top of the other, head supported on right hand, stiff and solemn he lay there in his gilded robe, the great face serene and majestic in the hour of bodily death as ever it had been during life. Though the temple was so small that there was barely room to circumambulate the image, to me, at least, the dimensions of the place were exactly right. As we knelt there in the gloom, with only two or three lighted candles flickering between us and the placid features of that enormous face, so deep was the silence, and of such inexpressible solemnity, that we seemed to be present at the very deathbed of the Master. Before many days had passed the Stupa and the Temple had become the twin centers of our spiritual existence. Every evening, at sunset, we sat and meditated in front of the Stupa, stirring only when it loomed a black shape against the star-filled depths of the sky. Every morning, long before dawn, having chanted our praises in that unsleeping ear, we sat and meditated beside the stone couch of the Recumbent Buddha. During the rest of the day we studied, talked with Mother Vipassana and, of course, continued our explorations.

Encounters: "China Baba"

Marie Beuzeville Byles, 1953 C.E.
The second day we walked about a mile along a dusty white new road with barley fields on either side to a hillock crowned by a banyan or bodhi tree into which a thatched shelter had been built. It was the hermitage of China Baba, a bhikkhu, who had made it his home for twenty-four years. A lengthy conversation took place with the one behind the closed door, and I heard a lot of "Australias" interspersed. This magic word at length caused the yellow-robed one to emerge. He was not very gracious and his eyes did not seem to shine with the light of loving kindness and serene bliss that I had expected. He soon went inside again refusing to be photographed, but after having given his permission for me to stay awhile near his shelter. I sat and meditated under the shadow of the banyan tree, and once again, as with guruji at Rajgir, I found it extremely easy to concentrate the thoughts. I had no doubt that, whatever else he lacked, he had acquired the art of stilling the thoughts, but meditation is only one step of the Eightfold Path to

347

Liberation. It was because the great seers, Alara and Uddaka, had been able to teach Gautama only this that he had left them, and sought by other means to find the way to enlightenment. When he at last did attain this and became the Enlightened One . . . the temptation then came to him to depart alone like this bhikkhu and enjoy the bliss he had found . . . He resisted it, and spent the rest of his long life mixing with people in their joys and sorrows, and showing them the Way to the serene peace and joy that he himself had found. It is not for us to judge another, but millions upon millions have rejoiced because Gautama, the Buddha, did not do as this bhikkhu had done.

Despite this veiled criticism, this hermit was the one pleasant memory left of Kusinara.

Maha Sthavira Sangharakshita (D. P. E. Lingwood), 1949 C.E.

Near the Chaitya grew an enormous peepul tree, and high up in the tree, half hidden by the dense foliage, there was perched a strange figure in a saffron-coloured loin cloth. As soon as he caught sight of us he let out a loud whoop, apparently of welcome, and with amazing agility swarmed chuckling and gibbering down the tree until he stood balancing himself only a few feet above our heads. We then saw that he was Chinese, and that his arms, and chest, which were bare, were covered with a multitude of burns. Though he seemed to know a little Hindi, his pronunciation was so uncouth that it was impossible for us to make out more than a few words. In response to his gesticulations, however, we looked up into the tree, and eventually saw among the branches a kind of rough platform, so clumsily put together from half a dozen planks as to seem like the nest of some enormous bird. It was here that the strange figure lived. As we afterwards learned, he had lived in the tree for a number of years, and though he moved about freely among the branches he never set foot on the ground. Periodically he applied lighted candles to different parts of his body and allowed them to burn down into the flesh. This was, of course, an extension of the Far Eastern Buddhist practice of burning wax cones on the head at the time of ordination, as a sign of one's willingness to suffer for the sake of Supreme Enlightenment, and was not without precedent in traditional Chinese Buddhism — or, indeed, without canonical sanction in the *White Lotus Sutra.* Whatever visiting Buddhists may have thought of these bizarre practices, the local Hindus were full of admiration, and Cheenia Baba, as they called him, was held in high esteem. Some of the villagers, indeed, would bring him candles to burn on himself in the belief that whatever prayers they offered up while he was so doing were sure to be granted.

Major Rowland Raven-Hart, 1956 C.E.

[A] thing I forgot to look for: an arboreal hermitage, of a Chinese monk who lived in a treetop.

A Few Notes About the Contributors

Arnold, Sir Edwin.
Winner of the Newgate Prize at Oxford in 1852, Sir Edwin Arnold (1832-1904) was principal of Poona College from 1856-61. In 1873, he became editor of the Daily Telegraph, for which he wrote a series of articles describing sites he had visited in India, among them Bodh Gaya. He published poems and several English translations of Sanskrit texts. He is known, above all, for *The Light of Asia*, a poem in blank verse relating the story of the Buddha's life.

Ashby, Lillian Luker:
Ashby's great-grandfather traded in Calcutta, her grandfather bred elephants and planted indigo in India, and her father was an officer in the Indian police. She married a British officer and together they lived for a short time in Gaya, near Bodh Gaya, where Ashby watched Hindu and Buddhist pilgrims pass by her house every day. In 1937, Ashby published her memories of Indian life in *My India: Recollections of Fifty Years*.

Asoka Maurya:
King of the Mauryan empire, Asoka ruled over most of what is now present-day India. In the early years of his reign, Asoka waged war against the Kalingas of Orissa. Though victorious, he was repulsed by the war's brutality and decided to embrace non-violence and the Buddhist dharma. He proclaimed his change of heart to the public in a number of stone inscriptions, engraved on cliff faces and pillars throughout his empire. Asokan pillars erected at or en route to several Buddhist pilgrimage sites fed legends, like the Asokavadana, which portrayed the king as an ideal Buddhist ruler and pilgrim.

Badiner, Allan Hunt:
Badiner lives in Big Sur, California. He has studied Buddhist meditation and dharma at Rockhill Hermitage in Sri Lanka, and with Ven. Dr. Havanpola Ratanasara in Los Angeles. His articles have appeared in *LA Weekly*, *Utne Reader*, and the *Yoga Journal*. He was the editor of *Dharma Gaia: A Harvest of Essays in Buddhism and Ecology* for Parallax Press, and he is consulting editor for *Tricycle, The Buddhist Review*. In 1988, Allan traveled with Thich Nhat Hanh on a pilgrimage to Buddhist India. *Buddha by Land: Pilgrimage to India* is the title of his forthcoming book from Parallax Press.

351

Blofeld, John:
An English Buddhist, Blofeld traveled extensively in Asia. He lived five years in Thailand and seventeen in China, where he married Chang Meifang. In 1956, when the 2,500th anniversary of the Buddha's *paranirvana* was celebrated, Blofeld went on pilgrimage to the places where the Buddha lived in India. He then traveled on to Sikkim, where he was initiated into Vajrayana Buddhism. Blofeld has written several books on Buddhism, including *Beyond the Godds: Taoist and Buddhist Mysticism and Mahayana Buddhism in South East Asia*.

Boucher, Sandy:
In addition to several volumes of short stories, Boucher is the author of *Turning the Wheel: American Women Creating the New Buddhism*, a collection of interviews she conducted with Buddhist women in America. A *vipassana* practitioner, Boucher now lives in Oakland, California.

Buchanan, Francis:
In 1807, Buchanan was hired by the Directors of the East India Company to make an extensive statistical survey of the Company's eastern territories. Buchanan took seven years to complete the survey, which was arranged by Montgomery Martin into a three-volume book entitled *Eastern India*.

Byles, Mary Beuzeville:
In 1953, Byles went on a kind of comparative pilgrimage. Traveling from Britain to India, she visited the places where the Buddha and Mahatma Gandhi had lived and taught. She published her thoughts and observations in *The Lotus and the Spinning Wheel*. She is also the author of *Journey into Burmese Silence* and *Footprints of Gautama the Buddha*.

Crane, Walter:
An Englishman, Crane expressed discomfort with what he called the "great Dependency" of the Indians on the British "autocractic system" and hoped that his travelogue, *India Impressions*, would help to "increase the interest of [his] own countrymen and women in India." Crane journeyed to India in 1906–7.

Crosette, Barbara:
Barbara Crosette is a UN Corresponent for The New York Times.

Cushman, Anne:

An associate editor of *Yoga Journal*, she went to India with Shantum Seth, who takes regular guided tours to the sites of the Buddha's life.

Dalai Lama:

The fourteenth Dalai Lama was born in 1935. The political and religious leader of the Tibetans, he was forced into exile in 1959, ten years after China's invasion of Tibet. Though exiled, he has continued to struggle for his people's freedom.

Del Mare, Walter:

In 1905, Del Mare published an account of his travels in India. He wrote the book in anticipation of the prince and princess of Wales' visit to India, and the curiosity about the subcontinent he expected their visit to arouse among the English.

Deussen, Paul:

Born in 1845, Deussen, a German philosopher, is the author of several books on German and Indian philosophy, including *The System of Vedanta* and *Outlines of Indian Philosophy*. He died in 1919.

Dharmapala, Angarika:

Dharmapala was born in Colombo in 1864. His given name was Don David Hevavitarana. Though Dharmapala was educated in Christian schools as a child, he clung to his Buddhist faith. At the age of fourteen, he heard about the Theosophical Society and its founders Madame Blavatsky and Colonel Olcott, who had expressed a deep interest in Buddhism and who would themselves become Buddhists during their visit to Sri Lanka. Dharmapala joined their society in 1884 and, at the behest of Madame Blavatsky, began to study Pali. Soon thereafter, he turned down a government job in order to devote his life to Buddhism. Visiting Bodh Gaya in 1891, he was horrified by the area's state of decay and resolved to fight for its restoration. To this end, he founded the Maha Bodhi Society in 1891 and, in 1892, the *Journal of the Mahabodhi Society*. His efforts to restore Bodh Gaya to Buddhist devotees involved Dharmapala in a lengthy legal battle with the site's Hindu management. He died in 1933, vowing to continue the fight for the Temple in his next rebirth.

The Dharmasvamin (Chag lo-Tsa-ba Chos-rje-dpal):

A Tibetan Buddhist monk who traveled to India during

the thirteenth century when the country was being overrun by Islamic armies, he dictated the narrative of his travels to a younger monk, Upasaka Chos-dar. 1234–36

Fa-hsien:

A Buddhist monk and the first of the great Chinese pilgrims to visit India, Fa-hsien was "distressed by the imperfect state" of Buddhist literature in China. In 399 C.E., he embarked on a search for Buddhist texts in the subcontinent, accompanied by a group of monks, among whom he names Hui-ching, Tao-cheng, Hui-ying, and Hui-wei. Fa-hsien traveled in India for fourteen years, returning to China in 414 C.E. to translate the texts he had acquired on his journey. He lived to the age of eighty-eight.

Fields, Rick:

Rick Fields is the author of *How the Swans Came to the Lake: A Narrative History of Buddhism in America* (Shambhala, third edition, 1992), and *The Code of the Warrior* (HarperCollins, 1991), and co-translator of *The Turquoise Bee: Love Songs of the Sixth Dalai Lama*. He is a contributing editor of *Tricycle* and editor-in-chief of *Yoga Journal* in Berkeley, California.

Forbes-Lindsay, C.H.:

The American Charles Harcourt Ainslie Forbes-Lindsay published an account of his travels to India in 1903. He is also the author of *Washington, the City and the Seat of Government.*

Ginsberg, Allen:

Among the most influential of the American beat poets, Ginsberg traveled to India with Gary Snyder, Joanne Kyger, and Peter Orlovsky in 1962–63. Ginsberg considered himself a Buddhist of sorts and traveled to Bodh Gaya, Rajagriha, and Nalanda during the course of his India journey. His thoughts and poems about the journey appear in his *Indian Journals.*

Hiuen Tsiang:

Born in China's Ho-nan province in 603 C.E., Hiuen Tsiang became a Buddhist monk at the age of thirteen. In 629 C.E., he set out for India on a search for Buddhist texts. At the city of Kan-suh, government officials tried to stop him from leaving China. However, he forded the river at night, with the help of two priests, and managed, by one device or another, to get past the five watchtowers standing between him and the border. He traveled extensively in India, returning to China in 645 C.E. to translate the many Buddhist texts he had brought back from his journey. His detailed travel accounts have been an invaluable source for nineteenth- and twentieth-century archaeologists attempting to retrace and unearth India's major Buddhist sites.

Huntington, John:

A professor in the Department of the History of Art at Ohio State University, Professor Huntington is the author of several books on Indian art. Between 1985 and 1986, he published a series of articles in *Orientalis* describing the eight canonical sites of Buddhist pilgrimage in India.

Hye Ch'o:

A Korean Buddhist, he traveled to India around 724 C.E., returning to China afterward to study with Vajrabodhi, a prominent master of Tantric Buddhism.

I-Ching:

The third of the three great Chinese pilgrims to India, I-Ching was born in 635 C.E. and entered the Buddhist order at the age of fourteen. Inspired by the pilgrims Fa-hsien and Hiuen Tsiang, I-Ching conceived a desire to visit India when he was eighteen. He left for the subcontinent nine years later, in 671 C.E., just forty-two years after Hiuen Tsiang. Though he visited Vaisali, Sarnath, Kusinagara, and Bodh Gaya and studied for some time at Nalanda, his travel writings dwell less on place than on Indian custom and religion. In 692 C.E., three years before returning to China with four hundred Buddhist texts, I-Ching sent these writings home in the hands of the Chinese priest Ta-ts'in.

Kawaguchi, Ekai:

A Japanese Buddhist monk, Kawaguchi left Japan on a journey to Tibet in the summer of 1897. While he claimed to be looking for Mahayana Buddhist texts, he had traveled to Tibet before on secret missions for the British government and may have been acting on behalf of the Japanese government during his 1897 voyage. En route to Tibet, Kawaguchi stopped briefly in Bodh Gaya. His ecstatic reaction to the site is described in his published travel account, *Three Years in Tibet*.

Kyger, Joanne:

Joanne Kyger is the author of 14 books of poetry, most recently *Just Space*, published by Black Sparrow Press, 1991. She currently teaches writing at the Naropa Institute in Boulder, Colorado. She lived in Japan from 1960 to 1964 during which time she also spent six months in India.

355

Lerner, Eric:

Emerging from the sixties in America with a feeling of dislocation, Lerner traveled to India in the early seventies to undertake an intensive meditation course. He stopped in Bodh Gaya between meditation retreats and published an account of his experiences in *Journey of Insight Meditation: A Personal Experience of the Buddha's Way.*

Macy, Joanna:

A professor of Philosophy and Religion at the California Institute of Integral Studies, Joanna Macy leads workshops on peace and environmental issues throughout the world. She is the author of *Despair and Empowerment in the Nuclear Age* and *World as Lover, World as Self.* Among her most recent projects is Nuclear Guardianship, a citizen effort to keep a mindful watch on the weapons and toxins produced by a militarized society.

Matthiessen, Peter:

Zen priest, environmentalist, and explorer, Matthiessen is the author of *The Snow Leopard, Nine-Headed Dragon River,* and, recently, *Killing Mr. Watson.*

Naravane, V. S.:

A professor of Indian studies, Naravane published his pilgrimage account as one in a collection of writings entitled *The Elephant and the Lotus: Essays in Philosophy and Culture.* He is the author of several books, including *Ananda K. Coomaraswamy, An Introduction to Rabindranath Tagore* and *Modern Indian Thought.*

Mukherji, Babu Purna Chandra:

An Archaelogist, Mr Mukherji conducted an exploration of the Nepalese Terai for the Archaelogical Survey of India in 1898. Hewas searching for the exact sites and remains of Lumbini and Kapilavastu, the Buddha's birthplace and childhood home.

Peiris, Noeyal:

A Sri Lankan Buddhist, Noeyal Peiris took a vow to bring relics of the Buddha back to Sri Lanka. The discovery of Kapilavastu in northern Uttar Pradesh was announced in the paper during Peiris's trip to India, and he immediately went to visit the excavations, arranging to bring relics from the site back to Sri Lanka, and, later, organizing a celebration of Vesakha, the Buddha's birthday, to be held at the newly unearthed Kapilavastu.

356

Raven-Hart, Major Rowland:

The English major described himself as a writer. In addition to his account of Buddhist pilgrim sites, published in 1956 and entitled *Where the Buddha Trod*, Raven-Hart produced several books on Sri Lanka, among them *Germans in Dutch Ceylon* and *Ceylon: History in Stone*, translated historic travelogues such as *The Pybus Embassy to Kandy*, and published a record of his voyages in the American South called *Down the Mississippi*. Though he was not himself a Buddhist, Raven-Hart's sympathies for the Buddha's teachings are evidently sincere. His travel accounts betray an extensive knowledge and fondness for birds and for Buddhist literature.

Sangharakshita, Maha Sthavira:

Born D. P. E. Lingwood, Sangharakshita traveled in 1949 to Sarnath and then Kushinagara, searching for a monk who would agree to ordain him into the Buddhist order. After being rebuffed in Sarnath, he received ordination at Kusinagara. Since then, he has written extensively on Buddhism and, as head of the Western Buddhist Order, has worked to disseminate knowledge of Buddhism throughout the world. He is based in Norfolk, England.

Schelling, Andrew:

Schelling is a poet, translator, essayist, and scholar of the languages and literature of India. He is on the faculty of the Jack Kerouac School of Disembodied Poetics at the Naropa Institute in Boulder, Colorado, where he is chair of the Department of Writing and Poetics. Schelling's books include *The India Book, For Love of the Dark One: Songs of Mirabai, Moon Is a Piece of Tea* and *Dropping the Bow: Poems from Ancient India*, which won the Academy of American Poets Prize for Translation in 1992. He has co-edited with Anne Waldman a recent anthology entitled *Disembodied Poetics: Annals of the Jack Kerouac School*.

Scidmore, Eliza Ruhamah:

Journeying from America, Scidmore spent a winter in India. Her travelogue, published in 1903, is titled *Winter India*. Scidmore's descriptions of Bodh Gaya and Sarnath reveal a profound respect for Buddhism, mingled with a sharp disdain for modern-day Hinduism. She is the author of several other books on the East, including *Jinrikisha Days in Japan* and *China: The Long-Lived Empire*.

Shoemaker, Michael Myers:

An American travel writer, Michael Myers Shoemaker is author of *Islands of the Seven Seas, Islam Lands,* and *Winged Wheels in*

357

France, among others. In 1912, he published *Indian Pages and Pictures*, a description of places, he suggests, less known to Americans. His chapter on the Buddha, focusing on his trip to Sarnath, speaks to the recently awakened Western interest in Buddhism.

Smith, Vincent:

Vincent Smith (1848-1920) wrote one of the first histories of early India, entitled *Early History of India, from 600 B.C. to the Muhammadon Conquest, Including the Invasion of Alexander the Great*. An historian and Indologist, Smith was involved with the Archaelogical Survey of India's exploration of the Nepalese Terai, where the Buddha's birthplace was believed to lie.

Snyder, Gary:

Snyder lives in the Northern Sierra Nevada and practices in the Lingji Ch'an Buddhist tradition. A Pulitzer Prize–winning American poet and essayist, Snyder traveled to India in 1962 with his wife at the time, Joanne Kyger, and the Beat poets Allen Ginsberg and Peter Orlovsky. Snyder published a description of his travels in a book entitled *Passage Through India*.

Tagore, Rabindranath:

Born in 1861, Tagore was educated privately. He grew up in Calcutta and at the age of twenty-four, moved to his father's estates, where he wrote most of his works. In 1901, he founded the Visva Bharati University (Santiniketan). Tagore received the Nobel Prize for Literature in 1913. Among his numerous novels, plays, and political works are *Gitanjali* (1912), *Nationalism* (1919), and *The Home and the World* (1919).

Terrell, Richard:

Terrell first traveled to India in 1943 as part of the Royal West African Frontier Force. In 1980, he returned to visit the Indian states of Bihar and Orissa, where his father had been the chief justice from 1928 to 1938.

Von Orlich, Captain Leopold:

The German von Orlich was born in 1804 and lived until 1860. The account of his travels to India is entitled *Travels in India: Including Sinde and the Punjab*.

Waldman, Anne:

The author of over thirty books of poetry and editor of several poetry anthologies, most recently *Kill or Cure* (1994), *Iouis*

(1993), and *Helping the Dreamer: New and Selected Poems* (1992), Waldman has performed her own works extensively here and abroad. With Allen Ginsberg, she is the founder of the Jack Kerouac School of Disembodied Poets at the Naropa Institute in Boulder, Colorado, where she currently teaches. She is also the co-editor with Andrew Schelling of a recent anthology entitled *Disembodied Poetics: Annals of the Jack Kerouac School.*

Webb, Sidney and Beatrice:
The Webbs were Fabian socialists, living in England at the end of the nineteenth and beginning of the twentieth centuries. Politically active, the Webbs worked and wrote extensively together. Among other accomplishments, the couple established the London School of Economics and Political Science. In 1911, the Webbs traveled to Japan, China, Burma, and India. Their experiences are recounted in their *Indian Diary.*

Wheeler, Kate:
Wheeler grew up in South America. She went to her first meditation retreat in 1977 and has been practicing ever since. A contributing editor to *Tricycle*, she is the author of *Not Where I Started From*, a collection of short stories published by Houghton Mifflin in 1993.

Wijayatilake, S. R.:
A court justice in Sri Lanka and a devout Buddhist, Wijayatilake went on pilgrimage with his family to the major Buddhist holy sites in India. In 1969, he published an account of his pilgrimage in *A Pilgrim Path.*

Credits

The editors are grateful for permission
to use the following material.

LUMBINI AND KAPILAVASTU

Arnold, Sir Edwin. *Light of Asia.* Chicago and New York: Rand, McNally & Company, 1890.

Beal, Samuel, translator. *The Romantic Legend of Sakya Buddha: A Translation of the Chinese Version of the Abhiniskramanasutra.* Delhi: Motilal Banarsidass, 1985. Excerpts reprinted by permission of Motilal Banarsidass.

Blofeld, John. *The Wheel of Life.* London: Rider, 1972. Excerpts reprinted by permission of Rider.

Cleary, Thomas, translator. From *The Dhammapada: The Sayings of the Budda* by Thomas Cleary. Copyright 1994 by Thomas Cleary. Used by permission of Bantam Books, a division of Bantam Doubleday Dell Publishing Group, Inc.

Cowell, E.B., translator. *Buddhist Mayayana Texts: The Buddha-Karita of Asvagosha.* New York: Dover Publications, Inc., 1969. Excerpts reprinted by permission of Dover Publications.

Crosette, Barbara. "A Nepalese Garden of Buddhist Legend" in the *New York Times,* Sunday, October 16, 1994. Excerpts reprinted by permission of The New York Times.

Fa-hsien. *The Travels of Fa-hsien (399-414 A.D.), or Record of the Buddhistic Kingdoms.* Re-translated by H.A. Giles. Cambridge: Cambridge University Press, 1923. Excerpts reprinted by permission of Cambridge University Press.

Huntington, John. "Sowing the Seeds of the Lotus: A Journey to the Great Pilgrimage Sites of Buddhism, Part IV" in *Orientalis,* vol. 16, no. 11, November, 1985. Excerpts reprinted by permission of John Huntington.

Matthiessen, Peter. *The Snow Leopard.* New York: The Viking Press, 1978. Used by permission of Viking Penguin, a division of Penguin Books.

Mukherji, Babu Purna Chandra. *Archaeological Survey of India: A Report on a Tour of Exploration of the Antiquities of Kapilavastu, Tarai of Nepal during February and March, 1899,* no. xxvi. With an introduction by Mr. Vincent Smith. Delhi: Indological Book House, 1969.

Naravane, V.S. *The Elephant and the Lotus: Essays in Philosophy and Culture.* Bombay: Asia Publishing House, 1965.

Nikam, N.A. and **Richard McKeon.** *The Edicts of Asoka.* Chicago: The University of Chicago Press, 1959. Excerpts reprinted by permission of the University of Chicago Press.

Peiris, Noeyal. *My Pilgrimage to the Lost City of Kapilavastu.* Colombo: International Center of Asoka Culture, 1978.

Raven-Hart, Rowland. *Where the Buddha Trod: A Buddhist Pilgrimage.* Colombo: H.W. Cave & Company, 1956.

Rockhill, W. Woodville, translator. *The Life of the Buddha and the Early History of His Order: Derived from Tibetan Works in the Bkah-Hgyur and Bstan-Hgyur.* London: Kegan Paul, Trench, Trübner & Co. Ltd., 1884.

Sangharakshita, Maha Sthavira (D.P.E. Lingwood). *The Thousand-Petalled Lotus.* London: William Heinemann Ltd., 1976.

Smith, Vincent. In *A Report on a Tour of the Antiquities of Kapilavastu Terai of Nepal during February and March, 1899* by P.C. Mukherji, Monographs of the Archaelogical Survey of India, Imperial Series, no. XXVI, pt.1, Calcutta, 1901. Reprinted, Varanasi, 1969.

Strong, J.S., translator. *The Legend of King Asoka: A Study and Translation of the Asokavadana.* Copyright 1984 by Princeton University Press. Reprinted by permission of Princeton University Press.

Tsiang, Hiuen. *Buddhist Records of the Western World.* Translated by Samuel Beal. Delhi: Oriental Books Reprint Corporation, 1969.

Warren, Henry C., translator. *The Life of the Buddha.* Delhi: Eastern Book Linkers, 1978.

Wijayatilake, S.R. *Buddhist India: A Pilgrim Path.* Colombo, Sri Lanka: The Colombo Apothecaries' Co., Ltd., 1969.

BODH GAYA

"The whole of the plinth and lower mouldings. . . ." Cited in *Boddha Gaya Temple: Its History* by Dipak K. Barua. Buddha Gaya: Buddha Gaya Temple Management Committee, 1981, pg. 77. Reprinted by permission of the Buddhagaya Temple Management Committee.

Arnold, Sir Edwin. *Light of Asia.* Chicago and New York: Rand, McNally & Company, 1890.

————. "East and West—A Splendid Opportunity" from the *Daily Telegraph.* Cited in *Boddha Gaya Temple: Its History* by Dipak K. Barua. Buddha Gaya: Buddha Gaya Temple Management Committee, 1981. Reprinted by permission of the Buddhagaya Temple Management Committee.

Ashby, Lillian Luker. *My India: Reflections of Fifty Years.* Copyright 1937 by Little, Brown and Company. By permission of Little, Brown and Co.

Blofeld, John. *The Wheel of Life.* London: Rider, 1972. Excerpts reprinted by permission of Rider.

Boucher, Sandy. Contributed by Sandy Boucher.

Ch'o, Hye. *The Hye Ch'o Diary: a memoir of the pilgrimage to the five regions of India.* Translation, text and editing by Han-sung Yang. Berkeley, California: Asian Humanities Press, 1984. Excerpts reprinted by permission of the Asian Humanities Press.

Cleary, Thomas, translator. From *The Dhammapada: The Sayings of the Budda* by Thomas Cleary. Copyright 1994 by Thomas Cleary. Used by permission of Bantam Books, a division of Bantam Doubleday Dell Publishing Group, Inc.

Cowell, E.B., translator. *The Buddha-Karita of Asvagosha.* New York: Dover Publications, Inc., 1969. Excerpts reprinted by permission of Dover Publications, Inc.

Cushman, Anne. "In the Footprints of the Buddha" in the *Yoga Journal,* July/August, 1994. Reprinted by permission of Anne Cushman.

Dalai Lama. *Freedom in Exile: The Autobiography of the Dalai Lama.* New York: Harper Perennial, 1990. Excerpt reprinted by permission of Harper Collins Publishers.

Del Mare, Walter. *India of Today.* London: Adam and Charles Black, 1905.

Deussen, Paul. From *Traveller's India.* Edited by H.K. Kaul. Delhi: Oxford University Press, 1979. Excerpts reprinted by permission of Oxford University Press.

Dharmapala, Anagarika. *Return to Righteousness: A Collection of Speeches, Essays and Letters of the Anagarika Dharmapala.* Edited by Ananda Guruge. Ceylon: The Anagarika Dharmapala Birth Centenary Committee, Ministry of Education and Cultural Affairs, 1965.

Dharmasvamin. *Biography of Dharmasvamin.* Translated by Dr. George Roerich. Patna: K.P. Jayaswal Research Institute, 1959.

Fields, Rick. "The Buddha Got Enlightened Under a Tree" in *Tricycle,* winter, 1992. Excerpt reprinted by permission of Rick Fields.

Forbes-Lindsay, C.H. *India Past and Present.* Philadelphia: Henry T. Coates & Co., 1903.

Forster, E.M. "Enclosed is a leaf. . . ." From *Selected Letters of E.M. Forster: Volume One, 1879-1920.* Edited by Mary Lago and N. Furbank. London: Collins, 1983. Reprinted by permission of King's College, Cambridge, and the Society of Authors as the literary representatives of the E.M. Forster Estate.

————. "The glory is . . . gone from Bodh Gaya." From *E.M. Forster's India* by G.K. Das. London and Basingstoke: Macmillan Press Ltd., 1977. Reprinted by permission of Macmillan Press Ltd.

Ginsberg, Allen. *Indian Journals: March 1962—May 1963.* San Francisco, California: Dave Haselwood Books & City Lights Books, 1970. Excerpt reprinted by permission of Allen Ginsberg.

Hanh, Thich Nhat. *Old Path White Clouds: Walking in the Footsteps of the Budda, 1991,* with permission of Parallax Press: Berkeley, California.

Huntington, John. "Sowing the Seeds of the Lotus: A Journey to the Great Pilgrimage Sites of Buddhism, Part IV" in *Orientalis.* Vol. 16, No. 11, November, 1985. Excerpt reprinted by permission of John Huntington.

I-Tsing. *A Record of the Buddhist Religion as Practised in India and the*

Malay Archipelago (A.D. 671-695) by I-Tsing. Translated by J. Takakusu. Oxford: Clarendon Press, 1896. Excerpts reprinted by permission of Oxford University Press.
Kawaguchi, Ekai. *Three Years in Tibet.* Kathmandu, Nepal: Ratna Pustak Bhandar, 1979.
Kyger, Joanne. *The Joanne and India Journals:* 1960-1964. Tombouctou, 1981.
Lerner, Eric. Excerpt from *Journey of Insight Meditation: A Personal Experience of the Buddha's Way* by Eric Lerner. Copyright 1977 by Schocken Books, Inc., reprinted by permission of Schocken Books, published by Pantheon a division of Random House, Inc.
Matthiessen, Peter. *The Snow Leopard.* New York: The Viking Press, 1978. Excerpts reprinted by permission of Penguin Books.
Poppe, Nicholas, translator. *The Twelve Deeds of Buddha: A Mongolian Version of the Lalitavistara.* Wiesbaden: Otto Harrassowitz, 1967. Excerpts reprinted by permission of Verlag Otto Harrassowitz
Scidmore, Elizabeth Ruhamah. *Winter India.* New York: The Century Co., 1903.
Siridhammasoka. Cited in *Boddha Gaya Temple: Its History* by Dipak K. Barua. Buddha Gaya: Buddha Gaya Temple Management Committee, 1981, pg. 197. Reprinted by permission of Buddhagaya Temple Management Committee.
Snyder, Gary. *Passage Through India.* San Francisco: Grey Fox Press, 1972. Excerpts reprinted by permission of Gary Snyder.
Strong, J.S., translator. *The Legend of King Asoka: A Study and Translation of the Asokavadana.* Copyright 1984 by Princeton University Press. Reprinted by permission of Princeton University Press.
Tagore, Rabindranath. "On Buddhadeva" in *The Visvabharati Quarterly.* Vol. 22, No. 3, Winter 1956-57. Excerpt reprinted by permission of *Visva-Bharati,* Santiniketan, West Bengal, India.
Tsiang, Hiuen. *Buddhist Records of the Western World.* Translated by Samuel Beal. Delhi: Oriental Books Reprint Corporation, 1969.
Waldman, Anne. Contributed by Anne Waldman.
Warren, Henry C., translator. *The Life of the Buddha.* Delhi: Eastern Book Linkers, 1978.
Wheeler, Kate. Contributed by Kate Wheeler.
Wijayatilake, S.R. *Buddhist India: A Pilgrim Path.* Colombo, Sri Lanka: The Colombo Apothecaries' Co., Ltd., 1969.

SARNATH
"It will have been observed. . . ." Cited in *Return to Righteousness: A Collection of Speeches, Essays and Letters of the Anagarika Dharmapala.* Edited by Ananda Guruge. Ceylon: The Anagarika Dharmapala Birth Centenary Committee, Ministry of Education and Cultural Affairs, 1965.
Blofeld, John. *The Wheel of Life.* London: Rider, 1972. Excerpts reprinted by permission of Rider.

Byles, Marie Beuzeville. *The Lotus and the Spinning Wheel.* London: George Allen and Unwin Ltd., 1963. Excerpts reprinted by permission of Harper Collins Publishers.

Cleary, Thomas, translator. From *The Dhammapada: The Sayings of the Budda* by Thomas Cleary. Copyright 1994 by Thomas Cleary. Used by permission of Bantam Books, a division of Bantam Doubleday Dell Publishing Group, Inc.

Cowell, E.B., translator. *The Buddha-Karita of Asvagosha.* New York: Dover Publications, Inc., 1969. Excerpts reprinted by permission of Dover Publications, Inc.

Cushman, Anne. "In the Footprints of the Buddha" in the *Yoga Journal,* July/August, 1994. Reprinted by permission of Anne Cushman.

Crane, Walter. *India Impressions.* London: Methuen & Co., 1907.

Dalai Lama. *Freedom in Exile: The Autobiography of the Dalai Lama.* New York: Harper Perennial, 1990. Excerpt reprinted by permission of Harper Collins Publishers.

Das Gupta, Surendranath. Cited in *The Modern Review,* December, 1931.

Daw Mya Tin, translator. *Dhammapada: Verses and Stories.* Sarnath, Varanasi: Central Institute of Higher Tibetan Studies, 1990. Excerpt reprinted by permission of the Central Institute of Higher Tibetan Studies, Sarnath, Varanasi, India.

Dharmapala, Anagarika. *Return to Righteousness: A Collection of Speeches, Essays and Letters of the Anagarika Dharmapala.* Edited by Ananda Guruge. Ceylon: The Anagarika Dharmapala Birth Centenary Committee, Ministry of Education and Cultural Affairs, 1965.

Duncan, Jonathan, Esq. "An Account of the Discovery of Two Urns in the Vicinity of Benares" in *Asiatic Researches,* Vol. 5. New Delhi: Cosmo Publications.

Fa-hsien. *The Travels of Fa hsien (399-414 A.D.), or Record of the Buddhistic Kingdoms.* Re-translated by H.A. Giles. Cambridge: Cambridge University Press, 1923. Excerpts reprinted by permission of Cambridge University Press.

Hanh, Thich Nhat. *Old Path White Clouds: Walking in the Footsteps of the Budda,* 1991, with permission of Parallax Press: Berkeley, California.

Huntington, John. "Sowing the Seeds of the Lotus: A Journey to the Great Pilgrimage Sites of Buddhism, Part IV" in *Orientalis,* vol. 17, no. 2, February, 1986. Excerpt reprinted by permission of John Huntington.

Naravane, V.S. *The Elephant and the Lotus: Essays in Philosophy and Culture.* Bombay: Asia Publishing House, 1965.

Raven-Hart, Rowland. *Where the Buddha Trod: A Buddhist Pilgrimage.* Colombo: H.W. Cave & Company, 1956.

Rhys Davids, Mrs., translator. *Psalms of the Early Buddhists: II-Psalms of the Brethren.* London: Published for the Pali Text Society by Henry Frowde, 1913. Excerpt reprinted by permission of Oxford University Press.

Rhys Davids, T.W., translator. *Buddhist Birth Stories or Jataka Tales.* Arno Press: New York, 1977.

Sangharakshita, Maha Sthavira (D.P.E. Lingwood). *The Thousand-Petalled Lotus.* London: William Heinemann Ltd., 1976.

Scidmore, Elizabeth Ruhamah. *Winter India.* New York: The Century Co., 1903.

Shoemaker, Michael. *Indian Pages and Pictures: Rajputana, Sikkim, The Punjab, and Kashmir.* New York and London: G.P. Putnam's Sons, 1912. Excerpt reprinted by permission of the Putnam Publishing Co.

Snyder, Gary. *Passage Through India.* San Francisco: Grey Fox Press, 1972. Excerpts reprinted by permission of Gary Snyder.

Tagore, Rabindranath. From *The Modern Review,* December, 1931.

Tsiang, Hiuen. *Buddhist Records of the Western World.* Translated by Samuel Beal. Delhi: Oriental Books Reprint Corporation, 1969.

Walshe, Maurice, translator. *Thus Have I Heard: The Long Discourses of the Buddha.* (London: Wisdom Publications, 1987) with permission of Wisdom Publications, 361 Newbury Street, Boston, MA. *Thus Have I Heard* will be reissued in 1995 as *The Long Discourses of the Buddha: A New Translation of the Digha Nikaya.*

Wijayatilake, S.R. *Buddhist India: A Pilgrim Path.* Colombo, Sri Lanka: The Colombo Apothecaries' Co., Ltd., 1969.

RAJAGRIHA

Arnold, Sir Edwin. *Light of Asia.* Chicago and New York: Rand, McNally & Company, 1890.

Blofeld, John. *The Wheel of Life.* London: Rider, 1972. Excerpts reprinted by permission of Rider.

Buchanan, Francis. *The History, Antiquities, Topography, and Statistics of Eastern India.* Vols. I-III London: Wm. H. Allen and Co. Leadenhall-Street, 1838.

Cleary, Thomas, translator. From *The Dhammapada: The Sayings of the Budda* by Thomas Cleary. Copyright 1994 by Thomas Cleary. Used by permission of Bantam Books, a division of Bantam Doubleday Dell Publishing Group, Inc.

Cowell, E.B., translator. *The Buddha-Karita of Asvagosha.* New York: Dover Publications, Inc., 1969. Excerpts reprinted by permission of Dover Publications, Inc.

Cushman, Anne. "In the Footprints of the Buddha" in the *Yoga Journal,* July/August, 1994. Reprinted by permission of Anne Cushman.

Dharmasvamin. *Biography of Dharmasvamin,* translated by Dr. George Roerich. Patna: K.P. Jayaswal Research Institute, 1959.

Fa-hsien. *The Travels of Fa-hsien (399-414 A.D.), or Record of the Buddhistic Kingdoms.* Re-translated by H.A. Giles. Cambridge: Cambridge University Press, 1923. Excerpts reprinted by permission of Cambridge University Press.

Ginsberg, Allen. *Indian Journals: March 1962-May 1963.* San Francisco, California: Dave Haselwood Books & City Lights Books, 1970. Excerpt reprinted by permission of Allen Ginsberg.

Hanh, Thich Nhat. *Old Path White Clouds: Walking in the Footsteps of the Budda,* 1991, with permission of Parallax Press: Berkeley, California.

Horner, I.B., translator. *The Book of the Discipline (Vinaya-Pitaka),* vol. 5. London: Luzac and Company Ltd., 1952.

Huntington, John. "Sowing the Seeds of the Lotus: A Journey to the Great Pilgrimage Sites of Buddhism, Part IV" in *Orientalis,* vol. 17, no. 7, July 1986. Excerpt reprinted by permission of John Huntington.

Macy, Joanna. Contributed by Joanna Macy.

Murcott, Susan. *The First Buddhist Women.* Berkeley, 1991, with permission of Parallax Press, Berkeley, California.

Poppe, Nicholas, translator. *The Twelve Deeds of Buddha: A Mongolian Version of the Lalitavistara.* Wiesbaden: Otto Harrassowitz, 1967. Excerpts reprinted by permission of Verlag Otto Harrassowitz.

Rabten, Geshe. *Echoes of Voidness.* Translated by Stephen Batchelor. Wisdom Publications: London, 1983. Excerpt reprinted courtesy of Wisdom Publications, 361 Newbury Street, Boston, MA.

Raven-Hart, Rowland. *Where the Buddha Trod: A Buddhist Pilgrimage.* Colombo: H.W. Cave & Company, 1956.

Rockhill, W. Woodville, translator. *The Life of the Buddha and the Early History of His Order, derived from Tibetan works in the Bkah-Hgyur and Bstan-Hgyur.* London: Kegan Paul, Trench, Trübner & Co. Ltd., 1884.

Sangharakshita, Maha Sthavira (D.P.E. Lingwood). *The Thousand-Petalled Lotus.* London: William Heinemann Ltd., 1976.

Schelling, Andrew, translator. "When Rajadatta the trader. . . ." in the *Teragatha.* Contributed by Andrew Schelling.

Strong, J.S., translator. *The Legend of King Asoka: A Study and Translation of the Asokavadana.* Copyright 1984 by Princeton University Press. Reprinted by permission of Princeton University Press.

Tsiang, Hiuen. *Buddhist Records of the Western World.* Translated by Samuel Beal. Delhi: Oriental Books Reprint Corporation, 1969.

Wijayatilake, S.R. *Buddhist India: A Pilgrim Path.* Colombo, Sri Lanka: The Colombo Apothecaries' Co., Ltd., 1969.

SRAVASTI AND SANKASYA

Blofeld, John. *The Wheel of Life.* London: Rider, 1972. Excerpts reprinted by permission of Rider.

Byles, Marie Beuzeville. *The Lotus and the Spinning Wheel.* London: George Allen and Unwin Ltd., 1963. Excerpts reprinted by permission of Harper Collins Publishers

Ch'o, Hye. *The Hye Ch'o Diary: a memoir of the pilgrimage to the five regions of India.* Translation, text and editing by Han-sung Yang. Berkeley, California: Asian Humanities Press, 1984. Excerpts reprinted by permission of the Asian Humanities Press.

Cleary, Thomas, translator. From *The Dhammapada: The Sayings of the Budda* by Thomas Cleary. Copyright 1994 by Thomas Cleary. Used by permission of Bantam Books, a division of Bantam Doubleday Dell Publishing Group, Inc.

Cowell, E.B. *The Jataka: Stories of the Buddha's Former Births.* London: The Pali Text Society, 1973. Excerpts reprinted by permission of the Pali Text Society.

Cushman, Anne. "In the Footprints of the Buddha" in the *Yoga Journal*, July/August, 1994. Reprinted by permission of Anne Cushman.

Daw Mya Tin, translator. *Dhammapada: Verses and Stories.* Sarnath, Varanasi: Central Institute of Higher Tibetan Studies, 1990. Excerpt reprinted by permission of the Central Institute of Higher Tibetan Studies, Sarnath, Varanasi, India.

Fa-hsien. *The Travels of Fa-hsien (399-414 A.D.), or Record of the Buddhistic Kingdoms.* Re-translated by H. A. Giles. Cambridge: Cambridge University Press, 1923. Excerpts reprinted by permission of the Cambridge University Press.

Huntington, John. "Sowing the Seeds of the Lotus: A Journey to the Great Pilgrimage Sites of Buddhism, Part III" in *Orientalis*, vol. 17, no. 3, March 1986. Excerpts reprinted by permission of John Huntington.

Murcott, Susan. *The First Buddhist Women.* Berkeley, 1991, with permission of Parallax Press, Berkeley, California.

Peiris, Noeyal. *My Pilgrimage to the Lost City of Kapilavastu.* Colombo: International Center of Asoka Culture, 1978.

Raven-Hart, Rowland. *Where the Buddha Trod: A Buddhist Pilgrimage.* Colombo: H.W. Cave & Company, 1956.

Rockhill, W. Woodville, translator. *The Life of the Buddha and the Early History of His Order, derived from Tibetan works in the Bkah-Hgyur and Bstan-Hgyur.* London: Kegan Paul Trench, Trübner & Co. Ltd., 1884.

Schelling, Andrew, translator. "One day [Nandaka] was searching . . . ."; "Reborn in this Buddha age. . ." in the *Teragatha*. Contributed by Andrew Schelling.

Tsiang, Hiuen. *Buddhist Records of the Western World.* Translated by Samuel Beal. Delhi: Oriental Books Reprint Corporation, 1969.

Walshe, Maurice, translator. Copyright Maurice Walshe. Reprinted from *Thus Have I Heard: The Long Discourses of the Buddha.* (London: Wisdom Publications, 1987) with permission of Wisdom Publications, 361 Newbury Street, Boston, MA. USA. *Thus Have I Heard* will be reissued in 1995 as *The Long Discourses of the Buddha: A New Translation of the Digha Nikaya.*

Wijayatilake, S.R. *Buddhist India: A Pilgrim Path.* Colombo, Sri

Lanka: The Colombo Apothecaries' Co., Ltd., 1969.

VAISALI
"Ananda, Vaisali is delightful. . . ." From *Thus Have I Heard: The Long Discourses of the Buddha.* (London: Wisdom Publications, 1987) with permission of Wisdom Publications, 361 Newbury Street, Boston, MA. USA. *Thus Have I Heard* will be reissued in 1995 as *The Long Discourses of the Buddha: A New Translation of the Digha Nikaya.*
Badiner, Allan Hunt. Contributed by Allan Hunt Badiner. From the forthcoming book, *Buddha by Land: Pilgrimage to India.* (Parallax Press).
Burlingame, E.W. *Buddhist Legends.* Cambridge, Massachusetts: Harvard University Press, 1921. Excerpt reprinted by permission of Harvard University Press.
Cleary, Thomas, translator. From *The Dhammapada: The Sayings of the Budda* by Thomas Cleary. Copyright 1994 by Thomas Cleary. Used by permission of Bantam Books, a division of Bantam Doubleday Dell Publishing Group, Inc.
The *Dipavansa.* Citation from *Buddhist Birth Stories or Jataka Tales* by Thomas William Rhys Davids. New York: Arno Press, 1977. Excerpt reprinted by permission of Ayer Press.
Hanh, Thich Nhat. *Old Path White Clouds: Walking in the Footsteps of the Budda,* 1991, with permission of Parallax Press: Berkeley, California.
Rockhill, W. Woodville, translator. *The Life of the Buddha and the Early History of His Order, derived from Tibetan works in the Bkah-Hgyur and Bstan-Hgyur.* London: Kegan Paul, Trench, Trübner & Co. Ltd., 1884.
Terrell, Richard. *A Perception of India.* Michael Russell, 1984. Excerpts reprinted by permission of Michael Russell, Ltd.
Tsiang, Hiuen. *Buddhist Records of the Western World.* Translated by Samuel Beal. Delhi: Oriental Books Reprint Corporation, 1969.
Waldman, Anne, translator. "I'm free. . . ."; "Once my hair was black. . . ."; "I was a prostitute with fees. . . ."; "Out of my mind. . . ." & "Homage to you Buddha. . . ." in the *Terigatha.* Contributed by Anne Waldman.
Walshe, Maurice, translator. Copyright Maurice Walshe. Reprinted from *Thus Have I Heard: The Long Discourses of the Buddha.* (London: Wisdom Publications, 1987) with permission of Wisdom Publications, 361 Newbury Street, Boston, MA. *Thus Have I Heard* will be reissued in 1995 as *The Long Discourses of the Buddha: A New Translation of the Digha Nikaya.*

KUSINAGARA: The Great Passing Away
Badiner, Allan Hunt. Contributed by Allan Hunt Badiner.
Blofeld, John. *The Wheel of Life.* London: Rider, 1972. Excerpts reprinted by permission of Rider.
Byles, Marie Beuzeville. *The Lotus and the Spinning Wheel.* London: George Allen and Unwin Ltd., 1963. Excerpts reprinted by permis-